T0153240

VIETNAM

VIETNAM

THE (LAST) WAR THE U.S. LOST

JOE ALLEN

FOREWORD BY JOHN PILGER

Haymarket Books

Chicago, Illinois

First published in 2008 by Haymarket Books
P.O. Box 180165
Chicago, IL 60618
773-583-7884
info@haymarketbooks.org
www.haymarketbooks.org

Trade distribution:
In the U.S. through Consortium Book Sales, www.cbsd.com
In the UK, Turnaround Publisher Services, www.turnaround-psl.com
In Australia, Palgrave MacMillan, www.palgravemacmillan.com.au
All other countries, Publishers Group Worldwide, www.pgw.com/home/worldwide.aspx.

This book was published with the generous support of the Wallace Global Fund.

Cover design by Eric Ruder
Cover photo of North Vietnamese fighters firing at American warplanes after they
bombed. Undated, photo by Mai Nam, © Associated Press.

Library of Congress Cataloging-in-Publication Data:
Allen, Joe, 1960-
Vietnam : the (last) war the U.S. lost/Joe Allen; preface by John Pilger.
Includes bibliographical references and index.
ISBN-13: 978-1-931859-49-3 (pbk. : alk. paper)
1. Vietnam War, 1961–1975—United States. 2. United States—Politics and government—
1945-1989. 3. Vietnam War, 1961–1975—Protest movements—United States. I. Title.
DS558.A43 2008
959.704'3--dc22
2008009123

Printed in Canada by union labor on recycled paper containing 100 percent post-
consumer waste in accordance with the guidelines of the Green Press Initiative,
www.greenpressinitiative.org.

10 9 8 7 6 5 4 3 2 1

union bug   recycle logo

CONTENTS

FOREWORD BY JOHN PILGER IX

INTRODUCTION: THE GHOSTS OF VIETNAM 1

1. FROM THE FRENCH CONQUEST TO
THE OVERTHROW OF DIEM 5

2. FROM THE OVERTHROW OF DIEM
TO THE TET OFFENSIVE 31

3. COLD WAR LIBERALISM AND THE
ROOTS OF THE ANTIWAR MOVEMENT 61

4. BLACK AMERICA AND VIETNAM 79

5. FROM THE BIRTH OF THE ANTIWAR
MOVEMENT TO 1968 101

6. THE U.S. WORKING CLASS
AND THE WAR 135

7. FROM QUAGMIRE TO DEFEAT 157

8. FROM WATERGATE TO
THE FALL OF SAIGON 177

CONCLUSION: THE LEGACY OF VIETNAM 203

NOTES 209

FURTHER READING 232

INDEX 236

This book is dedicated to all Vietnamese, Cambodians, Laotians, and Americans who continue to suffer death and deformity as a result of America's use of weapons of mass destruction in Southeast Asia from 1960 to 1975.

FOREWORD

BY JOHN PILGER

Hongai is a coal mining and fishing town on the shores of beautiful Ha Long Bay in northern Vietnam. For three days in June 1972, American fighter-bombers flew fifty-two sorties against Hongai, around the clock. People were evacuated to the mines and to caves in the hills while the pilots pulverized their homes, schools, hospitals, churches. The pilots deployed a new type of pellet bomb, the size of a grapefruit, which exploded into millions of minuscule darts. In the rubble of a school I found a note written by a young girl, describing how the fragments had peppered her sister. Designed to move through the body and extremely difficult to detect under X-ray, the darts caused internal injuries from which the victim would die a terrible death. This weapon of mass destruction, the forerunner of the cluster bomb, was first tested on the people of Hongai. This landmark was not reported in the United States. It was as if one of the heaviest and most concentrated aerial assaults in the modern era had never happened.

When I reached Hongai in 1975, most of the town lay in its debris, a Pompeii of war. I stood in St. Mary's Catholic Church, in the saddle of a hill, and all that remained was the altar. The church, which had dominated the town, had taken a direct hit, and its remains had been bombed repeatedly. None of the other churches stood. A health ministry official, Dr. Luu Van Hoat, told me that 10 percent of the town's children were deaf, and many might never regain their hearing. None of this was reported in the United States.

Apart from a few old Soviet aircraft, the Vietnamese nationalists had no air force. I met local people who had been members of militia and had put up a curtain of small-arms fire as the F-105s and Phantoms came in at 200 feet. Remarkably, they survived. However, further south, at Dong Loc, which had been bombed back to the Stone Age, leaving craters that merged into a swamp, I stood where an all-women anti-aircraft battery had brought down several aircraft. The eldest of them had been nineteen years old, and I stood among their graves. None of this was reported in the United States.

It was a decade later that I happened to read the results of an opinion poll in which people in the United States were asked how much they could remember about the war. More than a third could not say which side the American government had supported and some believed that Ho Chi Minh and his nationalists had been "our allies." This reminded me of something a friend of mine, Bob Muller, a former U.S. Marine officer paralyzed from the waist down as a result of the war, told me. As president of Vietnam Veterans Against the War, Bob spoke frequently on college campuses, where he was often asked: "Which side did *you* fight on?"

Today, this "historical amnesia" seems entrenched. This is not accidental, or a comment on the inadequacy of human memory. It merely demonstrates the insidious, enduring power of the dominant propaganda of the Vietnam War. This propaganda described the war as essentially a conflict of Vietnamese against Vietnamese, in which Americans had become "involved," mistakenly yet honorably. This falsehood soon became a presupposition that marked the limits of most "mainstream" debate. It was embraced both by "hawks" and "doves," conservatives and liberals, and at times, seemed to have a sacred immunity. It permeated the media coverage during the war and has been the overriding theme of numerous scholarly and journalistic retrospectives since the war. In fact, the longest war of the twentieth century was waged by the American government *against* the people of Vietnam, North and South, communist and noncommunist. It was an invasion of their homeland upon which the United States dropped the greatest tonnage of bombs in the history of warfare, pursued a military strategy deliberately designed to force millions to abandon their homes, and used banned chemicals in a manner that profoundly changed the environmental and genetic order, leaving a once bountiful land petrified. Some three million people were killed and at least as many were maimed and otherwise ruined. The American military commander, General William Westmoreland, declared that the object was to cause human devastation "to the point of national disaster for generations to come." That this was achieved as an epic crime by the Nuremberg standard is hardly known in the United States.

Therefore, it is not surprising that many Americans, especially the young, are confused about Vietnam, if they are called upon to think about it at all.

They may be aware that it was "a mistake" or even "wrong" and that it divided the nation, but their perspective, at best, is more than likely to be from the liberal Hollywood point of view, of angst-ridden "fallen heroes." They will have little if any notion of the culpability—the lies and the murderous policies and actions that caused and sustained the war, and which have caused and sustained subsequent invasions, notably the invasion of Iraq.

This is why Joe Allen's book is so needed, and so welcome. Indeed, the following pages amount to a masterpiece in which the author, unrelenting in his research, has reclaimed memory from the organized forgetting that has so bedeviled the very word "Vietnam."

The Westmoreland quotation above, which I had forgotten, is there, as are references to the splendid work of those like Marilyn Young, who mines illuminating statistics from a long-abandoned coalfield. "Nineteen million gallons of herbicide had been sprayed on the South during the war," she wrote. How many malformed children have I seen in the Mekong Delta over the years, the victims of "Agent Orange?" And we are reminded that the North was spared in relative terms compared with South Vietnam, said to be America's "ally." What I also appreciate about Joe Allen's work is that he demonstrates as a historian how a rapacious force as seemingly invincible as the United States can be defeated politically, if not militarily. While not claiming a likeness between the invasions of Vietnam and Iraq, he draws many valuable parallels of how they began. Rather than giving us "hope," he is giving us power: the power of information, meticulous, distilled, coherent, principled. His mighty primer should be on every curriculum. No, it should be in every home.

John Pilger
March 2008

INTRODUCTION

THE GHOSTS OF VIETNAM

"By God, we've kicked the Vietnam Syndrome once and for all."
—President George H. W. Bush, 1991,
in the aftermath the Persian Gulf War

The war in Vietnam resulted in the greatest military defeat ever suffered by the United States. Ever since, the U.S. ruling class and its intellectual pundits have worked hard to overcome what has become known as the Vietnam Syndrome—the fear on the part of American planners that any large-scale military engagement might become a "quagmire" and provoke mass domestic opposition. Virtually every foreign military intervention that followed Vietnam, from Ronald Reagan's 1983 invasion of the tiny Caribbean island of Grenada to George H. W. Bush's 1991 Gulf War and Bill Clinton's intervention in Bosnia, was presented as a step toward restoring the ability (and moral right) of the United States to engage unilaterally and without limit in overseas military action.

The 2003 U.S. invasion of Iraq (for which Afghanistan was a dress rehearsal) was meant to be a watershed event that would establish Washington's position as the world's sole and unassailable superpower. Instead, it has created a domestic and international crisis for the United States not seen since the war in Vietnam.

"There are so many cartoons where people, oppressed people, are saying, 'Is it Vietnam yet?'—hoping it is and wondering if it is. And it isn't," declared former Secretary of Defense Donald Rumsfeld in the summer of 2003, against critics invoking comparisons between the growing insurgency in Iraq and the war in Vietnam.[1] Despite Rumsfeld's assurances, and George Bush's (the first) before him, the comparisons keep on coming. Not a week goes by when a writer or politician isn't making some comparison between Vietnam and Iraq. The Vietnam Syndrome may have been "licked"—only to be replaced by the Iraq Syndrome.

Yet for the generation of Americans who have come of age in the three decades since the last U.S. troops left Vietnam, the history of the war is practically forgotten. The motivation that drove the United States to launch one of the most destructive wars of the twentieth century, and the reasons that millions of ordinary Americans came to actively oppose it, are also largely forgotten or distorted.

President Lyndon Johnson once described Vietnam, in his own particularly racist and vulgar way, as a "raggedy-ass little fourth-rate country."[2] How such a country could defeat the most powerful government in the world had to be hidden from both the oppressed of the world and the American people. That is the job of the popular media, establishment historians, and their friends in Hollywood. It is one of the great ironies of American society that one can watch many of the war in Vietnam–related films produced by Hollywood (with some notable exceptions, of course) and actually know less about the war than before walking into the theater.[3] History, it is said, is written by the victor. In the case of Vietnam, history has been written, or rewritten (at least outside of Vietnam), by the loser that still remains the dominant economic and military power in the world.

This is a very small book that attempts to cover a wide range of issues related to the Vietnam era. It is meant to be an introduction for that generation of Americans that has grown up in the post–Vietnam era, who have become politicized by the war in Iraq, and wonder what it will take to end that war, now approaching its fifth anniversary.

This book is not meant to be a substitute for reading many of the fine books by radical historians or memoirs of soldiers and activists, which are listed at the end of the book. I have tried my best to provide an overview of the three decades of United States intervention in Vietnam, as well as the profound political ramifications of that intervention at home. Because of limited space, I have concentrated on the key moments of the antiwar movement, a huge subject, so that readers may take away from it the most important political lessons while not getting lost in the minutiae.

An introduction to the Vietnam era is also necessary because even the best histories of the war have serious omissions and sometimes such a narrow focus that a reader is prevented from getting a thorough understanding of the war and the antiwar movement, or of the relationship between the two. For example, some histories begin the war in Vietnam in 1965, even though the U.S. role in Vietnam goes back many years before that. Many histories ignore the importance of the civil rights and Black Power movements in generating opposition to the war, or the rebellion of American soldiers, sailors, and airmen that put the final nail in the coffin of the U.S. war effort.

But the most glaring omission of many war-in-Vietnam histories is the triumphant, three-decade struggle of the Vietnamese people to free their country from foreign domination. Though it was the longest national liberation struggle of the twentieth century, inspiring millions around the world in the 1960s and 1970s, too few people outside of Vietnam understand or appreciate the Vietnamese national liberation movement today. This book attempts to integrate all these issues into one narrative. The lessons of the war in Vietnam are many, and it is up to readers to discover for themselves which of them may provide a guide to bringing an end to the current American wars in Iraq and Afghanistan today.

There are many people who have encouraged me at different points in time to write and complete this book. I would like to thank Sharon Smith and Christian Appy for critically reading the chapter on the war in Vietnam and the American working class, and Keeanga Taylor and Michael Letwin for their comments on Black America and Vietnam. Joel Geier put aside a lot of time to help me think through the origins of the New Left and the antiwar movement. Historian Mike Gillen sent me a chapter of his unpublished dissertation on the opposition of American merchant marines to transporting French troops to reconquer Vietnam after World War II. I want to thank them both. But above all, I would like to thank my editor, Paul D'Amato, and the Haymarket staff, in particular Dao Tran, without whom I never would have completed this project.

Joe Allen
Chicago
March 2008

CHAPTER ONE

FROM THE FRENCH CONQUEST
TO THE OVERTHROW OF DIEM

To answer the question "Why did the U.S. get involved in Vietnam?" we need to go back to before the large-scale landing of U.S. troops in 1965 and look at the history of the struggle for Vietnamese independence and the communist movement that led it to victory twice—first over the French, then over the Americans.[1]

THE FRENCH CONQUEST

> "When France arrived in Indochina, the Annamites
> [Vietnamese] were ripe for servitude."
> —Paul Doumer, Governor General of Indochina

Vietnam was an independent nation until the French conquered it during the latter half of the nineteenth century. While French missionaries and businessmen had been going to Vietnam since the early 1600s, converting inhabitants to Catholicism and establishing commercial ties with the country, it was in the mid-nineteenth century that the fundamental direction of French policy toward Indochina rapidly changed. The French no longer simply wanted the concessions they had won in the past; they wanted complete control of the whole country. France's rivals—Britain, Belgium, Germany, the Netherlands, and Portugal—were all engaged in a struggle to carve up and colonize those parts of the globe that could serve them as sources of raw materials, markets, and profitable investments. As the British consolidated their position in India and China (sidelining French interests there), the French made their move into Indochina in order to reap the potential fortunes to be made there.

The French were aided in their conquest of Indochina by a policy of appeasement pursued by the Vietnamese royal court under the unpopular Emperor Tu Duc (1847–1883) of the ruling Nguyen family. Tu Duc's regime faced a growing revolt of the peasantry, which the royal family perceived as a greater threat to its rule than the French hovering off the coast. This was a serious miscalculation. Tu Duc signed away the country piece by piece to the French, beginning in 1863, when the French captured six Vietnamese provinces around Saigon. In 1874, Tu Duc made more territorial concessions, and finally, in 1882, the French fleet captured Hanoi. The French were now in control of the whole country.[2]

The first thing the French did when they completed their conquest of Vietnam was to abolish Vietnam as a political entity. It was a classic case of divide and conquer. France divided Vietnam into three administrative provinces: Tonkin in the north, Annam in the center, and Cochinchina in the south. Tonkin and Annam were considered "protectorates," where Vietnamese royal power was allegedly still intact, while Cochinchina was ruled directly as a colony. In practice, the difference between a protectorate and a colony was pure fiction—the French ran everything. They chose the emperor, along with a host of advisers, and Frenchmen dominated the colonial bureaucracy.[3]

The Vietnamese economy was reorganized for the benefit of the French and their Vietnamese collaborators. The chief architect of France's policies in Vietnam was Paul Doumer, who was appointed governor general of Indochina and arrived in 1897. His goal from the day he arrived was to make Vietnam a "profitable colony" for France. "Indochina began to serve France in Asia on the day that it was no longer a poverty-stricken colony," Doumer claimed. "Its strong organization, its financial and economic structures…are being used for the benefit of French prestige."[4] Doumer established monopolies for the production and marketing of alcohol, salt, and opium. French businessmen, whose monopolies were interlocked with the powerful Bank of Indochina, became very wealthy.

French colonial policies had their biggest impact on rice farming, the source of livelihood for the vast majority of people. The French and their collaborators stole most of the best land for themselves within a generation of the conquest. Tens of thousands of acres of land were taken away from the Vietnamese and given to the French at dirt-cheap prices. Many of the French owned 3,000- to 7,000-acre estates. Despite this robbery, most Vietnamese still owned something. After 1900, the French theft of land increased. By the 1930s, over half the peasants in Tonkin and Annam were landless, while in Cochinchina, 75 percent were landless and the rest owned next to nothing.[5] Tenant farmers and sharecroppers had to pay anywhere between 50 percent and 70 percent of their crops to landlords and, in addition, provide free gifts and services.

France's investments in industry and rubber plantations also had an enormous impact on Vietnam, much of it coming after World War I. The bulk of it was in the booming rubber plantations, where one hundred thousand to two hundred thousand Vietnamese were annually tricked or forced to work. The conditions were slave-like. Michelin rubber plantations were called slaughterhouses. "Rubber, the second largest Vietnamese export after rice, was produced by virtually indentured workers so blighted by malaria, dysentery and malnutrition that at one Michelin company plantation, twelve thousand out of forty-five thousand workers died between 1917 and 1944."[6] Similar conditions were also found in the mines, which were called death valleys. Miners as well as rubber workers had to pay for the shacks that they lived in and for their tools. Punishment was severe for the smallest of infractions and those who attempted to escape were subjected to torture and hunger.[7]

How much were Vietnamese workers paid for their hard labor? According to French colonial statistics, a fully employed worker had an average annual income of forty-eight piasters in the late 1920s, which was barely enough for a person to buy enough rice to live on for a year. Or, as Vietnamese historian Ngo Vinh Long put it graphically: "Even a dog belonging to a colonial household cost an average of 150 piasters a year to feed." In addition, many workers were cheated out of their wages by their bosses, and often paid in rice and vegetables (sometimes rotten) from the company store. By 1929, before the worldwide depression hit, there were nearly two hundred twenty thousand workers in the industrial and commercial sectors of the economy.[8]

The French not only brought economic exploitation to Vietnam; they also brought their *mission civilisatrice* (civilizing mission), a mixture of paternalism and racism aimed at molding the Vietnamese in the image of the French. As one enthusiastic supporter of French imperialism put it, it was the duty of France to bring "into light and into liberty the races and peoples still enslaved by ignorance and despotism."[9] This mission of delivering people into "light" really meant fostering cultural repression, directed particularly at the Vietnamese peoples' language, and political repression, directed against any organized dissent.

Before the French conquest, 80 percent of the Vietnamese population was functionally literate in the Chinese ideographs used for written Vietnamese. The French banned the Chinese characters and introduced either French or *quoc ngu*, the Latin alphabet, for the Vietnamese language. This proved to be a disaster. On the eve of the Second World War, less than one fifth of school-age Vietnamese boys were attending school. "The Vietnamese can speak their tongue but neither read nor write it. We have been manufacturing illiterates," commented one former governor general.[10]

Political repression was the rule in Vietnam. Any form of organized dissent against the colonial authorities was ruthlessly repressed. The handful of wealthy Vietnamese who sent their children to school in France had a rude awakening upon their return to Vietnam. Rights and privileges that they enjoyed in France ended in Vietnam. The colonial police confiscated books and newspapers deemed "subversive." One student was so enraged by his treatment upon his return to Vietnam that he told a judge at his trial that French injustice "turned me into a revolutionary."[11] The French *sûreté* (colonial police) hunted dissidents, tortured them, and imprisoned them at the notorious island fortress of Poulo Cordone with its infamous "tiger cages."

NATIONALISM AND COMMUNISM

> "At first, patriotism, not yet communism, led me to have confidence in Lenin, in the Third International."
> —Ho Chi Minh

By the beginning of the twentieth century, France was the master of all of Indochina. However, as historian James Gibson points out, "In attempting to grind colonial rule so deeply into Vietnamese culture, the French aroused resistance. Colonialism ruled Vietnam, but at the same time it created contradictions that weakened it."[12] Modern Vietnamese nationalism appeared in the first decade of the new century out of a dissident section of the mandarin class.

While the bulk of mandarins served the puppet emperors of the French, some began to question their role in colonial Vietnam. "Who lost Vietnam?" first arose as a burning question among the disaffected mandarins, who looked to the past for inspiration, while simultaneously looking to the modern West for knowledge to create a resistance movement. Two strains of thought emerged. Phan Boi

Chau, who believed that a strong emperor backed by the Chinese and Japanese could defeat the French, represented the first. His thinking was essentially feudal in outlook and aimed at restoring the power of the emperor, supported by his mandarins, in an independent Vietnam. He had almost nothing to say about the vast economic and social changes brought by French imperialism. Constantly hounded by the French *sûreté*, he lived in exile until he was arrested in 1925 at the age of fifty-eight. Tens of thousands of Vietnamese followed his trial and were angered by the death sentence that was handed down by French judges. It was later commuted. Phan Boi Chau died under house arrest in 1940.

Phan Chu Trinh represented a second current of emerging Vietnamese nationalism. He was the son of a rich landowner. Early in his life, he rallied to the side of dissident Empéror Ham Nghi. Later, he accompanied Phan Boi Chau to Japan, where he broke with him over the question of Japan's real intentions toward Indochina. Phan Chu Trinh returned to Vietnam and opened a modern school to teach children of both sexes, and he railed at the French for their hypocrisy. While he attacked the French, Phan Chu Trinh also believed that with the help of the French bureaucracy Vietnam could become a modern society. In 1908, the French closed his schools, arrested him, and sentenced him to death, but his death sentence was commuted to life in prison in Poulo Cordone. Released from prison after three years, Phan Chu Trinh symbolized resistance to the French for many educated Vietnamese. When he died in 1926, sixty thousand people marched in his funeral procession.[13]

While Phan Boi Chau and Phan Chu Trinh inspired many people who would later come to be involved in nationalist politics, their political movements remained small. The main reason for this was that their politics appealed to a very thin layer of educated middle-class Vietnamese. The end of both of their political lives in the 1920s coincided with a major turning point in the consciousness of the Vietnamese people. According to historian David Marr, "The twentieth-century history of Vietnam must be understood within the context of fundamental changes in political and social consciousness among a significant segment of the Vietnamese populace in the period of 1920–1945."[14] The major beneficiary of this would be the Communist Party (CP), led by Ho Chi Minh, which built up a mass base by linking the Vietnamese national struggle with the economic and social concerns of the peasantry, the intellectuals, and, to a lesser degree, the small working class.

Ho Chi Minh grew up in a nationalist household with a father who was also a disaffected mandarin. Ho's father hated both the French and the mandarin system. In 1908, when he was fifteen years old, Ho participated in demonstrations against the French. The savage repression that followed began to radicalize him and he started to attract the attention of the French police. Fearing arrest, he decided to leave the country in 1911. He got a job aboard a French ocean liner and headed for France. He would not return to Vietnam for thirty years. In 1917, he moved to Paris. By then the patriotic euphoria that gripped the European countries at the beginning of the First World War had been replaced by widespread antiwar sentiment. The revolutionary left began to revive and the impact of the Russian Revolution was just beginning to be felt. The very large Vietnamese community in France—numbering one hundred thousand people—was alive with political debate. Ho was at the right place at the right time. (He was then known as Nguyen Ai Quoc or Nguyen "the patriot.") Drawn to activists in the French Socialist Party, Ho very quickly became the leading Vietnamese activist in France.

In 1919, the Versailles peace conference met to discuss the settlement at the end of the First World War. Ho Chi Minh went there to petition for the rights of Vietnam. He was drawn to U.S. president

Woodrow Wilson's Fourteen Points program, which included the right of nations to self-determination. Ho stopped short of calling for independence for Vietnam, but in his appeal to the Versailles conference, he called for more democratic rights for the Vietnamese people, along with the release of all political prisoners. Ho tried to meet with the American delegation, but was turned away. Ho Chi Minh learned, like many colonial nationalists, that Wilson's call for self-determination was meant for European countries, not colonial peoples. Yet Ho Chi Minh's advocacy for the Vietnamese people at Versailles gained him enormous prestige that would last for decades.[15]

A year later, Ho was the Indochinese delegate to the French Socialist Party conference in Tours. The party was about to split between a majority who wanted to affiliate to the Communist International (Comintern) in Moscow and a minority that did not. While at the conference, Ho got a copy of Lenin's "Thesis on the National and Colonial Question." It had an enormous impact on him, primarily because, unlike the national chauvinist Second International, the thesis supported the right of oppressed nations to self-determination. "At first, patriotism, not yet Communism, led me to have confidence in Lenin, in the Third International. Step by step, along the struggle, by studying Marxism-Leninism parallel with participation in practical activities, I gradually came upon the fact that only socialism and communism can liberate oppressed nations," he told an interviewer in 1960. Ho joined the new French Communist Party and, after several more years of political activity in France, he left for Moscow in 1924.[16]

When Ho Chi Minh arrived in Moscow, the Comintern had been gradually degenerating into an arm of the emerging Stalinist bureaucracy's foreign policy. Stalin's new theory of "socialism in one country," the political expression of the rising bureaucracy, transformed socialism from one of working-class internationalism to one of nationalist state-led development. These changes had their most devastating impact on the Far East. Lenin had warned in his 1920 Comintern thesis that revolutionaries should not "merge" with "bourgeois democracy in the colonial and backward countries," and "should under all circumstances uphold the independence of the proletarian movement." Lenin warned specifically not to "give communist coloring to bourgeois-democratic liberation trends in the backward countries."[17] Stalin followed precisely the opposite policy in China.

China was in a revolutionary ferment in the mid-1920s. Instead of calling on Chinese workers to seize power in alliance with the rebellious poor peasants—as the Bolsheviks had done in Russia—Stalin compelled the Chinese Communist Party (CCP) to join Chiang Kai-shek's Kuomintang under an agreement that virtually tied the CCP's hands politically. Though the Kuomintang represented China's small corrupt and reactionary capitalist class, Chiang was feted for years by the Russian CP and given lavish aid and training to build up his army. China needed first to complete a bourgeois-nationalist phase of the revolution, it was now argued, before workers could fight for socialism. This "alliance" resulted in revolutionary workers and communist militants being massacred by Chiang in 1927.[18]

Ho Chi Minh was in China as a Comintern representative and witnessed Chiang Kai-shek's massacre, but he never raised any criticisms of Stalin's policies. He was to remain an uncritical Stalinist for the remainder of his life. Indeed, his communism was essentially radical nationalism with a red gloss. While in China, Ho trained several hundred Vietnamese in schools set up by the Comintern; they were to become the seeds of the Vietnamese communist movement.[19]

Meanwhile, political struggles began to revive in Vietnam in the mid-1920s. Several revolutionary groups emerged to organize peasants, workers, and intellectuals against the colonial regime. The small working class began to flex its muscles, starting with a strike movement begun in 1928 by Saigon brewery workers that was soon joined by petroleum workers, rubber workers, textile workers, and railroad workers. The worldwide economic depression, starting with the Wall Street stock market crash of 1929, hit Vietnam especially hard with widespread hunger and unemployment. Anger began to boil to the surface. It was symbolized by a failed rebellion of indigenous colonial troops in Vietnam.

Feeling the pressure to catch up with political developments in Vietnam, the fractured Vietnamese communist movement met in February 1930 at a unification conference in Hong Kong. During the conference, the three Vietnamese Communist Parties merged into one Indochinese Communist Party (ICP).[20] Ho Chi Minh convened the meeting. Among the points in its political program were the overthrow of French imperialism, complete independence of Vietnam, confiscation of wealth held by the French, the implementation of the eight-hour day, abolition of unjust taxes, universal education, and equality of the sexes.

The ICP immediately faced savage repression, resulting in the imprisonment and deaths of thousands of people. In the mid-1930s, the French made some concessions by opening up the election process. The French Popular Front government led by the socialist Léon Blum, which came to power in July 1936, ordered the release of thousands of Vietnamese political prisoners. In 1938, thousands marched in May Day parades led by the ICP and it began to emerge as a serious political force. In 1939, the atmosphere turned sharply with the election of a right-wing government in France. In Vietnam, repression against nationalists and communists was the order of the day. What was legal just a short time before was now illegal. The ICP was driven underground and some members fled to China. Vo Nguyen Giap, who led the Vietnamese troops from 1946–1980, lost almost all his immediate family, who died in prison. The French executed Ho's second wife. Yet a small Communist Party was still intact and world events were about to take a dramatic turn.[21]

WAR AND REVOLUTION

> "I have a government that is organized and ready to go. Your statesmen make eloquent speeches about helping those with self-determination. We are self-determined. Why not help us? Am I any different from Nehru, Quezon—even your George Washington? I, too, want my people free."
> —Ho Chi Minh, to an American OSS agent, summer 1945

For most Europeans and Americans, the Second World War began with the German invasion of Poland in 1939 or the Japanese attack on Pearl Harbor in December 1941. For the people of East Asia, it started with the Japanese invasion of China in 1931. While Japan proved itself to be just as ruthless in oppressing the people of East Asia as the Europeans and Americans were, its stunning military victories in the end destroyed the foundation of the old colonial empires.

It should be kept in mind that on the eve of the war almost all countries in East Asia, with the exception of Japan, were either colonies or semi-colonies ruled indirectly by one of the colonial powers. While Britain retained formal dominance in the area, the United States and Japan were challenging it. After the bombing of Pearl Harbor, the Japanese launched a massive invasion into most of Southeast Asia, sweeping away two hundred years of colonial rule in a matter of a few weeks. Japan tried to disguise its imperialism in grand slogans like, "Asia for Asians" and "East Asia co-prosperity sphere." Despite the false promise of liberation made by the Japanese, this was a stunning turn of events, nowhere more deeply felt than in Vietnam.[22]

In May 1940, Hitler attacked France. Within a month, the French government surrendered and a puppet government headed by the aging Marshal Philippe Pétain was set up in Vichy, France. The French colonialists in Vietnam were initially confused about what to do after the collapse of the French government. After a small skirmish with Japanese troops on September 22, 1940, French Governor General Jean Decoux surrendered Indochina to the Japanese, who were given unfettered access to Vietnam's ports and were allowed to station troops. However, the Japanese left the French in charge of administration. This was unique among the colonies occupied by the Japanese, where the former Dutch, British, and American colonialists were imprisoned by the Japanese. The French were collaborating with the Japanese in Indochina just as they collaborated with the Germans in occupied France. Now Vietnam had two masters, the Japanese and the French, both of whom were determined to destroy any opposition.

Ho Chi Minh returned to Vietnam in 1941, after thirty years abroad, to take direct charge of the struggle against the French and the Japanese. The ICP dissolved itself into "a broad National Front uniting not only workers, peasants, the petit bourgeois and the bourgeois, but also a number of patriotic landowners." The League for the Independence of Vietnam, known as the Vietminh, set as its goal the "overthrow of the Japanese fascists and the French imperialists" and the establishment of "a revolutionary government of the Democratic Republic of Vietnam."[23] Three years of guerrilla war ensued.

Other crucial events in 1941 would dramatically affect events in Vietnam. Following the German invasion of Russia and the Japanese attack on Pearl Harbor, the major players in the war dramatically changed. A "Grand Alliance of the Four Great Democracies"— Britain, China, the Soviet Union, and the United States—was formed to fight the Axis powers. This meant that the United States in particular had to cloak its imperialism in the guise of anticolonialism to combat Japanese influence in the Pacific. The United States argued that the right of nations to self-government agreed to in the Atlantic Charter must be applied to the world, not just Europe. Meanwhile, the Soviet Union instructed members of the Comintern to support the Allies in the "antifascist" war. This shift meant that the Vietminh developed a small but important working alliance with the United States in the war against Japan.[24]

While the French and the Japanese worked together to try to destroy the Vietminh, its popularity grew throughout the country. During the Japanese occupation, a famine broke out that could have easily been stopped if the Japanese and the French had moved stored rice and grain to needed areas. Instead, they allowed the famine to rage out of control. The Vietminh organized peasants and city residents to raid rice storage facilities and, as a result, their reputation soared even higher. However, in Tonkin, a major center of Vietminh resistance, a quarter of the population—two million people—died in the famine. It was one of the great acts of colonial genocide in the twentieth century.

In July 1944, Allied troops marched into Paris and the Vichy government collapsed. Eight months later, the Japanese unilaterally ended French rule in Indochina. The war was decisively turning against the Axis powers, and total defeat was only a short time away. The Japanese, in a last-ditch effort to rally support, proclaimed an "independent Vietnam," with Emperor Bao Dai as its head of state. It was at this time that the first agents of the American Office of Strategic Services (OSS, the immediate predecessor agency to the CIA) arrived in Vietnam. Their mission was to provide military training to the Vietminh, while the Vietminh agreed to help locate and rescue downed Allied pilots in Vietnam. Many of the OSS agents developed enormous sympathy for the Vietnamese struggle for independence and a deep hatred for the French and colonialism.

The Vietminh moved quickly to take advantage of the fast-changing situation. Writes historian Marilyn Young:

> During the five-month interlude between the Japanese coup and the end of the Pacific War, the Vietminh base in Cao Bang expanded to include six provinces in northern Vietnam. In this "liberated zone,"

entirely new local governments were established, self-defense forces recruited, taxes abolished, rents reduced and, in some places, land that belonged to French landlords was seized and redistributed. Above all, the Vietminh acted to alleviate the famine then raging in the North by opening local granaries and distributing rice.[25]

The August Revolution began on August 13, 1945, when the Vietminh issued orders to its military wing and a call to the Vietnamese people to immediately launch a general insurrection. Between August 14 and 18, the Vietminh took power over the administrative centers of almost every village and district and in twenty-seven provinces. The big cities of Hanoi, Hue, and Saigon took a few more days to fall, but it was virtually a bloodless revolution. On August 30, Emperor Bao Dai, installed as the figurehead of "independent Vietnam," abdicated his office. "I prefer to be a citizen of an independent nation rather than to be a king of an enslaved country," he remarked.[26] He then handed over the gold seal and sword symbolizing royal power to a representative of the provisional government of the Vietminh and declared the abolition of the monarchy.

On September 2, Ho Chi Minh proclaimed the independence of Vietnam and the formation of the Provisional Government of the Democratic Republic of Vietnam to a crowd of two hundred thousand people in Hanoi, including members of the American OSS. Vietnam was one of the first colonies to declare independence following the end of the war. The opening line of Ho's speech paraphrased the American Declaration of Independence—"All men are created equal. They are endowed by their Creator with certain inalienable rights: among these are Life, Liberty, and the pursuit of Happiness."[27] Ho was more than just paying homage to the American Revolution; he was hoping to rely on the Americans to keep the French from returning to Vietnam. After all, in the minds of the Vietminh, they had been loyal allies in the war, while the French collaborated with the Japanese. Who should better curry America's favor?[28]

If the story had ended there, with the United States recognizing Vietnam's independence, then more than fifty eight thousand Americans and three million Vietnamese would not have died in the following two wars. It was not to be.

THE FIRST WAR IN VIETNAM

> "Cochinchina is burning, the French and the British are finished here, and we [the Americans] ought to clear out of Southeast Asia."
> —OSS Lieutenant Colonel Peter Dewey's last message to OSS command, September 1945

A ravaged postwar France was in no position to reassert its colonial prerogatives in Indochina; to accomplish this, they needed and got the help of the British and the Americans. For all the U.S. talk of self-government, it was going to support recolonization. Why? As U.S. policy makers shifted their attention from the defeat of the Axis powers to a looming confrontation with the Soviet Union in Europe, they needed a strong and loyal France. At the May 1945 United Nations conference in San Francisco, Roosevelt's secretary of state Edward Stettinius made clear to France's foreign minister that the United States did not question "French sovereignty over Indochina."[29] The foot in the door for the French return was the landing of Allied forces to force the surrender of Japanese troops, a landing that the Vietminh initially welcomed.

At the Potsdam conference in July 1945, the Allies agreed that Chinese nationalists were to occupy and accept the surrender of Japanese troops north of the 16th parallel (a line that ran about midpoint between north and south of the country), while British troops were to do the same south of the 16th parallel. Chinese nationalist troops started entering Vietnam in late August 1945, just before Ho's declaration of independence. By mid-September there were more than two hundred thousand Chinese troops in Tonkin. In the south,

British General Douglas Gracey arrived in Saigon on September 22, 1945, with a detachment of Indian troops. At this time, no government in the world recognized Vietnam's independence or Ho's government in Hanoi.

The British, who were acutely aware of the possibility of their own empire coming apart at the end of the war, had a vested interest in helping the French reestablish their presence in Indochina. Soon after the British arrived, they released and rearmed 1,500 French troops who had been imprisoned by the Japanese and were kept in custody by the Vietminh. Soon after their release, French soldiers—with the support of Gracey—attacked Vietminh offices. French residents began assaulting and killing Vietnamese on the streets of Saigon. The Vietminh counterattacked on September 24, 1945. OSS Lieutenant Colonel Peter Dewey was killed that night outside of Saigon—the first American to die in Vietnam. In his last message to OSS command, he issued his warning that "we ought to clear out of Southeast Asia."[30]

Gracey needed more troops to get control of Saigon and to begin to take the surrounding countryside from the Vietminh. While he conducted negotiations with the Vietminh, his Indian troop strength was increased to ten thousand soldiers, and the first one thousand French combat troops under Marshal Leclerc arrived armed and equipped by the Americans. The Vietminh, realizing that the talks with Gracey were a cover for bringing more troops, attacked the Franco-British forces but were driven out of Saigon. To augment British and French forces even further, Gracey authorized the arming of Japanese prisoners of war to help suppress the Vietminh.

Gracey's coup should go down as one of the great acts of deceit and betrayal in modern history. He sponsored a coup against the Vietminh (who had been allies in the war against the Japanese) to put the French (who had collaborated with the Japanese and the Germans) back in power with the help of the recently defeated enemy—

Japanese soldiers. Gracey's shameless actions were all taken with the connivance of the U.S. government.[31]

But the Vietminh also helped create confusion by initially welcoming the British landing. For this, they were denounced by the Vietnamese Trotskyist International Communist League, who at the war's end organized dozens of working-class Popular Action Committees throughout Saigon that called for armed resistance against the landing of Allied troops, and for the arming of workers and peasants. Two days after Gracey's troops landed in Saigon, the Vietminh police chief in Saigon began rounding up and arresting Trotskyists. The Vietminh wanted to negotiate with the imperialists, urging a "moderate" course, and was explicitly opposed to turning the national struggle into a class struggle against the Vietnamese landlords and capitalists. In the months that followed, the Vietminh murdered the leadership of the Trotskyist movement, thereby gaining unchallenged control of the nationalist movement.[32]

Despite Gracey's coup, the French were very far from regaining full control of their colonial possession. The Vietminh still controlled most of the country, and the Chinese nationalists had a huge presence in Tonkin. Jean Sainteny, the French envoy, and Marshal Leclerc decided to enter into negotiations with the Vietminh to buy time to build up their strength. Ho Chi Minh and the Vietminh then made a series of disastrous decisions. In March 1946, they agreed to French terms. The substance of the agreement was that Vietnam would only get minimal rights inside the French Union, while Cochinchina would hold a referendum to decide its fate. The French military would reenter Hanoi and the Chinese would leave. Ho justified all this by saying it was a way of getting rid of the Chinese: "I'd rather sniff French shit for five years than eat Chinese for a thousand."[33]

However, a double cross was in the works. While Ho and a Vietminh delegation were heading to France in 1946, the French resurrected Bao Dai and proclaimed him emperor of a new nation based in Cochinchina. The French then refused to recognize the tiny ministate, the Democratic Republic of Vietnam (DRV) in Tonkin. In October 1946, after a clash between French and Vietminh military forces, the French Prime Minister Georges Bidault ordered the shelling of Haiphong, killing six thousand Vietnamese. The order to shell Haiphong was cosigned by the French deputy prime minister and head of the French Communist Party Maurice Thorez. The first war in Vietnam had begun with the support of the French Communist Party.

U.S. aid to the French began in 1947 with financial credits totaling $160 million. During Truman's second administration, from June 1950 through December 31, 1952, "539,847 tons of American military equipment, valued at $334.7 million, was funneled to the French.... The total cost for such U.S. war materiel sent during the Truman administrations to the French in Indochina amounted to $775.7 million."[34] By the end of the war in 1954, it was tallied that the United States had financed almost 80 percent of the French war effort ($2.763 billion).[35] The United States also provided three hundred airforce maintenance personnel.[36]

Ho's government was forced to abandon Hanoi without receiving diplomatic recognition—not even from Russia. Ho Chi Minh was forced to acknowledge that all his maneuverings had achieved disaster. "We apparently stand quite alone; we shall have to depend on ourselves."[37]

The French had early success, but then got bogged down. The Vietminh had the allegiance of the population, particularly the peasantry—something that the French could not break. The war was unpopular in France. To ease the opposition, French officials didn't impose conscription and instead relied heavily on forty thousand Legionnaires, more than half of whom fought for the Nazis in the

Second World War. Indeed, a majority of France's more than five hundred thousand troops in Indochina in 1953 were not French (only 80,000 were) but Vietnamese and North African. The French were able to control the cities and towns, but the Vietminh (which had an estimated 290,000 troops in 1953) held sway in the country-side.[38] In 1949, the war shifted decisively against the French. Because of the Chinese Revolution, the Vietminh would now be able to re-ceive direct military aid from Mao Zedong's government.

In 1950, Russia and China finally recognized Ho Chi Minh's gov-ernment, breaking its diplomatic isolation. On the military front, the French continued to suffer heavy losses. By 1953, the French ca-sualty rate totaled 148,000, despite claims that victory was around the corner.[39] The war was becoming increasingly unpopular in France. Hoping for a decisive victory over the Vietminh, in late 1953 they picked a spot for what they hoped would be a decisive con-frontation. It was a remote outpost on the Laotian border called Dien Bien Phu. What the French got instead was a 57-day siege—in which they were outmanned, outgunned, and outgeneraled by Vo Nguyen Giap—that ended in their complete defeat and surrender on May 7, 1954. After nine bloody years, the French war was over.

THE GENEVA CONFERENCE AND ACCORDS

"The Geneva Conference…was merely an interlude between two wars—
or, rather, a lull in the same war."
—Stanley Karnow

As the battle raged at Dien Bien Phu, a conference was already planned to take place in Geneva, Switzerland, in July 1954 to deal with issues left over from the recently finished Korean War. The at-tendees at this conference were the United States, Britain, France, Russia, and China. Vietnam was added to the agenda following the French surrender. However, the "Geneva Conference produced no durable solution to the Indochina conflict, only a military truce that awaited a political settlement, which never really happened. So the conference was merely an interlude between two wars—or, rather, a lull in the same war." [40]

It had been originally part of France's plan that after their anticipated victory at Dien Bien Phu they would go to Geneva in a position of strength and get a settlement beneficial to themselves and their Vietnamese collaborators. Now, the Vietnamese nationalists were in a position of strength. Yet at Geneva, Ho Chi Minh would once again make a series of disastrous decisions that would only delay Vietnam's independence and set the stage for the next war.

President Eisenhower's secretary of state, John Foster Dulles, a fanatical anticommunist, represented the United States. Dulles was committed to preventing any other nationalist movements from taking power. The Chinese Revolution of 1949 had already humiliated the United States and the three-year Korean War had left the Americans with an unhappy stalemate. The United States had contemplated direct intervention at Dien Bien Phu to save the French, and was continuing to make threats to intervene after the French surrender. While the economic importance of Vietnam was not significant, it assumed a vital political importance that would underpin U.S. policy for the next twenty years. According to Dulles, if nothing was done to halt communism in Indochina, "it was only a question of time until all of Southeast Asia falls along with Indonesia, thus imperiling our western island defense." [41] Dulles was therefore committed to denying the Vietminh the full fruits of their victory. In this, an unlikely ally, the Chinese, would help Dulles.

The Chinese policy at Geneva, formulated by Chou En-lai, was motivated by a desire to avoid a further military conflict with the United States after having fought a very bloody war in Korea with them for three years. The irony of this situation is that the United

States was in an extremely difficult position to intervene in Vietnam in the mid-1950s. It had just finished a very unpopular war in Korea, the French were on the run, and the potential U.S. allies in Vietnam were weak and discredited by collaborating with the French and the Japanese. Nonetheless, the Chinese brought enormous pressure to bear on the Vietnamese to make major concessions.

The Geneva Accords signed by the Vietminh delegation and the French agreed to the following: Vietnam would be divided into two troop regroupment zones along the 17th parallel, with a demilitarized zone separating them. The divide was stipulated as strictly temporary, pending elections in two years to decide who would run a unified Vietnam—while Laos and Cambodia would become independent countries. Though the United States never signed the accords, it said that it would abide by them. But the United States was only buying time; its own intelligence at the time admitted that in any freely held election Ho Chi Minh and the Vietminh would win 80 percent of the vote. U.S. policy set out to stop the mandated elections and build an anticommunist state in South Vietnam.[42]

FROM NATION-BUILDING TO ASSASSINATION

"South Vietnam is today a quasi-police state characterized by arbitrary arrests and imprisonment, strict censorship of the press, and the absence of an effective political opposition…."
—William Henderson in *Foreign Affairs*, January 1957

The United States set out to build an anticommunist state in South Vietnam in direct violation of the Geneva Accords, though at the time it was not clear at all whether it would succeed in its efforts. While the United States initially did succeed in creating a ministate in South Vietnam, the regime it created proved so unpopular and unstable that only the direct intervention of American troops could keep it from collapsing.

For the French, the settlement at Geneva was the road out of Indochina. They left behind a devastated country and corrupt allies grouped around Emperor Bao Dai and a colonial army officer corps. The United States quickly stepped into this situation and used the remnants of the French colonial state to begin building a new one. The United States convinced Emperor Bao Dai to appoint Ngo Dinh Diem as president of the new Republic of Vietnam. Diem was a Catholic mystic who had been living in the United States, and had cultivated powerful friends such as Cardinal Spellman and Senator John F. Kennedy.[43]

The state that the United States built in South Vietnam during the 1950s was a brutal, corrupt dictatorship around the Diem family—very similar to the regimes of the Duvaliers in Haiti, the Somoza family in Nicaragua, and the Marcoses in the Philippines. Diem's brother, Nhu, would become head of the secret police, while his other brother was the Catholic bishop of Hue. Though Diem was praised by many liberals in the United States as the best hope for freedom and democracy, he saw himself as a modern day emperor. In his own words, "A sacred respect is due to the person of the sovereign. He is the mediator between the people and heaven as he celebrates the national cult." During another interview he described himself as a "Spanish Catholic," at a time when Spanish Catholics were closely identified with Francisco Franco's fascist dictatorship.[44] He held a rigged referendum on his rule in 1955, after which he announced that he had won 98.2 percent of the vote.[45]

Diem's immediate goal was gaining control of his capital city. The CIA sent a team led by Colonel Edward Lansdale to help Diem launch a war for the control of Saigon, defeating a bizarre collection of gangsters and armed religious groups. Then Lansdale turned his attention to covert action in North Vietnam. He helped create the flight of nearly one million Catholic refugees to South Vietnam.

Many of these refugees became the political base, along with landowners, former French collaborators, and the local bourgeoisie, for Diem's anticommunist government. Diem then unleashed a wave of terror against supporters of the Vietminh. Tens of thousands were jailed or killed, virtually wiping out their presence in many areas by the late 1950s. Diem's government's own figures— which most likely underestimated the numbers—reported that they had placed up to twenty thousand Vietminh supporters in detention camps and had jailed 48,250 people between 1954 and 1960.[46] In one district of 180,000 people, 7,000 were imprisoned and another 13,000 simply disappeared.[47]

Diem carried out a counterrevolution in the countryside by using the power of the state to return the rich landlords to power. At the same time, U.S. military and economic aid poured into the country, creating a garrison state and a new corrupt business class loyal to Diem. As opposition grew to Diem in the late 1950s, he increased the repression, symbolized by Law 10/59, that allowed the Saigon government to jail any oppositionists under the allegation of "communist activity." By 1960, Diem's regime was so corrupt, isolated, and hated by the mass of the population that widespread opposition began to emerge. Former Vietminh cadre began to rebuild their decimated ranks in the countryside and resume the armed struggle. Opposition to Diem exploded on the street, led by Buddhist monks who had suffered at the hands of Diem's strident Catholic regime.[48]

During the latter half of the 1950s, Ho Chi Minh and his Workers' Party (formerly the Vietminh), spent the bulk of their time consolidating their regime in the northern half of the country. Their response to the atrocities committed by Diem and the open disregard for the Geneva Accords was to publicly commit themselves to their implementation. This, however, became increasingly impossible to do. Tens of thousands of Vietminh fighters, political organiz-ers, and their families, who went north after the accords were signed, as well as those who remained in the south, were a constant pressure on Ho's regime to do something.

In 1959, Ho Chi Minh finally committed to liberate the south from Diem's dictatorship and his U.S. master. In 1960, the National Liberation Front (NLF) of South Vietnam was formed, an umbrella organization combining opponents of the Diem regime with the supporters of the Communist Party, which was the paramount po-litical formation within it. It was committed to a program of demo-cratic reform and eventual reunification of the country. This program was to be achieved by armed struggle in the countryside based on the support of the rural population. Very quickly the NLF (later derisively called the Viet Cong by U.S. forces) became a serious political force. In 1960, the NLF had five thousand armed guerrillas, which by the end of 1961 had grown to fifteen thousand. The CIA reported that, a year later, the NLF was in control of most of the South Vietnamese countryside.

John F. Kennedy, one of Diem's earliest supporters, assumed the U.S. presidency in 1961, and quickly realized that Diem was facing disaster. Kennedy's response was to increase the number of military and civilian advisers and pressure Diem to broaden the base of his government. But Diem refused to share power and increased the re-pression inside the country.

The Kennedy administration turned South Vietnam into a labo-ratory for counterinsurgency techniques. These included a massive project to evaluate the effectiveness of herbicidal warfare. Operation Ranch Hand was begun by dropping defoliants from airplanes in 1962 and didn't stop until eight years and one hundred million pounds of herbicides later. Its slogan was: "Only we can prevent forests."[49] The "strategic hamlet" program, a policy of using massive military incursions to clear the guerrillas from an area, round up the remaining population at gunpoint, and herd them into guarded compounds, began in March 1962. The aim was to drain the ocean (the people) of the fish (the guerrillas). But the pilot project, dubbed Operation Sunshine, resulted in the NLF taking over the areas where the population had been resettled.[50]

Diem's government continued to spiral downward, its base of support becoming unsustainably thin. It was clear that Diem had to go or the NLF would soon be in power. However, Diem was also becoming aware that the Americans wanted to get rid of him. In a final effort to save himself, he had his brother Nhu approach the North Vietnamese about a political rapprochement. That was the last straw for Kennedy. He ordered the CIA to overthrow Diem's government. Diem was overthrown by his own military on November 2, 1963. Diem and his brother Nhu were assassinated. Two weeks later, Kennedy was assassinated in Dallas. During Kennedy's tenure in office the number of American military "advisers" grew from eight hundred to sixteen thousand seven hundred.[51]

CHAPTER TWO

FROM THE OVERTHROW OF DIEM
TO THE TET OFFENSIVE

From the end of the Second World War to 1965, the United States attempted to prevent the triumph of the nationalist forces in Vietnam without the large-scale use of its own troops. U.S. administrations tried to do this by first supporting the French in their failed effort to reconquer their former colony, which, under the leadership of the Vietminh, had declared independence following the end of the war. After the defeat of the French at the battle of Dien Bien Phu in 1954, the U.S. strategy was to partition Vietnam along the 17th parallel and create an anticommunist puppet state in the southern half of the country around the figure of Ngo Dinh Diem.

The Geneva Accords had stipulated that the country would quickly be reunited after national elections. U.S. policy, however, aimed at making the 17th parallel a permanent dividing line. As historian Marilyn Young notes, U.S. propaganda in support of its intervention in Vietnam "cast Vietnamese who lived and worked north of the 17th parallel as more foreign to South Vietnam than the Americans, for the Americans were invited as guests, while North Vietnam was an enemy country."[1] Though the war was one of Vietnamese national liberation against American aggression, U.S. propaganda persistently presented the war as one between North Vietnam and South Vietnam. While this strategy was initially successful, by the early 1960s it was in complete disarray, as the population of South Vietnam turned increasingly to open rebellion against the Diem regime.

By the end of 1963, the Kennedy administration decided that Diem had to go in order to forestall the collapse of the Saigon government. Diem and his brother Nhu, head of the secret police, were overthrown and assassinated in a military coup directed by the CIA and U.S. ambassador to South Vietnam Henry Cabot Lodge.[2] Despite the removal of the Diem family, who had become a political liability, the Saigon government continued to spiral downward and the revolutionary movement led by the National Liberation Front of South Vietnam (NLF) continued to move forward. Diem's removal from power set off over a year of political instability that would eventually lead to the direct U.S. invasion of South Vietnam in 1965.

REGIME CHANGES IN SAIGON

> "The emergence of an exceptional leader could
> improve the situation and no George Washington is in sight."
> —General Maxwell Taylor, U.S. ambassador to South Vietnam, September 1964

Lyndon Johnson became president of the United States after the assassination of John F. Kennedy in November 1963. Johnson inherited two things from the Kennedy administration concerning Vietnam. One was a rapidly deteriorating situation in South Vietnam, with an NLF victory on the immediate horizon. The second was a coterie of advisers who had presided over America's deepening involvement in Vietnam and who were now arguing for an even more dramatic escalation of U. S. involvement. Among these advisers were Defense Secretary William McNamara, Secretary of State Dean Rusk, and National Security Advisers Walt Rostow and McGeorge Bundy. These were the men who would eventually take the United States into total war in Vietnam, but in the meantime they struggled with finding the "right man" to lead the Saigon government.

Despite the removal of Diem, the Saigon government remained on the verge of collapse. It was plagued by a series of military coups following Diem's assassination, sponsored by the United States, which further weakened it politically and militarily. Diem's immediate successor was General Duong Van Minh, known as "Big Minh." Many people in South Vietnam initially greeted his government with much approval and hope. Minh infuriated the Americans by making a rapprochement with the Buddhist forces that had organized massive demonstrations against the Diem regime. He began talking about possibly opening talks with the NLF. Minh also began to describe his government as "noncommunist" as opposed to "anticommunist," and raised the possibility of his government adopting a diplomatic position of "neutrality" in world affairs. This was clearly not what the Americans wanted from a military coup.[3]

Soon after, the Americans spearheaded another military coup, this time organized by the Military Assistance Command—Vietnam, the main body that U.S. military aid and "advisers" were organized through in Vietnam. This coup, at the end of January 1964, has gone down in the history books as the "Pentagon Coup," and it brought to power General Nguyen Khanh. Nguyen seemed to be what the Americans wanted. He was committed to fighting the war against the NLF, and seemed wholeheartedly to accept military and political strategies emanating from the U.S. embassy. However, he immediately ran into a renewed wave of antiwar activity from the Buddhists and radical students of South Vietnam. Nguyen was completely thrown off balance by this and began to talk about a negotiated end to the war. In fact, the CIA learned that Nguyen had contacted the NLF in December 1964, and had had more serious contacts with them in January and February 1965. Clearly, he also had to go.[4]

The Americans, led by the new U.S. ambassador, Maxwell Taylor, a retired general who returned to government service under Kennedy, brought enormous pressure to bear on Nguyen, who subsequently left Vietnam for exile in France. Power now passed to the military triumvirate of Generals Nguyen Cao Ky, Nguyen Chanh Thi, and Nguyen Van Thieu. The leading figure was Ky, who became prime minister (Thieu became chief of state). Ky would hold onto power until 1967, when elections excluding anyone holding "procommunist" or "neutralist" views delivered Ky's position to Thieu, who won with only 35 percent of the vote. Ky first came to the attention of the United States by working for the CIA in covert operations against North Vietnam in the early 1960s. He would later embarrass the United States by telling reporters that his only real hero was Hitler. Ky and Thieu were both trained by the French and had fought against their own people in the First Vietnam War. If this wasn't enough to prove their loyalty to the Americans, they pledged, on March 1, 1965, that they would never negotiate with the NLF or the North Vietnamese. They also made it clear that they would follow the lead of Washington on all military, political, and diplomatic affairs.[5]

While military coups wracked Saigon throughout 1964 and 1965, a much deeper crisis was brewing in South Vietnam. By mid-1964, the various military and political strategies developed by the United States for combating the NLF were at a dead end. "Viet Cong" forces—as the United States insisted on calling the nationalists—controlled 40 percent to 50 percent of the countryside. U.S.-sponsored counterinsurgency tactics, rather than strengthening the regime, were turning the mass of the peasantry against it. The strategic hamlet program, in which peasants were forcibly uprooted from their traditional villages and burial grounds and concentrated into walled camps, was a disaster. These villages were essentially concentration camps designed to separate the peasant population from the guerrillas. Where they were not torn apart by internal dissention, they were overrun by NLF fighters. Army of the Republic of Vietnam troops (ARVN–Diem's forces) deserted in droves, unwilling to defend the regime. Marine pacification expert Lieutenant Colonel William R. Corson admitted that the role of the U.S. puppet regime in South Vietnam was "to loot, collect back taxes, reinstall landlords, and conduct reprisals against the people."[6]

Historian James Gibson summed up the situation:

> Strategic hamlets had failed…. The South Vietnamese regime was incapable of winning the peasantry because of its class base among landlords. Indeed, there was no longer a "regime" in the sense of a relatively stable political alliance and functioning bureaucracy. Instead, civil government and military operations had virtually ceased. The National Liberation Front had made great progress and was close to declaring provisional revolutionary governments in large areas.[7]

Finding the "right man" would not do away with these fundamental issues that at the end of the day strengthened the NLF and weakened the already weak Saigon government—class inequality, the absence of basic democratic rights, and a strong desire for the reunification of Vietnam.

The war was quickly moving beyond being a proxy war funded by the United States to becoming a full-fledged American war. By 1962, the Kennedy administration had boosted the number of U.S. military advisers to more than fifteen thousand and had authorized them to lead combat missions. By this time, U.S. pilots were also bombing North Vietnam. Despite all this, the South Vietnamese government continued to lose the war against the NLF. In the face of these mounting defeats, U.S. intelligence reported that the Saigon government was on the verge of abandoning its five northern provinces altogether.[8] A fundamental shift in American policy was about to take place.

MANUFACTURING AN EXCUSE FOR WAR

> "A lie is a lie...and it's supposed to be a criminal act if said under oath,
> but Mr. Johnson wasn't under oath when he said it."
> —Senator William Fulbright, chairman of the Senate Foreign Relations
> Committee, on the Tonkin Gulf incident[9]

The new escalation of American involvement in Vietnam was taking place during a presidential election year. The 1964 election would ultimately pit the sitting Democratic President Lyndon Johnson, running as a "peace candidate," against the right-wing Republican Senator Barry Goldwater, who was considered by many people to be a dangerous right-wing extremist. "We are not about to send American boys nine or ten thousand miles away from home to do what Asian boys ought to be doing for themselves," Johnson assured his supporters. [10] But despite these promises, the Johnson administration was planning behind the scenes to introduce hundreds of thousands of U.S. ground troops into South Vietnam after the election. "Just let me get elected," Johnson told a meeting of the Joint Chiefs of Staff at the end of 1963, "and then you can have your war."[11] Like many of the decisions made about U.S. policy toward Vietnam, this one was concealed from the public. This was the beginning of the famous "credibility gap" that developed between what the Johnson administration stated as its policy toward Vietnam and what it actually did.[12]

The large-scale introduction of U.S. combat troops would mark a fundamental shift in American policy. Most Americans at this point were unaware of the deep involvement of their country in the war in Vietnam. Sending tens of thousands, if not hundreds of thousands of U.S. troops to Vietnam, as some in the Johnson administration and the military were contemplating, would require both public support and some form of congressional authorization. A resolution had already been drafted in early 1964 by the State Department for that purpose, but was shelved because of election year considerations.[13] What was required was an "incident" to arouse both public and congressional support for war, preferably an attack on U.S. forces.[14] The incident that they were looking for came in early August 1964 in the Gulf of Tonkin off the coast of Vietnam, and it came about as a result of one of the many covert operations the United States was carrying out against North Vietnam.

On July 30, 1964, the CIA and South Vietnamese military were engaged in covert operations against North Vietnam called "34A Ops." All covert operations against North Vietnamese were run by a secret White House committee called the 303 Committee. The purpose of these operations was to identify and destroy North Vietnamese coastal radar stations. To do this, U.S. Navy destroyers were ordered to patrol well within what the North Vietnamese regarded as their territorial waters to force the North Vietnamese to turn on their radar. These patrolling operations were called "DeSoto." Once these sites were identified, the CIA agents and South Vietnamese commandos would move in and destroy them. On August 2, the navy destroyer USS *Maddox* was attacked by North Vietnamese patrol boats while on one of these DeSoto patrols. The *Maddox* sank one North Vietnamese patrol boat, while fighter jets from the U.S. aircraft carrier *Ticonderoga* damaged two others.[15] On August 3, 1964, U.S. naval forces carried out more South Vietnamese raids during the night.

During the following night, the *Maddox* reported that it was under persistent attack from North Vietnamese patrol torpedo boats, but its radar could find no target except the USS *Turner Joy*, which it almost fired on. The *Turner Joy* did not hear any torpedoes, nor did its radar find any targets, but it fired anyway. Commodore John J. Herrick, the commander of the two-destroyer flotilla in the Tonkin Gulf, reported it "doubtful" that U.S. forces were fired upon, blaming the incident on "freak weather effects on radar and overeager sonarmen." Reporting "no actual visual sightings by *Maddox*," Herrick recommended a "complete evaluation before further action taken."[16] While Herrick was doubtful about the whole encounter and wanted, in his own words, a "complete evaluation," Johnson had the incident that he desired. Though Johnson remarked later that, "For all I know, our navy was shooting at whales out there," he wasn't about to admit it then. [17] Johnson immediately announced that American ships had been involved in an unprovoked attack in international waters and ordered U.S. aircraft to "retaliate" against North Vietnam on the night of August 4.

Johnson also called for congressional approval of the Tonkin Gulf Resolution. On August 7, 1965, the Senate voted 98 to 2 and the House of Representatives voted 441 to 0 in favor of the resolution. [18] The resolution allowed Johnson "to take all necessary measures to repel any armed attack against the forces of the United States and to prevent further aggression."[19] Congress did not repeal it until 1971. Johnson then had the legal authority to wage the expanded war that he wanted in Vietnam. He waited until after the November 1964 election to invade South Vietnam. The marines landed in Danang on March 8, 1965—the beginning of a U.S. troop buildup that would eventually number more than five hundred thousand soldiers. Seven years of war followed, as the strongest military machine on earth unleashed its savage fury on one of the poorest countries in the world.

THE PRICE OF EMPIRE

> "Surrender anywhere threatens defeat everywhere."
> —Lyndon Johnson, 1964

Why did the United States choose the course of total war in Vietnam? Why did they believe they could win a war against a nationalist movement that defeated the French a decade earlier? Inside the

Kennedy and Johnson administrations it was recognized that the client regime created by them was highly unstable and enormously unpopular. In sharp contrast, the popularity of the NLF was acknowledged and its military capabilities taken very seriously. Why didn't the U.S. government accept something short of total victory—such as the various proposals for a coalition government and neutrality in Saigon? The NLF itself was prepared to accept such a proposal. In fact, Charles De Gaulle, president of France, was proposing such a plan for all of Southeast Asia at the time.

The Johnson administration chose war because anything less than a total victory of U.S. imperialism would be seen as a defeat. As Lyndon Johnson put it in 1964, "Surrender anywhere threatens defeat everywhere."[20] This wasn't some peculiar perspective of Johnson and his advisers; it flowed from the position that the United States found itself in after the Second World War as the guardian of the capitalist world. The United States emerged from the war as the dominant capitalist country, with a string of military bases circling the globe. Like the British Empire in the nineteenth century, it would find itself embroiled in conflicts and wars in remote parts of the globe in order to ensure that its "credibility" was not undermined. The failure of the United States to intervene could be taken as a sign of weakness by its chief rival, the USSR, or by indigenous national liberation movements. Vietnam was the weakest link in the chain of American imperialism during the Kennedy and Johnson years.[21]

Soon after Kennedy's inauguration in 1961, General Edward Lansdale met with Kennedy and Walt Rostow and presented a report on the deteriorating situation in South Vietnam. The thrust of Lansdale's report was to urge increased support for the Diem regime. Kennedy, turning to Rostow, said: "This is the worst one we've got, isn't it?"[22] After the botched Bay of Pigs invasion of Cuba and after being bullied by Russian Premier Nikita Krushchev at the Vienna summit, Kennedy was determined not have another defeat on his hands. Kennedy wanted to reestablish U.S. "credibility" in the world. In his own words, "Now we have a problem in making our power credible, and Vietnam is the place."[23]

Kennedy escalated U.S. involvement in South Vietnam to the point where the United States was essentially fighting a proxy war on the ground. After the Cuban missile crisis in October 1962, the Vietnam question became magnified even more through the lens of superpower rivalry. "The Cuban crisis did not so much ease the Cold War as direct it into channels, ones less likely to produce nuclear conflict," according to military historian Michael Sherry.[24] The stabilization of a pro-American regime in Saigon or a victory of the National Liberation Front would have a dramatic impact on the ability of the United States to influence Third World nations.

The Kennedy administration set the course from which Johnson could not stray. In March 1965, John McNaughton, assistant secretary of defense, was asked by his boss, Robert McNamara, to summarize U.S. political strategy and war aims in Vietnam. McNaughton began by attacking any support for a political settlement in Vietnam that would lead to a U.S. withdrawal. This, he argued, would "be regarded in Asia, and particularly among our friends, as just as humiliating a defeat as any other form." He went on to summarize U.S. war aims: "U.S. aims: 70 percent—To avoid a humiliating defeat (to our reputation as a guarantor). 20 percent—To keep SVN (and then adjacent) territory from Chinese hands. 10 percent—To permit the people of SVN to enjoy a better, freer way of life."[25] This sentiment was also echoed by Ambassador Maxwell Taylor. "If we leave Vietnam with our tail between our legs," he wrote, "the consequences of this defeat in the rest of Asia, Africa and Latin America will be disastrous."[26]

While the United States believed it faced enormous difficulties in Vietnam, it was sure that it could overcome these difficulties through the sheer weight of its enormous economic and military power. Rostow exuded the arrogance of this way of thinking when he wrote in 1964 that victory in Vietnam "flows from the simple fact that at this stage in history we are the greatest power in the world—if we behave like it."[27] Michael Sherry sums up the mindset of the Kennedy and Johnson administrations: "What defined the arrogance of leaders was not blindness to such difficulties but confidence that they could overcome them. They were both desperate and arrogant—but not about the same things: fearful about South Vietnam, but sure about American power."[28]

While Vietnam did not have any direct economic or strategic importance to the United States—without a great natural resource like oil or a command of vital sea lanes, like the Panama Canal—it took on great political importance. Success or failure there involved what American political leaders would call "credibility," "resolve," or "commitment" at different points in time. War in Vietnam was the price to be paid for having a global empire and an arrogant leadership who believed that they could bully anybody into line. Though it tried to justify its intervention in Vietnam by saying that it was fighting foreign "communist aggression" against South Vietnam directed by Moscow and Beijing, the only aggressors and foreigners in Vietnam were Americans.

THE AMERICAN WAY OF WAR

> "The American way of war is particularly violent, deadly and dreadful. We believe in using 'things'—artillery, bombs, massive firepower."
> —General Fred C. Weyand, assistant to General William Westmoreland, commander of U.S. forces in Vietnam

Every major war has one or two enduring images that last long after the conflict has faded into history. The war in Vietnam has left us with a kaleidoscope of images. Among them: the massive B-52 carpet-bombings of North Vietnam; Vietnamese children running naked with their flesh scorched by napalm; American soldiers burning down villages with Zippo lighters; and the summary execution of a suspected Viet Cong fighter by the Saigon police chief. This kaleidoscope of images is the memory for most people of the "deadly and dreadful" war that America brought to Vietnam.[29]

When the United States invaded and occupied South Vietnam beginning in 1965, the NLF controlled most of the countryside. Regular combat units of the North Vietnamese Army had been fighting alongside NLF forces for over a year in South Vietnam, making their way there by the Ho Chi Minh Trail—an elaborate network that comprised twelve thousand miles of paths and roads connecting North and South Vietnam. The invasion brought U.S. troops face to face with an experienced regular army led by the hero of Dien Bien Phu, General Vo Nguyen Giap, and a well-entrenched guerrilla movement in the South. In attempts to defeat such a formidable opponent, the United States constructed a killing machine of extreme proportions under the command of U.S. Army General William C. Westmoreland.

Westmoreland was a graduate of West Point and Harvard Business School, a former commander of the 101st Airborne Division, and superintendent of West Point. He first arrived in Vietnam in June 1964 and he eventually commanded one of the largest expeditionary forces in American history, which, by late 1967, numbered nearly five hundred thousand men with a colossal support apparatus. Each month, the United States spent nearly $2 billion on the war and delivered more than one million tons of supplies. American engineers built a massive road network, deep-water ports, and nearly one hundred airstrips to facilitate the war effort. This was augmented by bombing missions carried out from U.S. bases in Thailand and Guam, and from aircraft carriers in the South China Sea. It was the best trained, funded, equipped, and most mobile military force in the world. Yet despite the incredible destructive power it brought to bear in Vietnam, it failed miserably.

Westmoreland's war strategy was deeply flawed. His proposed fighting a "war of attrition." The object, in Westmoreland's own words, was to decimate the North Vietnamese population "to the point of national disaster for generations to come," while in South Vietnam his aim was to kill off resistance fighters faster than the population could replace them. The goal was simply to pulverize the enemy into submission. The Pentagon called this strategy the "meat grinder." This was to be achieved through massive bombing of North Vietnam and "search-and-destroy" missions in the south that would flush out the NLF and destroy them with American air power. It was hoped that this strategy would buy time for the Saigon government to become a viable political and military entity.[30]

Right away, the attrition strategy ran into trouble on several fronts. First, the massive U.S. troop presence and bombing campaigns actually increased the hostility of the mass of the population toward the Saigon government and their American masters. Instead of the huge American army intimidating the NLF and North Vietnamese, U.S. atrocities increased the number of Vietnamese willing to join the resistance and fight back. Despite a promise of a quick victory over the NLF, between 1965 and 1967 (during the massive buildup of U.S. forces), a clear-cut military victory eluded the United States, while the initiative of the war remained in the hands of the NLF and North Vietnamese Army (NVA). In 1967, with nearly five hundred thousand U.S. troops on the ground, roughly 80 percent of the contacts between American troops and NLF/NVA forces were still at the time and place of the nationalists' choosing.[31]

But even where the United States was able to fight at a time and place chosen by its commanders, there were problems. In Operation

Starlight, a large-scale military engagement in August 1965, combined massive U.S. air, land, and sea power allowed six thousand marines to kill 573 defenders while losing only 46 of their own. The problem was that three-quarters of the Vietnamese fighters escaped to fight another day. Moreover, as soon as the marines departed, the NLF moved right back in.[32] These early battles—especially the Battle of Ia Drang in November 1965—taught the Vietnamese the necessity of mostly using quick hit-and-run tactics, and, when fighting pitched battles, only to engage American forces at close quarters to make it hard for them to take advantage of their air superiority.

The failure of the attrition strategy was best symbolized by Operation Junction City. Carried out in the first three months of 1967, it was the largest American operation of the war to that date. More than thirty five thousand American and South Vietnamese troops swept along the Cambodian border northwest of Saigon, hoping to destroy longstanding NLF bases of support. Despite the huge number of highly mobile U.S. troops involved in the operation, they failed to engage the NLF in any significant fights. When large American forces swept through an area, the NLF would carefully avoid any contact. After the Americans left the area, the NLF would move back in. This would be repeated many hundreds of times during the course of the war. It was an attrition strategy—only it was the NLF's. By 1967, the Joint Chiefs of Staff and the CIA reluctantly acknowledged that a "long and costly" war lay ahead for the United States in Vietnam.[33]

Historian Gabriel Kolko sums up well the dilemma of America's military strategy in Vietnam, "The Americans won a large number of battles, and the PLAF [People's Liberation Armed Forces] and PAVN [People's Army of Vietnam] lost enormous numbers of men, but the revolution throughout this period dominated the overall military situation." Ultimately, Westmoreland's strategy of a war of attrition "failed because firepower and mobility were not decisive in military, much less political, terms."[34] U.S. forces were never able to dominate the field strategically, though they could dominate tactically, that is, within individual battles once engaged.

While the Johnson administration privately knew that their strategy was failing and a long war was forecast, they gave upbeat assessments of the war, always portraying victory as being "within our grasp."[35] The government fed the public a steady diet of good news about slow but steady progress, deploying statistics and graphs like business executives. Out of the White House, Walt Rostow ran the weekly meetings of the Psychological Strategy Committee, whose job was, according to journalist Dan Oberdorfer, to "win the hearts and minds of the American people" by inundating them with the proper facts.

> [Rostow] was a zealot about the war. If he saw a government report indicating progress or refuting an argument of critics, he wanted it released or leaked at once. To *Business Week* magazine went computer data charts of attacks initiated by the Viet Cong and the North Vietnamese (which showed the trend of battle to be down) and the "kill ratio" charts (the other side had suffered four times as many deaths). To the *Christian Science Monitor* went the population data from the computerized Hamlet Evaluation Survey.... The *Los Angeles Times* hit the jackpot of sorts with the leak of "authoritative reports from field commanders" to the president covering junks searched, hamlets secured, population controlled, comparative battle deaths, Communist combat battalions, Communist weapons lost, defectors received, and even "overland road haul (in thousands of short tons)." All the numbers rose or fell in the appropriate direction, but the readers...could only guess what they meant or did not mean.[36]

At the end of 1967, Westmoreland toured the United States with a message of progress. In Washington, D.C., at the National Press Club, he stated, "With 1968, a new phase is starting.... We have reached an important point where the end comes into view."[37] The U.S. embassy in Saigon sent out invitations to its New Year's Eve party saying, "Come see the light at the end of the tunnel."[38] Unbeknownst to the partygoers at the embassy that night, the light at the end of the tunnel was not an American victory, but the freight train of the Tet Offensive coming straight at them.

RACISM AND TOTAL WAR

> "The only thing they told us about the Viet Cong was they were gooks.
> They were to be killed. Nobody sits around and gives you their historical
> and cultural background. They're the enemy. Kill, kill, kill.
> That's what we got in practice. Kill, kill, kill."
> —A Vietnam veteran, on basic training

What was the American war like for the majority of people in South Vietnam, where the bulk of the fighting took place? While Westmoreland's war of attrition would ultimately prove unable to break the will of the Vietnamese people, it did unleash incredible destruction on them. According to antiwar critic Noam Chomsky:

> In a very real sense the overall U.S. effort in South Vietnam was a
> huge and deliberately imposed bloodbath. Military escalation was
> undertaken to offset the well-understood lack of any significant so-
> cial and political support for the elite military faction [the Saigon
> government] supported by the United States.[39]

This "huge and deliberately imposed bloodbath" consisted first and foremost of large-scale bombing. Bombing was, and still is, one of the great sacred cows of the American way of war.[40] America's massive industrial infrastructure allowed it to build a huge air force and a virtually limitless amount of ordnance during the Cold War. The B-52, which was originally designed for dropping nuclear weapons on Russia, was refitted for conventional warfare in Vietnam, with devastating results. The United States dropped more than one million tons of bombs on North Vietnam and more than four million tons on the south. Stunningly, the amount of bombs dropped by the United States on South Vietnam, in the air war alone, was double the tonnage it used in all of the Second World War. Life was made unbearable in the South Vietnamese country-side. While it is probably an underestimate, the U.S. Senate Subcommittee on Refugees reported the civilian casualties at four hundred thousand dead, nine hundred thousand wounded, and 6.4 million refugees by 1971. It concluded "that there is hardly a family in South Vietnam that has not suffered a death, injury or the anguish of abandoning an ancient homestead."[41]

The Vietnamese people were subjected to virulent racism by the occupying U.S. Army. The Vietnamese were regularly referred to as "gooks," "slants," and "dinks" by American troops. Racism started with the top brass; General Westmoreland believed that the "Oriental doesn't value life in the same way as a Westerner."[42] While this could be dismissed as the casual bigotry of a son of a rich southern family, in other cases officials' statements bordered on the genocidal. Colonel George S. Patton III, son of the notorious Second World War general and a combat commander in Vietnam, sent out Christmas cards in 1968 that read, "From Colonel and Mrs. George S. Patton III—Peace on Earth." Printed on the cards were photographs of Viet Cong soldiers dismembered and stacked in a pile.[43] This racism worked its way down to the troops through basic training. As one combat veteran recalled basic training, "The only thing they told us about the Viet Cong was they were gooks. They were to be killed."[44]

It was during search-and-destroy missions that the most direct contact took place between American soldiers, Vietnamese civilians, and NLF supporters. For historian Christian Appy, "search and destroy was the principal tactic; and the enemy body count was the primary measure of progress" in Westmoreland's war of attrition.[45] "Search and destroy" was coined as a phrase in 1965 to describe missions aimed at flushing the Viet Cong out of hiding in order to deploy air power against them, while the body count was the measuring stick for the success of any operation. Competitions were held between units for the highest number of Vietnamese killed in action, or KIAs. Army and marine officers knew that promotions were largely based on confirmed kills. The pressure to produce confirmed kills resulted in massive fraud. One study revealed that American commanders exaggerated body counts by 100 percent.[46]

The emphasis on maximum kills naturally resulted in atrocities. Civilian casualties, in any case, were inevitable in a conflict in which the occupier faced not a traditional military, but one "embedded" in the local population and dependent on its support. "As much as the military command might deny its significance," writes Appy, "the widespread local support for the full-time main forces of the NLF and NVA was the central disadvantage faced by American soldiers."[47] Villagers would supply the NLF with soldiers, food, and assistance in the planting of land mines. What many U.S. soldiers feared most were land mines and ambushes. Soldiers would become demoralized by weeks of mundane patrolling and then they would be hit unexpectedly by the explosion of land mines or an ambush. Enraged soldiers would go back to the nearest area they had just been through and brutalize the villagers in a racist fury. The effect of fighting a total war on an entire population was to create a situation where all Vietnamese people were seen as fair game to kill. The most famous case of this (but by no means the only one) was the My Lai massacre in March 1968, where Charlie Company, led by Captain Ernest Medina and Lieutenant William Calley, murdered more than 350 unarmed women and children. An army psychiatrist reported later that, "Lt. Calley states that he did not feel as if he were killing human beings, rather they were animals with whom one could not speak or reason."[48]

My Lai was not an aberration—smaller, unreported My Lais happened throughout the war. James Duffy, a machine-gunner on a

Chinook helicopter for Company A of the 228th Aviation Battalion, 1st Airborne Division, served from February 1967 to April 1968. Testifying at the Winter Soldier Investigation, held in Detroit in 1971, he reported an incident he was involved in:

> I swung my machine gun onto this group of peasants and opened fire. Fortunately, the gun jammed after one or two rounds, which was pretty lucky, because this group of peasants turned out to be a work party hired by the government to clear the area and there was GIs guarding them about fifty meters away. But my mind was so psyched out into killing gooks that I never even paid attention to look around and see where I was. I just saw gooks and I wanted to kill them. I was pretty scared after that happened because that sort of violated the unwritten code that you can do anything you want to as long as you don't get caught. That's, I guess that's what happened with the My Lai incident. Those guys just were following the same pattern that we've been doing there for ten years, but they had the misfortune of getting caught at it.[49]

When the Americans decided that an area could not be "pacified," they would turn it into a "free-fire zone," where anyone could be shot on sight, and which was subject to constant artillery barrages. In other areas, the Americans would literally plow the land down using huge Rome plows—giant bulldozers. The most famous case of this was the "Iron Triangle." A 32-mile perimeter 22 miles north of Saigon and an NLF bastion of support, it was first flattened by B-52s and artillery fire beginning in January 1967, and then the plows moved in and bulldozed everything in sight. Despite this, the NLF built a vast area of tunnels and was operating in the area again within six months.[50] If bombing and plowing couldn't deny an area to the NLF, the United States would use defoliants, such as the highly toxic Agent Orange and other herbicides, to destroy jungle cover and food. The United States dropped more than one hundred million pounds of herbicides across Vietnam during the war, with long-lasting effects on the Vietnamese and American soldiers. The United

States simply turned whole swaths of Vietnam into dead zones. The mindset of the military command can be summed up by the slogan painted on the wall of the U.S. Army's 9th Division helicopter headquarters during Operation Speed Express: "Death is our business and business is good."[51]

The bitterness and demoralization among troops also encouraged a growing resistance to the war, which took various forms, including going AWOL (Absent Without Leave), avoiding combat, "fragging" officers (tossing fragmentation grenades at them), and even active political resistance. This development contributed greatly to the eventual defeat of the United States in Vietnam. This will be one of the subjects taken up in a later chapter.

THE NLF: SURVIVING THE AMERICAN ONSLAUGHT

> "For better or worse, our endeavor was meshed into an ongoing historical movement for independence that had already developed its own philosophy and means of action. Of this movement, Ho Chi Minh was the spiritual father....
> And yet, this struggle was also our own."
> —Truong Nhu Tang, founding member of the
> National Liberation Front of South Vietnam

The United States invasion of South Vietnam in 1965 saved the Saigon government from collapse. It prevented both the formation of a coalition government committed to peace and U.S. withdrawal and an outright NLF victory. During the previous four years, the various pacification and counterinsurgency programs instigated at the behest of the U.S. government not only failed to dislodge or erode the NLF's base of support, they in fact fuelled it. In the two-and-a-half years following the American invasion, the NLF continued to control a significant section of the countryside in the face of massive American firepower. What accounted for the ability of the NLF to survive the American onslaught?

One reason was the longevity and depth of popularity of the nationalist cause. "We fought against the Chinese for twelve centuries.
We fought against the French for one hundred years. And, finally,
when the war was lost by the French in 1954 at Dien Bien Phu, the
Vietnamese were liberated from foreign oppression," according to
Father Chan Tin, a Vietnamese Catholic priest. "But it was at that
precise moment that the Americans came to Vietnam; little by little
at first, then, more and more as an invasion. An invasion of the
American army. Five hundred thousand of them in Vietnam and
this war became a war of genocide. The people of North Vietnam
and South Vietnam fight only for freedom, independence and national unity."[52] The NLF was only the latest political formation in the
long struggle against foreign oppression. The Diem regime and its
successors were seen by the mass of the population as puppet
regimes for foreign domination of their country by the Americans.
The Saigon government could not escape this "colonial taint" to its
rule, and the U.S. invasion only made this more glaring. For Diem
Chu, the editor of *Trinh Bay* magazine, "This war is a war against the
American imperialist. This is our war for independence."[53]

To most people in the countryside, the NLF was merely the latest
name for the Vietminh, which had been fighting for the independence of Vietnam and land reform in the countryside since the 1940s.
This continuity of struggle was reinforced by Vietminh veterans
who had regrouped after the 1954 armistice in the north and were
now returning home to the south to reignite the struggle against
Diem and his successors. In 1959–60, about 4,500 Vietminh veterans returned to the south; by 1961 the number rose to more than
6,200.[54] As one peasant from a village near Hue recalled, "Some of us
thought they had died. We were surprised to see them return, and we
were very happy to hear them say that they wanted to organize the
liberation in the area."[55] These returning veterans and those that

survived the repression of the Diem years set up NLF committees in thousands of villages across South Vietnam. These people ("living heroes" as one peasant called them) had an authority that the Saigon government couldn't challenge.

Another reason was repression, itself a reflection of the fact that Diem's regime lacked a popular base. "Had Ngo Dinh Diem proved a man of breadth and vision we would have rallied to him. As it was, the South Vietnamese nationalists were driven to action by his contempt for the principles of independence and social progress in which they believed," recalled Truong Nhu Tang.[56] This was an expression of middle-class and bourgeois alienation from Diem that only got worse under his successors. The Saigon government was hopelessly corrupt, undemocratic, and violently repressive. By the mid to late 1960s, there were thousands of political prisoners in South Vietnam. Elections were a sham, there was no viable course for reforming the Saigon government, and, as a result, many reformers joined the armed struggle because they had no other recourse.[57]

The third reason for the continued survival of the NLF was its ability to respond to the economic interests of the oppressed peasantry. The vast majority of the population lived in villages in the countryside where the key issue was land reform. The Vietminh had reduced rents and debts, and had leased communal lands, mostly to the poorer peasants. Diem brought the landlords back to the villages. People who were farming land they held for years now had to return it to landlords and pay years of back rent. The South Vietnamese Army enforced this rent collection. This produced a fury in the countryside. "I knew the rich oppressed the poor.... So I joined the Liberation Front," explained a landless peasant in 1961.[58] "Everywhere [Diem's] army came," another peasant remarked, "they made more friends for the V.C." "Cruel," exclaimed another peasant, "like the French."[59]

"The divisions within villages reproduced those that had existed against the French: 75 percent support for the Front, 20 percent trying to remain neutral, and 5 percent firmly pro-government," says historian Marilyn Young. [60] As the NLF came to control an area, the rich fled to the cities, "leaving the poorer element as almost the sole dwellers in the countryside," stated an American report, which concluded that "the war became in a real sense a class war." [61] This class war only intensified under the occupation, as the Saigon rich grew fat off the war while the poorer peasants suffered under the weight of American firepower. The failure of the Americans to alter class relations in the countryside was recognized by Robert Komer, the head of the pacification effort, who reported in February 1967, "By themselves none of our Vietnam programs offer high confidence of a successful outcome." [62]

The United States had a large and lumbering military machine in Vietnam, very capable of inflicting incredible destruction. In Quang Ngai province—referred to by the U.S. Army as "Indian country" because of the NLF's wide support—the Americans destroyed 70 percent of the villages. [63] The growing and increasingly destructive American presence in Vietnam pushed many who had been previously neutral in the conflict between the NLF and the Saigon government and its American backers to join the NLF. An American education expert from the International Volunteer Services (IVS) recounts one summer evening in 1967 when he was visiting a Vietnamese teacher and four of her students came to see her. "They were startled to see an American, but soon overcame their fears. 'We've come to say good-bye,' they told their Vietnamese teacher. 'We're leaving tonight.' Their teacher knew immediately what they meant. They were going to join the Front. 'Why are you joining?' the IVS man asked. 'We must fight for our country,' they answered. 'We must fight the Americans who have taken away our sovereignty. We must fight them because their presence is destroying our native land, physically and culturally and morally. To fight now is the only way to prove our love for our country, for our Vietnamese people.'"[64]

TET OFFENSIVE: THE TURNING POINT

"To say that we are closer to victory is to believe, in the face of the evidence, the optimists who have been wrong in the past.... It is increasingly clear to this reporter that the only rational way out, then, will be to negotiate, not as victors, but as an honorable people...[who] did the best they could."
—Walter Cronkite

While General Westmoreland was touring the United States in 1967 talking about the "thinning of the ranks of the Viet Cong" and the coming end of the war, an earthquake was building beneath his feet—the Tet Offensive.[65] Tet was the turning point in the American war in Vietnam. It had a dramatic effect on domestic U.S. politics. From Tet on the question was no longer when would the United States win the war, but how quickly could the United States get out of Vietnam.

Tet was the Lunar New Year, a major holiday in Vietnam. It is celebrated by relatives traveling long distances to visit one another. Since the American bombing campaign had driven many people into the cities, a great many people traveled to the largest cities. Fireworks of various sorts marked the Tet holiday, and it was normal that many strangers would be around. This made it a perfect time for a military offensive in the cities. The plans for Tet were drawn up a year before in Hanoi with the personal approval of Ho Chi Minh. While there had been military offensives in the past around Tet, the one planned for February 1968 was nothing less than an effort to shift the course of the war against the United States.

The offensive itself actually began in late 1967—during the dry season in Vietnam—when the North Vietnamese and the NLF launched military feints to draw American military forces away from the major cities. Up until Tet, the war had been primarily confined to the countryside. The French newspaper *Le Monde* reported in January 1968 that a "sustained and general offensive" had the Americans pinned back in defensive positions.[66] On January 20, the North Vietnamese Army began a siege of the U.S. Marine base at Khe Sanh near the Laotian border. Westmoreland was convinced that the Vietnamese wanted to repeat at Khe Sanh the victory they had at Dien Bien Phu fifteen years earlier. Johnson was so nervous about the situation that he had a model of Khe Sanh in the White House and made his generals pledge that Khe Sanh could be held no matter what. He reportedly barked at his generals: "I don't want any damn Dinbinphoo!"[67]

Westmoreland and Johnson's obsession with Khe Sanh, a base of little strategic value, revealed how much they were misreading the battlefield. While the NVA was laying siege at Khe Sanh and Westmoreland correspondingly rushed troops to reinforce his besieged forces, the NLF moved into place elsewhere. In January, tens of thousands of NLF troops moved into the larger provincial towns and cities. They smuggled weapons and explosives in coffins, burying them in cemeteries for future use. As one American journalist observed, once in the cities "the Viet Cong were absorbed into the population by the urban underground like out-of-town relatives attending a family reunion."[68] It is a testament to the deep roots and widespread sympathy for the nationalist movement that no one tipped off the Saigon government or the Americans that such a large military buildup was taking place.

But it is also a testament to the bureaucratic complacency of American planners, who had in their possession an appeal to the People's Army that recommended "strong military attacks in coordination with the uprisings of the local population to take over towns and cities."[69] Writes Oberdorfer:

The inertial force of habit and of bureaucracy overpowered the evidence at hand. Belief in a tremendous impending attack would have required tremendous countierefforts. Personal plans would have to be altered; holidays and furloughs canceled; daily habits of comfort and convenience in previously safe cities abandoned. If an official reported "progress" last month and the months before that and had been praised for his tidings of success, how did he justify reporting an impending crisis now? Official assessments of Communist weakness would have to be discarded or explained away; public predictions would have to be eaten. It could not be done.[70]

On the night of January 29–30, the main part of the offensive began, when seventy thousand NVA/NLF soldiers attacked 34 of 44 provincial capitals, 64 district capitals, and many military installations. More than one hundred targets were hit all over South Vietnam, including the American embassy in Saigon, the citadel of American power. Hue, the ancient capital of Vietnam, fell to the combined forces of the North Vietnamese Army and the NLF.[71] "The feat stunned U.S. and world opinion," according to liberal anticommunist historian Stanley Karnow.[72] In Saigon, one thousand NLF troops took the city and managed to hold it for three weeks against a combined U.S.–ARVN force of eleven thousand. Westmoreland tried to portray the offensive as the death rattle of the NLF, similar to the Battle of the Bulge by the Germans in the final phase of the Second World War in Europe. After the first reports of the attacks on Saigon and other cities, Westmoreland still considered them diversionary to the main enemy effort at Khe Sanh.[73]

The United States responded with what one reporter called "the most hysterical use of American firepower ever seen,"[74] particularly air power. "The Viet Cong had the government by the throat in those provincial towns," explained one U.S. military adviser. "Ordinary methods would have never gotten them out, and the government did not have enough troops to do the job, so firepower was substituted."[75] The nationalists held Hue for three weeks, and it was only retaken after being virtually destroyed by the Americans. "Nothing I saw during the Korean War, or in the Vietnam War so far," wrote Robert Shapen, who toured Hue after its destruction, "has been as terrible, in terms of destruction and despair, as what I saw in Hue."[76] Ben Tre in Kien Hoa province was obliterated by U.S. firepower. "We had to destroy the town to save it," the commanding officer in charge of recapturing Ben Tre told reporters[77]—"coining one of the most notorious phrases of the war and a fitting motto for the U.S. counterattack against the Tet Offensive," writes historian David Hunt.[78]

While American firepower pushed back the Tet Offensive, the costs were high. During the offensive, South Vietnamese (ARVN) forces were severely mauled at the hands of the NVA and the NLF. The Americans suffered nearly four thousand casualties between January 30 and March 31. American military forces were clearly demoralized after Tet, beginning the process of decay and rebellion that would reach crisis proportions in the remaining years of the war. A March 3 State Department report dismally concluded: "We know that despite a massive influx of 500,000 U.S. troops, 1.2 million tons of bombs, 400,000 sorties per year, 200,000 KIA in three years, 20,000 U.S. KIA, etc., our control of the countryside and the defense of the urban levels is now essentially at pre-August 1965 levels. *We have achieved a stalemate at a high commitment.*"[79] (Emphasis added.)

Yet it should be noted that the Tet Offensive was also extremely costly for the nationalist forces, especially for the NLF. The anticipated urban uprisings that the attacks were meant to inspire did not happen. Moreover, in addition to the tremendous casualties inflicted in the battle by U.S. forces to retake the cities from the NLF and NVA, the absence of NLF fighters in the villages exposed their rural bases to attack. Writes Marilyn Young:

> In Long An province, for example, local guerrillas taking part in the May–June offensive had been divided into several sections. Only 775 out of 2,018 in one section survived; another lost all but 640 out of

1,430. The province itself was subjected to what one historian has called a "My Lai from the Sky"—non-stop B-52 bombing.[80]

Nevertheless, the political effect of Tet in domestic U.S. politics was swift and dramatic. While Johnson's personal popularity had been declining for two years, Tet decimated his credibility with the American public. Six weeks after the Tet Offensive began, "public approval of [Johnson's] overall performance dropped from 48 percent to 36 percent—and, more dramatically, endorsement for his handling of the war fell from 40 percent to 26 percent."[81] Eugene McCarthy, a relatively obscure first-term U.S. senator from Minnesota, who was for American withdrawal from Vietnam, nearly defeated Johnson in the February New Hampshire Democratic primary. Soon afterward, Robert Kennedy, a much more substantial threat to Johnson's renomination by the Democratic Party, announced that he too would be running for president on an antiwar platform. Robert McNamara, secretary of defense and an architect of the war in Vietnam, was replaced by Clark Clifford. Clifford, a longtime Washington lawyer and adviser to Democratic presidents, began a massive review of U.S. war policies in Vietnam that would quickly convince him of the need for the United States to get out. Johnson was besieged.

The final blow to Johnson came from the very same people who had just recently endorsed his war policies, the U.S. State Department's Senior Informal Advisory Group—popularly known as the "wise men." The wise men were a group of the most senior advisers on foreign policy in the United States, many of whom were architects of the postwar world, including Dean Acheson, Truman's secretary of state, John J. McCloy, former American high commissioner for occupied Germany, and many others. They met with Johnson on March 18 and told him that his policies were in a shambles and that U.S. interests demanded that the United States begin withdrawing from Vietnam. Johnson was stunned.[82] The sentiment of the American ruling class can be summed up by Walter Cronkite, dean of American broadcast journalism, who made a fresh report on Vietnam on February 27 in which he suggested that the U.S. "negotiate, not as victors, but as an honorable people…[who] did the best they could."[83] Johnson addressed the nation on March 31 and announced that he would not seek reelection as president.[84]

The presidential race was now wide open. The antiwar movement began to surge in the United States and American politics began to be dominated by the question of withdrawal. Yet, the Tet Offensive was only the opening shot of a year in which the U.S. ruling class faced its most severe challenges in a generation. In April, Martin Luther King Jr. was assassinated and one hundred cities rose in rebellion. Robert Kennedy was assassinated after winning the California primary in June. Chicago Mayor Daley's police's brutal attack on antiwar demonstrators at the Democratic convention drew the world's attention to political repression in America. While in Vietnam, the U.S. military started to report major disciplinary problems with its troops that marked the beginning of a soldiers' rebellion never before witnessed on such a scale in American history.

In November 1968, Richard Nixon won the presidency over Hubert Humphrey, Johnson's vice president, by almost the same margin he had lost eight years before against Kennedy. Nixon won largely due to the impression given by his campaign that he had a "secret plan" to end the war in Vietnam. Yet the war would continue for another four years as the United States fought a savage, bloody retreat from Vietnam.

CHAPTER THREE

COLD WAR LIBERALISM AND THE ROOTS OF THE ANTIWAR MOVEMENT

When did Americans first become opposed to their government's policies in Vietnam? Tom Wells, in his voluminous history of the antiwar movement, *The War Within*, begins in 1964 with the Tonkin Gulf incident and the ensuing dissent of Senators Morse and Gruening over the Tonkin Gulf resolution. Nancy Zaroulis and Gerald Sullivan, in their history, *Who Spoke Up?*, see opposition to the war in Vietnam in the course of 1963, entering the fringes of a peace movement that had focused primarily on issues of nuclear disarmament and testing. Socialist Fred Halstead's *Out Now* starts his history of the Vietnam antiwar movement within a general discussion of the state of the "old peace movement" in 1960. But it is H. Bruce Franklin, however, in his extremely important essay, "The Antiwar Movement We Are Supposed to Forget," who recognizes how early the opposition to U.S. involvement in Vietnam really began: "The first American opposition came as soon as Washington began warfare against the Vietnamese people by equipping and transporting a foreign army to invade their country—in 1945."[1]

In September 1945, the triumphant Vietminh constituted themselves as the Democratic Republic of Vietnam and declared Vietnam independent from France. "But in the following two months," writes Franklin, "the United States committed its first act of warfare against the Democratic Republic of Vietnam. At least eight and possibly twelve U.S. troopships were diverted from their task of bringing American troops home from World War II and instead began transporting U.S.-armed French troops and Foreign Legionnaires from France to recolonize Vietnam."[2] This provoked immediate opposition from the seamen of the troopships, members of the merchant marine. According to Franklin, "The enlisted crewmen of these ships, all members of the U.S. Merchant Marine, immediately began organized protests."[3]

All eighty-eight enlisted members of the crew of the troop transport ship *Pachaug Victory,* for example, wrote a protest letter on November 2, 1945, to the War Shipping Administration in Washington, D.C. Several weeks later, crew members of the *Winchester Victory* sent the following cable to President Truman and New York Republican Senator Robert Wagner: "We, the unlicensed personnel [non-officers] of the S.S. *Winchester Victory*, vigorously protest the use of this and other American vessels for carrying foreign combat troops to foreign soil for the purpose of engaging in hostilities to further the imperialist policies of foreign governments when there are American troops waiting to come home. Request immediate congressional investigation into this matter."[4]

Things didn't end there. When they arrived in Vietnam, the crew members were stunned to be saluted by Japanese soldiers recently rearmed by the British (who were the first Allied troops to arrive in Vietnam) to suppress the Vietminh. "The entire crew of four troopships," Franklin says, "met together in Saigon and drew up a resolution condemning the U.S. government for using American ships to transport troops 'to subjugate the native population' of Vietnam."[5]

During the course of 1946, as already noted, full-scale war broke out for control of Vietnam, with the French side getting large-scale material support from the United States. The Viet Nam Friendship

Association (VNFA) organized a "Celebration of the Second Anniversary of the Independence of the Republic of Viet-Nam" in New
York City in September 1947—the first stateside protest against the
war in Vietnam. VNFA Chairman Robert Delson declared "the
founding of the newest Republic in the world—the Democratic Republic of Viet Nam…an event which history may well record as
sounding the death knell of the colonial system."[6] Norman
Thomas, the six-time presidential candidate of the Socialist Party,
told those assembled, "It is only by direct and indirect aid…from
the United States that a colonial imperialism can be maintained in
the modern world."[7]

This opposition to America's Vietnam policy took place at a particular moment in U.S. history, between the end of the Second World
War and before the onslaught of the Cold War, when the United States
portrayed itself as the anticolonial superpower. There seemed to be an
obvious contradiction in the minds of many people in being against
colonialism and supporting French colonialism in Vietnam. With the
outbreak of the Korean War in 1950, this embryonic opposition to the
U.S. support for the French recolonization of Vietnam was completely overshadowed by the slaughter on the Korean peninsula.

The war in Korea was highly unpopular, but it coincided with the
rise of McCarthyism in the United States, making any opposition to
the war impossible to organize beyond small pockets of besieged individuals. Yet, the unpopularity of the war in Korea, which came to
an end in 1953, restrained the ability of the United States to save its
French allies in their doomed war in Vietnam as it entered its ninth
bloody year. When Vice President Richard Nixon raised the specter
of the U.S. intervening to save the French—on the eve of their disaster at Dien Bien Phu—opposition came from surprising places. An
American Legion division, which represented 78,000 veterans, demanded that, "The United States should refrain from dispatching

any of its Armed Forces to participate as combatants in the fighting in Indochina or in Southeast Asia."[8]

Senator Ed Johnson, who became notorious in the 1930s as governor of Colorado for mobilizing the National Guard to prevent Mexican immigrants from entering the state, declared on the Senate floor: "I am against sending American GIs into the mud and muck of Indochina on a blood-letting spree to perpetuate colonialism and white man's exploitation in Asia."[9] In May 1954, 68 percent of Americans surveyed in a Gallup poll were against sending U.S. troops to Indochina. That same month, the French were defeated at Dien Bien Phu, spelling the end of the French era in Indochina. The American era in Vietnam, however, was just beginning.

What effect did the withdrawal of the French and the direct intervention of the Unites States in the affairs of Vietnam have on those critics of American policy in Vietnam? The onslaught of the Cold War began in earnest in 1947 with President Harry Truman's announcement of American military aid to Greece and Turkey. In what became known as the Truman Doctrine, he declared, "It must be the policy of the United States to support free peoples who are resisting attempted subjugation by armed minorities or by outside forces."[10] These alleged "armed minorities" and "outside forces" were the fictitious "international communist conspiracy" that justified direct American military intervention or CIA covert operations around the globe. Critics of American foreign policy, many of whom considered themselves quite left-wing in the 1930s, joined the U.S. government in its "crusade against communism." Robert Delson, for example, a left-wing socialist in the 1930s who toasted the "Democratic Republic of Vietnam" in 1947, later played an important role in "developing" allies in many Third World countries. "We were concerned that the United States not be caught flat-footed in the postwar necessity to create non-communist governments in Asia," he later explained, after he became a well-established Park Avenue attorney and legal counsel for Indonesia in the United States.[11]

Norman Thomas went from denouncing U.S. support for French colonialism in 1947 to cofounding, in the fall of 1955, the American Friends of Vietnam, which was primarily "concerned with the political objective of committing the United States to a massive aid program on Diem's behalf," according to journalist Robert Scheer.[12] The most important figure of this milieu was Joseph Buttinger, a former left-wing Austrian socialist in the 1930s, who emigrated to the United States in the late thirties and became the key figure in founding the American Friends of Vietnam.

The American Friends of Vietnam—referred to as the "Vietnam Lobby"—spent more than six years lobbying the U.S. government on behalf of Diem and his little police state. Among the "friends" of the bloodthirsty dictator were Massachusetts Senator John F. Kennedy, historian Arthur Schlesinger, and the powerful Catholic Cardinal Spellman of New York, sometimes referred to as the "American Pope."[13] Thomas and other "State Department Socialists"[14] provided a left-wing cover for American foreign policy in this era, stifling any criticism of it from the left. Just a few years earlier, American merchant mariners, socialists, and politicians were denouncing U.S. policy for supporting "imperialism," "colonialism," and "white man's exploitation." All this disappeared under the crushing weight of the Cold War and McCarthyism, when most political tendencies supported either the United States or the USSR in the global struggle.

There were only a handful of revolutionary socialists in a small number of countries who resisted, but they were marginal in influence. "The years when the United States was steadily escalating its military presence and combat role in Vietnam—1954 to 1963— were also the years when fundamental critiques of U.S. foreign policy had become marginalized," notes H. Bruce Franklin.[15] With the

Communist Party destroyed by the Cold War repression and Krushchev's revelations of Stalin's atrocities, and with many self-described socialists supporting America's anticommunist crusade, left-wing critics of U.S. foreign policy were reduced to a handful. It would take the emergence of new generation of American radicals to throw off the deadening weight of anticommunism.

Anticommunism has been a feature of American society since the Russian Revolution of 1917, but it was from the eve of the Second World War through the mid-1950s that a "Red Scare" increasingly tightened its grip around all the major institutions of American society. Leading the charge was the House Committee on Un-American Activities, known by its mangled acronym HUAC. Created by Congress in the late 1930s, its first chairman was anti-union, Jim Crow Democrat Martin Dies of Texas. The committee used what Dies called "the light of pitiless publicity" to destroy the people brought before it.[16] In 1940, the Alien Registration Act, or Smith Act, was passed by a Democratic Party–controlled Congress and signed into law by the "great" liberal President Franklin Roosevelt. The Smith Act made it illegal "to advocate, abet, advise, or teach the duty, necessity, desirability, or propriety of overthrowing or destroying any government in the United States by force or violence." The act furthermore criminalized the publication or distribution of "any written or printed matter" advocating the government's overthrow.[17] It was primarily directed at left-wing organizations like the Communist Party and the Socialist Workers Party.[18]

After a brief pause during World War II, the Red Scare gained momentum and ferocity with each passing year. In 1947, President Harry Truman instituted a loyalty-security program for federal government employees, which included among other things loyalty oaths.[19] The Red Scare reached its most deadly phase under Senator Joseph McCarthy, when political dissent was literally crushed in the United States.[20] McCarthy discredited himself during the course of

1954—in the infamous "Army-McCarthy" hearings—and was soon censured by his Senate colleagues and later died in 1957. While the notorious HUAC continued to receive the largest amount of money allocated for any congressional committee, in the latter years of the 1950s, "the nation tired of security checks, loyalty oaths, and unending investigations."[21]

The tide began to turn. Starting in 1956, the Supreme Court made a series of rulings that curbed state sedition laws, limited the application of the notorious Smith Act, and struck down the ability of the secretary of state to deny passports on the grounds of someone's beliefs or associations.[22] The civil rights movement began to affect the much-reduced number of HUAC hearings. In September 1958, a Black witness at a HUAC hearing in Los Angeles "demanded of the Committee why it wasn't investigating the efforts being made in Little Rock, Arkansas, to nullify the Supreme Court's ruling on school integration."[23] Another Black witness at a HUAC hearing in Newark, New Jersey, in 1958, when asked where he was born responded, "I was born in the state where yesterday the Reverend Martin Luther King was arrested by the courthouse at Montgomery, Alabama."[24] Committee hearings were getting rowdier as opponents jeered committee members and supported witnesses. The Newark hearings had to recess on the first day because the audience became too boisterous. Similar incidents occurred across the country.

Throughout the spring of 1960, the country witnessed a new, more militant stage of the civil rights movement. Beginning in Greensboro, North Carolina, more than fifty thousand young Black and white people participated in sit-ins against segregation at lunch counters, theaters, parks, and swimming pools throughout the country but mostly concentrated in the South and border states.[25] These sit-ins captured the imagination of northern students, drawing many of them to the South, and led directly to the formation of the Student Nonviolent Coordinating Committee (SNCC).

"In May 1960…white students in San Francisco proved that the nonviolent tactics of the southern movement could be used effectively against other kinds of unjust authority."[26] They also gave people hope and the courage to fight back. The previous year HUAC had made itself intensely unpopular by issuing subpoenas to nearly a hundred schoolteachers in the Bay Area. Due to public pressure HUAC canceled its planned hearings—in and of itself a sign of the changing times—but the names made their way to the state government and several teachers lost their jobs. When HUAC announced they were returning in May 1960 to complete their work, "Bay Area students," according to historians Seth Cagin and Philip Dray, "were ready for them."[27]

HUAC scheduled its hearings to begin on May 12 at San Francisco's ornate City Hall. Several hundred students organized by SLATE (the left student government party) and the Young People's Socialist League (YPSL—the much more left-wing youth group of the Socialist Party USA), drawn mostly from the University of California at Berkeley and San Francisco State campuses, marched from Union Square to City Hall, where they were told there was no room for them in the hearing.[28] At that point twelve of the subpoenaed witnesses were ejected from the room after insisting that the students be let in. The next day, more than two hundred students came to City Hall and rallied in the marble rotunda watched over by fifty San Francisco police sent there on emergency duty. Once again the students were told there was no room for them in the hearing.

Word spread through the crowd that there were seats available but were reserved for HUAC guests. One committee investigator later said that he issued passes to friends of HUAC because, "We wanted some decent people in here."[29] Students began chanting, "first come, first served," and surged toward the hearing room door. Police unreeled fire hoses and washed protestors down the marble stairs, while other cops beat and arrested students. Some tried to hold onto banisters yelling, "We won't go!" and "Abolish the committee." For thirty minutes students battled the police. Captured on film by television crews, the incident shocked people around the country. "I was a political virgin," one student later recounted, "but I was raped on the steps of City Hall."[30]

HUAC tried red-baiting the students and later made a laughable forty-minute film called *Operation Abolition* that tried to portray the students as "Communist dupes." It backfired. When shown around the country, with HUAC supporters on hand to answer questions, the audience jeered and laughed at it, particularly when the narrator of the film identified the civil rights anthem *We Shall Overcome* as a "Communist song."[31] "The San Francisco demonstrations," according to Cagin and Dray, "marked a dramatic collapse in the ability of official red-baiters such as HUAC to inspire fear among Americans with liberals views. The Cold War hibernation was over."[32]

The hibernation was over, but the repressive atmosphere still persisted, particularly on many college campuses. The difference was that students were now ready to challenge it. In the fall of 1964, while much of the country was focused on the race for the presidency, veterans of Freedom Summer returned to Berkeley to find that "the freedom of students to organize and collect funds for their various political causes (both off campus and on) on a stretch of university property that has always been used for such purposes...had been denied to them by the university administration."[33] Campus police arrested Jack Weinberg, a member of the Independent Socialist Club, after he set up a table for the Congress of Racial Equality (CORE), one of the leading civil rights organizations. Almost immediately, dozens, then hundreds, and eventually thousands of students surrounded the police car with Weinberg in it. This was the beginning of the Berkeley Free Speech Movement(FSM). For two days students, led by veteran of Mississippi Freedom Summer Mario Savio, used the police car as a platform to organize against the university's policies on political activity. The FSM foreshadowed the movement to come against the war in Vietnam. In the end, the university relented and lifted its arcane restrictions on political activity on campus. The FSM was also another mile marker in the radicalization of the generation that would provide the first foot soldiers of the antiwar movement. "By the end of 1964, there existed a few thousand young people who had already begun to consider and adopt radical ideas and who had become activists to one degree or another."[34]

LIBERALISM AT WAR

"For in your time we have the opportunity to move not only toward the rich society and the powerful society, but upward to the Great Society. The Great Society rests on abundance and liberty for all. It demands an end to poverty and racial injustice, to which we are totally committed in our time. But that is just the beginning."
—President Lyndon Johnson, University of Michigan, May 22, 1964

The escalation of the American war against the Vietnamese people during the course of 1964 and 1965 coincided with the high point of liberal reform in the United States in the post–Second World War period. This would have an enormous impact on the future politics of the antiwar movement. Lyndon Johnson, like his predecessor Franklin Roosevelt, would appear to be an odd advocate for liberal reform, but both ultimately shifted the Democratic Party in an effort to capture and disarm the powerful political movements that arose during their respective presidencies.

Johnson came from more modest beginnings than the aristocratic FDR. Born on a farmhouse in central Texas, he rose to power and influence in the Texas Democratic Party, which was dominated by the corrupt oil industry and practiced Jim Crow as ruthlessly as in any other state that belonged to the former Confederacy. In his early career as a congressman, Johnson was a supporter of Roosevelt and his New Deal, but he moved in a more conservative direction after

FDR's death in 1945, hoping to win a U.S. Senate seat in Texas. In 1948, he finally succeeded in an election that was widely rumored then, and is now acknowledged, to have been stolen by him through ballot-box tampering in the border counties.

Johnson methodically planned and executed his rise to majority leader of the U.S. Senate in the 1950s, the most conservative era of politics since the 1920s.[35] Though he privately harbored presidential ambitions, these were thwarted by the public's image of him as a notorious Beltway insider. As Johnson biographer Robert Caro puts it, he had "a seemingly bottomless capacity for deceit, deception and betrayal."[36] While this may be true of all American presidents, it was an image that stuck with Johnson. He was placed on the 1960 presidential ticket with John Kennedy as a concession to the Dixiecrats,[37] but he hated being vice president and was isolated by the Kennedys while in office. After assuming the presidency following Kennedy's assassination in Dallas, Johnson's ambition to be a "great president" (modeled on FDR) came to full bloom.

In January 1964, Johnson formally announced his "war on poverty" during his State of the Union speech before a joint session of Congress. In March, he created, by executive order, the Office of Economic Opportunity (OEO), the agency that would oversee the large number of programs that came to symbolize the war on poverty—from Head Start to the Job Corps. Its director would be Kennedy brother-in-law Sargent Shriver, who had recently been in charge of the Peace Corps. Johnson summarized the ultimate goal of all his administration's efforts (an expanded welfare state, civil rights, and continued economic growth) to create what he called a "great society." This rebirth of liberal reform after a decade and a half of political reaction came in response to the increasingly powerful Black freedom struggle that transformed the political landscape of the country. The end of Jim Crow and the creation of a Black electorate in the South required the national Democratic Party to shift its political orientation specifically to capture the new Black vote. Johnson recognized the consequences of this when he confided to one of his closest aides, Bill Moyers, after signing the 1964 Civil Rights Act, "I think we just delivered the South to the Republican Party for a long time to come."[38]

The pace and costs of Johnson's reform quickened after his triumph in the 1964 presidential elections. According to liberal historian Irving Bernstein, Johnson would push through Congress during the course of 1965 "a broad array of domestic legislation: Medicare, the Elementary and Secondary Education Act, the Higher Education Act, the Voting Rights Act, the immigration law, the Water Quality Act…along with other statutes of lesser consequence."[39]Nothing like it had happened in nearly three decades. Many of these reforms, however, would be soon undone by the spiraling costs of the war in Vietnam.

GUNS AND BUTTER

Johnson wanted to fight, in the words of Vietnam-era reporter and author David Halberstam, "a war without a price, a silent, politically invisible war"[40]—particularly for America's prospering middle class. He hoped to do this in several ways: First, by keeping in place the many draft deferments that disproportionately benefited the middle and upper middle classes, the best-known being deferments for full-time college and graduate students; second, by not calling up the reserves.

The reserve forces of the various branches of the U.S. military and the National Guard had become, by and large, a refuge for the white middle class from active duty military service during the fifties and sixties.[41] In stark contrast to George W. Bush's invasion and occupation of Iraq, only once during the entire war in Vietnam were the reserves mobilized. In the early days of the war, Halberstam argues, Johnson "was not about to call up the reserves, because the use of the reserves would blow it all. It would be self-evident that we were really going to war, and that we would in fact have to pay a price."[42]

Johnson believed he could deliver "guns and butter" (high military spending and rising incomes) through an expanding social welfare state and other government fiscal policies that kept the historic growth in the economy booming.[43] As Johnson arrogantly declared, "As long as I am president we will do both."[44] This strategy, however, unwound very quickly.

The scale and cost of the war spiraled beyond the control of Johnson's war planners. Johnson hoped for a "short war,"[45] but the Vietnamese resistance destroyed that notion. In February 1965, the United States began Operation Rolling Thunder, its sustained bombing campaign of North Vietnam that would continue through 1968. The initial reports of the operation were dismal for U.S. war planners. Army Chief of Staff General Earle Wheeler concluded, "Outwardly, the North Vietnamese government appears to be uninfluenced by our air strikes." CIA Director John McCone, looking at the same data drew the same conclusion, "If anything, the strikes...have hardened their attitude."[46]

Meanwhile, when it became clear that the Vietnamese were not accepting the defeat that American planners expected them to accept, Defense Secretary Robert McNamara proposed a massive increase in U.S. troops on the ground. This was to be done with as much secrecy as possible. National Security Action Memorandum No. 328, signed by Johnson, declared the following: "The President desires that with respect to the actions in paragraphs 5 through 7 [increases in ground forces], premature publicity be avoided by all possible precautions."[47] Of course, this would be no secret to the Vietnamese, who could see the vast numbers of American troops pouring into their country—the buildup was meant to be kept secret from the American public.

To fill the combat divisions being sent to Vietnam, monthly draft calls were to be doubled from 17,000 to 35,000, because, as we have noted, Johnson refused to mobilize the reserves.[48] Troop levels continued to escalate, year in and year out, from then on. Ironically, the draft became one of the flashpoints for opposition to the war.

Both the House and the Senate had large Democratic Party majorities as a result of the 1964 elections, and each year they funded the war in Vietnam, though it began to produce some unease among the leading Senate Democrats. But the unease of Senate Democrats such as majority leader Mike Mansfield or William Fulbright, chairman of the Senate Foreign Relations Committee, never turned into outright opposition to the war. Vice President Hubert Humphrey, previously one of the most liberal members of the Senate, tried to reassure them that everything was under control and wouldn't go any further. Typical was a pitch Humphrey made to Senator Gaylord Nelson in 1965 during the first stages of the buildup: "You know, Gaylord, there are people at State and the Pentagon who want to send three hundred thousand men out there. But the president will never get sucked into anything like that."[49] He got sucked into that and much more. Johnson's "short, politically invisible war" was very visible and the political costs were only beginning to accrue.

It was up to Defense Secretary Robert McNamara to hide and falsify the growing costs of the war. His projections for the length of the war seem absurd in retrospect. He ordered the comptroller of the Defense Department to project the total cost of the war based on the war ending on June 30, 1967—eight years before it actually came to an end. In late 1966, McNamara estimated that the war so far had cost $20 billion and that the federal deficit instead of being $1.9 billion was actually $9 billion. By mid-1967 McNamara "could no longer hide the cost or the devastating impact on the federal budget."[50] The war would top out at nearly $30 billion in 1968, with the U.S. running historic budget deficits to pay for it. Johnson finally proposed a tax increase in 1967 to cover the cost of the war, but it was too little, too late.

The immediate economic effect of the war was the great inflation that began in 1966 (and would last for the next seventeen years), eating away at workers' wages and producing a strike wave against the employers, as well as a revolt of the rank and file inside the unions. *Life* magazine's August 26, 1966, cover story "Strike Fever," decried what it called the "rampant new militancy" and the "dilemma of labor leaders."[51] That summer, aircraft mechanics belonging to the International Association of Machinists (IAM) struck several major airlines, grinding 60 percent of the country's air traffic to a halt. They defied their leaders as well as Johnson's calls to return to work, remaining out on strike for five weeks. The slogan of the striking machinists was "We're working under chain-gang conditions for cotton-picking wages."[52] The strike had many of the same features that would appear in union struggles in the later sixties and early seventies.

END OF THE GREAT SOCIETY

In November 1966, the first major elections took place since the large-scale landing of U.S. troops in Vietnam. It was a referendum on Johnson's handling of the war, and the Democrats across the country suffered a huge defeat, with the Republicans winning back much of what they lost in 1964. They gained forty-seven seats in the House and three in the Senate as well as eight governorships (Ronald Reagan won his first term as governor of California) and 677 state legislative positions.[53]

Though the Democrats maintained majority control of both the House and Senate, a conservative coalition of southern Democrats and Republicans would ensure that there would be no more liberal initiatives. The Great Society in essence died on the battlefield of Vietnam. Richard Nixon, who was reemerging as the leading Republican in the country, was licking his chops at the Republicans' political prospects for 1968 if the war continued into a presidential election year. "No power on earth [can keep the Republican Party] from trying to outbid the Democrats for the peace vote," declared Nixon.[54]

How do we explain the Republicans' victories? After all, despite their criticism of Johnson, the Republicans were as committed to victory in Vietnam as the Democrats. But in America's suffocating two-party system, displeasure with the incumbent party is expressed by voting for the other party, almost irrespective of its formal positions.

There were few opportunities for the public to vote for clear antiwar candidates or express clear antiwar positions. In the few campaigns there were, it was obvious that antiwar protests had created sizeable opposition to the war. In California, two editors and the publisher of the left-liberal magazine *Ramparts* ran as antiwar candidates in three separate Democratic congressional primaries.[55] All three received more than 40 percent of the vote in their races while facing the wrath of the Democratic establishment. The best known of these was Robert Scheer, the foreign affairs editor of the magazine and author of the popular pamphlet *How the United States Got Involved in Vietnam*, who ran against Johnson supporter and incumbent congressman Jeffrey Cohelan in the Democratic primary for California's Seventh Congressional District. Cohelan was a former Teamsters union official in the Bay Area and received a 95 percent approval rating from the liberal Americans for Democratic Action (ADA).[56] Scheer got 45 percent of the vote despite the campaigning of Vietnam War "critics" like Fulbright and Bobby Kennedy for Cohelan.

The most telling expression of antiwar sentiment took place in Dearborn, Michigan, where the residents in the then predominately mixed-income, white suburb of Detroit, participated in a referendum on the war initiated by former autoworker and long-time revolutionary socialist John Anderson.[57] The referendum read: "Are you in favor of an immediate ceasefire and withdrawal of United States troops from Vietnam so that the Vietnamese people can settle their own problems?" Forty-one percent voted yes and a future study revealed that the vote correlated inversely to peoples' class position, with blue-collar workers voting against the war in much larger proportions than managers or professionals.[58] It was an example of how mass antiwar sentiment was spreading on the ground regardless of the maneuverings of the major parties.

CHAPTER FOUR

BLACK AMERICA AND VIETNAM

"I have an intuitive feeling that the Negro servicemen have a better understanding than whites of what the war is about."
—General William C. Westmoreland

"Our criticism of Vietnam policy does not come from what we know of Vietnam, but from what we know of America."
—Bob Moses, SNCC leader

The Vietnam antiwar movement emerged in response to the escalation of the U.S. war against the Vietnamese people in the spring of 1965, but the political basis for the emergence of such a movement was laid a decade before. To put it simply: There would have been no mass antiwar movement in the United States without the civil rights movement.[1] It broke the deadening grip of McCarthyism over American society, allowing for the reemergence of mass political struggle. Beginning with the Montgomery bus boycott in 1955 through the passage of the Voting Rights Act of 1965, there had been a decade of rising struggle by African Americans to tear down the American system of apartheid known as "Jim Crow." To understand why the Black liberation struggle was so crucial to the development of the antiwar movement, it is necessary to look at the relationship of African Americans to U.S. foreign policy and the American military on the eve of the civil rights era.[2]

African Americans have fought in every war waged by the United States. In every instance, the nation rewarded them for their sacrifices with continued bigotry and oppression—despite politicians' promises of full citizenship and the encouragement of most Black leaders to serve in the military. This bitter legacy (which included Black soldiers being lynched in their uniforms[3]) has meant that African Americans have been generally less supportive of America's foreign wars. The rhetoric that the United States fights its wars to spread "freedom and democracy" abroad—when Blacks had neither at home—was particularly unconvincing. According to historian Michael Honey, during the Second World War, "Many [Blacks] doubted the antifascist rhetoric of the war."[4] In Memphis, Tennessee, in 1942, for example, a poll conducted among Black residents of city revealed that, "75 percent of the respondents thought that they would be better treated than they currently were if Japan conquered the United States (although only 55 percent said this when interviewed by a white)."[5]

Despite such sentiments, millions of African-American men reported for induction into the U.S. military after receiving their draft notices, and served in segregated and largely noncombat roles during the war. Leading Black newspapers and politicians advocated a strategy of "Double Victory"—a victory over fascism abroad and Jim Crow at home. But a surprising number of Black men resisted military service in spite of the pressure to serve. Such politically diverse individuals as Elijah Muhammad, the leader of the Nation of Islam, and Bayard Rustin, the future organizer of the 1963 March on Washington, went to prison for refusal to do military service.[6] The young Malcolm Little (later known as Malcolm X) was declared 4-F (ineligible for military service) after confiding to a military psychiatrist (feigning mental illness) that, "I want to get sent down South…and kill up crackers."[7] Blues pioneer Willie Dixon fought a tumultuous and successful court battle to stay out of the army in 1942. "I told them [the Court]," Dixon recalled, "I didn't feel I had to go because of the conditions that existed among my people."[8]

After the war, President Harry Truman desegregated the armed forces in the face of bitter opposition from the military brass and most of the congressional leadership. Why did Truman, a lifelong supporter of Jim Crow, choose at that moment to do it? He had three major reasons. The 1948 election was a four-way race for the presidency and the unpopular Democrat Truman was running for the presidency not only against the Republican Governor Thomas Dewey of New York (his chief rival), but also two other parties that fielded candidates who threatened to steal a sizeable chunk of Truman's voting base. The first was the States' Rights Party lead by Governor Strom Thurmond of South Carolina. Thurmond's party was a breakaway party of southern Dixiecrats opposed to the mild language supporting civil rights in the Democratic party's platform.[9] As a result, Truman wrote off most of the South from his campaign strategy. The other was the Progressive Party, led by former vice president Henry Wallace. The Progressive Party was actively supported by the Communist Party and, according to Paul Robeson's biographer, Martin Duberman, "generated considerable excitement and respect within the Black community."[10] Truman feared that Wallace might win just enough Black votes in key northern states to throw the election to Dewey.

At the same time, a campaign to desegregate the military was initiated by the leading Black trade unionist in the country, A. Phillip Randolph, the president of the Brotherhood of Sleeping Car Porters, who had previously threatened Roosevelt with a "March on Washington" in 1940 and wrested from him an executive order banning discrimination in the defense industries. All this, combined with the United States's emerging rivalry with "communist" Russia for influence in the restless colonial world, meant that a Jim Crow military had to go. Such glaring racism at home made it difficult for the United States to project itself abroad as the free, equal, and democratic alternative to Soviet totalitarianism (not to mention German Nazism). "The existence of discrimination against minority groups in this country," wrote Secretary of State Dean Acheson in 1946, "has an adverse effect on our relations with other countries." He continued:

We are reminded over and over again by some foreign newspapers and spokesmen, that our treatment of various minorities leaves much to be desired. While sometimes these pronouncements are exaggerated and unjustified, they all too frequently point with accuracy to some form of discrimination because of race, creed, color, or national origin. Frequently we find it next to impossible to formulate a satisfactory answer to our critics from other countries; the gap between the things we stand for in principle and the facts of particular situations may be too wide to be bridged.[11]

In July 1948, Truman by executive order declared "equality of treatment and opportunity" in all of the armed forces without regard to race, color, religion, or national origin. With the coming of the highly unpopular Korean War in 1950, the United States fielded its first integrated combat units since the revolutionary war against Great Britain in the eighteenth century. The abolition of Jim Crow, however, didn't end racism or discrimination in the military. It would soon be discovered by Black soldiers and supporters that "integration" and racism could easily coexist. But through the 1950s and early 1960s, the military was the only major institution in American society that didn't hang Jim Crow on its front door—it had no segregated bathrooms, sleeping quarters, training facilities, or combat units.

In the South, where the marines and the army had some of their largest training bases, this meant that the military stuck out quite conspicuously from the surrounding communities. For a number of years, Blacks held the military in relatively high regard. This dramatically changed with the beginnings of the war in Vietnam. The desegregation of the armed forces, however, was the only significant victory for African Americans immediately following the Second World War. Soon the government-sponsored repression of communists, socialists, and union militants, known interchangeably as the "Red Scare" or "McCarthyism," also targeted civil rights activists, snuffing out the beginnings of a civil rights struggle.

The purge of radicals could not have been accomplished without the collaboration of leading figures of established Black organizations like A. Phillip Randolph or Walter White of the NAACP. According to historian Manning Marable, "By serving as the 'left wing of McCarthyism'...[they] retarded the black movement for a decade or more."[12] This began to change with the Montgomery bus boycott in 1955 and the sit-in wave of the early sixties that created two new organizations—the Southern Christian Leadership Council (SCLC) and Student Non-violent Coordinating Committee (SNCC) and the rebirth of the Congress on Racial Equality (CORE). All three organizations were committed to some form of mass action against Jim Crow (though they were very divided on what that meant) and became the organizational vehicles for the radicalization of a new generation of activists, both Black and white.

These organizations in turn were influenced by events taking place in the former colonial world, or what has been referred to as the "Third World," for over a generation. It has largely been forgotten that the Black freedom movement was keenly interested in the struggles in Europe's subjugated colonies in Asia, Africa, and the Middle East. After all, the position of African Americans, particularly in the southern United States, bore striking similarities to the conditions of colonial people throughout the world: domination by a white supremacist government, absence of any democratic rights, deep levels of poverty, and routine use of state violence against government critics. India held a particular interest from the 1920s until the country's independence in 1947, particularly its best-known leader, Mahatma Gandhi. "For more than two decades," according to Bayard Rustin biographer John D'Emilio, "the African-American press paid attention to Gandhi, daring as he did to challenge the world's greatest imperial power."[13] W. E. B. Du Bois, a founder of the NAACP and the editor of its magazine *The Crisis*, began writing about India and Gandhi as early as 1919. He declared to his readers,

"We are all one—we the Despised and Oppressed, the 'niggers' of England and America."[14] One of the major reasons that Martin Luther King Jr. and others were interested in the "nonviolent" tactics of Gandhi was their seeming vindication in winning that country's independence. Richard Wright, the famous Black American writer, traveled to Africa in the 1950s, recording the swelling movement for freedom in his book *Black Power*.[15]

The 1955 conference in Bandung, Indonesia, of Third World and nonaligned nations (which included "communist" China but not "communist" Russia) was attended by an array of African-American writers, activists, and intellectuals.[16] The Bandung conference inaugurated the "nonaligned" movement. The more radical nationalisms that emerged during the late 1950s and 1960s, personified by Kwame Nkrumah of Ghana, Gamel Abdel Nasser of Egypt, Ben Bella of Algeria, Patrice Lumumba of the Congo, and Fidel Castro of Cuba, had a twofold impact on the civil rights movement. They created an opening for various currents of Marxism and Socialism to be embraced by a large numbers of Blacks for the first time since the 1930s, and they nurtured a growing suspicion toward the role of the United States in the Third World, particularly after the 1961 murder of Lumumba by Belgian forces (with CIA complicity) and the failed U.S.-sponsored attempt to topple Castro in the Bay of Pigs invasion.[17]

The early stages of the civil rights movement took place largely in the South but had a profound impact on national politics. The two great legislative victories of this movement were the Civil Rights Act of 1964 and the Voting Rights Act of 1965. This is the same period when the movement also went into crisis. According to Ahmed Shawki, 1965 "marked an important turning point in the Black liberation movement. The hegemony exercised by the 'old guard' leaders like Martin Luther King Jr., was finally broken."[18] In its place emerged a more diverse movement with competing organizations that was moving to the left and embracing the sometimes more radical ideas of Black Power. While the reasons for this radicalization were many, the two major issues were the movement's relationship to the Democratic Party and the Vietnam War.[19]

The 1964 Democratic convention was a major milestone for militants in the movement. SNCC initiated the formation of the Mississippi Freedom Democratic Party in April 1964 to challenge the segregationist delegation from Mississippi for seats at the upcoming August convention in Atlantic City. After initially getting liberal support for their challenge, a phalanx of well-known liberals, at the bidding of the Johnson White House and led by Vice President Hubert Humphrey, the UAW's Walter Reuther, and liberal attorney Joseph Rauh (supported by Martin Luther King Jr. and Bayard Rustin) pleaded with and threatened the MFDP leaders to withdraw their challenge. The MFDP, whose best-known leader was Fannie Lou Hamer, were offered two delegates as a "compromise." They rejected this insulting proposal and sat in the seats of the Mississippi delegation until removed by the police. "The events at the 1964 convention," according to CORE historians Meier and Rudwick, "not only discredited the both the Democratic Party leadership and white liberal elements in the eyes of many militants but indicated that the Negroes themselves were deeply divided."[20]

The war would divide the civil rights movement even further. The "NAACP and Urban League leaders…held that the Vietnam conflict was irrelevant to the black protest and mixing the two issues would only lose substantial support for the Negroes' cause."[21] The radical wing of the movement, on the other hand, saw the war diverting "attention and funds away from solving the country's leading domestic problem [poverty]. Others went further and regarded the war as cut from the same cloth as domestic racism, charging that both represented attempts of the 'white power structure' to keep a colored race in a colonial status."[22] The war in Vietnam also coincided with the civil rights movement moving to the North and West, into the large industrial cities where a majority of the Black population now lived and worked in the heart of the U.S. economy. These very same cities were rocked by rebellions every summer—"long, hot summers"—beginning with Harlem in New York City in 1964. These same cities also contributed a sizeable number of Black combat troops to the regular army and marines.

According to sociologist Jack Bloom, these rebellions "had an immense political impact; they shifted both the geographical and the political focus of the Black movement. They went beyond the matter of civil rights to raise a wide variety of political, economic, and social issues.... Finally, their impact on Blacks themselves was profound."[23] An openly revolutionary current led by the Black Panthers would soon to be formed out of these urban insurrections. "In fact, the Black struggle found its most radical manifestations in the ghettos of the North and in the auto plants of Detroit and other manufacturing centers."[24] These struggles also pushed King to the left; his declared opposition to the war in Vietnam in April 1967 would help turn antiwar protests into a mass movement and significantly impact the American war effort. For the first time in the modern history of the United States, large numbers of Black men were radicalized before they entered active military service and combat.

Malcolm X was one of the first of the new Black leaders of the 1960s to consistently attack U.S. foreign policy.[25] He said, for example, at an August 10, 1963, Black Front Unity rally in New York:

> As Muslims, we don't go to war. We don't get drafted. We don't join anybody's army. We don't teach you not to go, because they'd put us in jail for sedition. I would never tell you not to go. I wouldn't be that dumb. But I sure will tell you, if you're dumb enough to go, that's up to you. If you're dumb enough to fight for someone who means you no good; if you're dumb enough to fight for something that you have never gotten; if you are dumb enough to be as dumb as your other brothers who went into Korea and came back and still caught hell; if you're dumb enough to follow in the footsteps of your older brothers during World War II,

who fought all over the South Pacific, like Isaac Woodard, who came back here to this country and got his eyes punched out by police right here in this country; if you are dumb enough behind what you know about the white man today to let him stick his uniform on you and send you overseas to fight, well, you go the hell on and fight.

But I'm not that dumb. For me—and I can only speak for myself—I'll go to jail. I'll go to prison. Stick me in jail. Let me go to prison. But don't give me your uniform, and don't give me your rifle, because I might use it on someone that you don't intend on me to use it. Don't never put me in your airplane and fill it with bombs and tell me to go bomb the enemy. Why, I don't have far to go to find that enemy.[26]

In many ways Malcolm's break from the Nation of Islam was directly tied to his growing criticism of American foreign policy, particularly the role of the United States in Vietnam, though this was not openly stated at the time. When asked his opinion about John Kennedy's assassination in Dallas in November 1963, he responded by declaring that the "chickens have come home to roost." He went on to add, "Being an old farm boy myself, chickens coming home to roost never make me sad; they've always made me glad."[27] He was soon suspended (in reality, expelled) from the Nation of Islam. According to Shawki, "Malcolm X attributed John F. Kennedy's assassination to the hate and violence produced by a society that whites themselves had created."[28] It's important to add that part of that "violence" that Malcolm had in mind was also the "violence" of American foreign policy in the former colonial world. Three weeks previous to Kennedy's assassination, long-time U.S. ally Ngo Dinh Diem, the dictator of South Vietnam, and his brother Nhu, were toppled and murdered in a Kennedy-sponsored military coup. In effect, Kennedy—the assassin of Diem—was assassinated in Dallas. As Malcolm later put it, "They put in Diem over there. Then they killed him. Yes, they murdered him, murdered him in cold blood, him and his brother. When the puppet starts talking back to the puppeteer, the puppeteer is in bad shape."[29]

He believed that the United States, like the French before them, would be defeated in Vietnam, and subsequent events proved him right.

From that point up until his assassination February 1965, Malcolm X made only a few comments dealing specifically with Vietnam—because it was still largely a hidden war. Malcolm mostly made reference to Vietnam along with events in Africa, particularly in the Congo. But he quickly developed a keen understanding of the reactionary nature of U.S. foreign policy and put himself squarely on the side of those fighting U.S. and European domination. Many of his ideas were formed during his extended 1964 tour of the Middle East and Africa after his expulsion from the Nation of Islam. Malcolm called Washington, D.C., the "citadel of imperialism,"[30] and attacked the Kennedy administration–created Peace Corps as "neo-missionaries."[31] When Malcolm was asked directly about Vietnam, he would say, "They are trapped, they can't get out. If they pour men in, they'll get in deeper. If they pull men out, it's a defeat."[32]

In a January 1965 speech at the Palm Gardens in New York, Malcolm saluted the fighting prowess of the "oppressed people of South Vietnam": "Little rice farmers, peasants, with a rifle—up against all the highly mechanized weapons of warfare—jets, napalm, battleships, everything else, and they can't put those rice farmers back where they want them. Somebody's waking up."[33]

Just days before his assassination, when asked during a late-night newspaper interview with a South African reporter how far he would take violence in ending white minority rule in South Africa, Malcolm X responded, "All the way. I believe that the only solution to the South African problem is the same solution that was used in Algeria or the one that is being used right now in Vietnam."[34] Malcolm was assassinated before the large-scale landing of American troops in Vietnam—when the war was still a proxy war, and still largely on the margins of American consciousness; but he planted the seeds of opposition to the American war in Vietnam among a growing number of radicalizing Blacks.

After the U.S. invasion of South Vietnam in March 1965, the war became a major political issue in the United States. "For black Americans," according to Manning Marable, "the war had a direct impact upon every community." Three things in particular had an impact on the Black community: the disproportionately high casualty rate among Black soldiers, the draft, and growing identification of the struggle for Black freedom at home with the national liberation struggle of the Vietnamese and other oppressed people. In the twenty years following the Second World War, the number of African Americans in the U.S. military tripled from 107,000 in 1949 to over 303,000 in 1967. One out of seven soldiers stationed during the entire Vietnam War era were Black. Black soldiers who were not allowed to be in combat units or who fought in segregated ones up until the Korean War were now overrepresented in them with correspondingly disproportionate high casualty rates. The enlisted men in the marines and the army, which did the bulk of the ground combat, were respectively 9.6 percent and 13.5 percent Black. During January through November 1966 alone, Blacks made up 22.4 percent of the army's casualties. To say the least, it was shocking to most African Americans to find that double their percentage in the U.S. population was being killed or wounded in Vietnam.[35]

It would be the radical wing of the civil rights movement that first declared their opposition to the war in the Black community. "In fact, many Black civil rights activists first voiced the anti-imperialist consciousness toward which many antiwar activists would inevitably move."[36] The Mississippi Freedom Democratic Party (MFDP), whose ultimately failed effort to unseat the segregationist delegation from Mississippi at the 1964 Democratic convention radicalized many, issued a flyer in July 1965 against Black participation in the war in Vietnam. "No one," the MFDP flyer declared, "has a right to ask us to risk our lives and kill other Colored People in Santo Domingo and Vietnam, so that the White American can get richer. We will be looked upon as traitors by all the Colored People of the world if the Negro people continue to fight and die without cause."[37]

In January 1966, SNCC became the first civil rights organization to publicly declare its opposition to the war. As SNCC historian Clayborne Carson put it, "Most SNCC workers opposed U.S. involvement in Vietnam as soon as they became aware of it. The current of pacifism that still existed in SNCC, combined with SNCC workers' generalized distrust of the motives of the federal government and their sympathy for Third World struggles against white domination, made this opposition inevitable."[38] This may be true, but during the course of 1965, as the war escalated in Vietnam and individual SNCC members spoke out against the war, the organization as a whole took no position. It was only in November 1965, after a contentious staff meeting, that the Executive Committee was authorized to draft and issue an antiwar statement on behalf of SNCC that represented all factions. The issuance of such a statement was given greater urgency after SNCC member Sammy Younge, a twenty-one-year-old naval veteran, was murdered while trying use a "whites only" bathroom in Tuskegee, Alabama, on January 3, 1966. "On the day of his death, Younge had been threatened with a knife by a registrar in the Macon County Courthouse as he took forty Blacks to register."[39] Within days SNCC issued a blistering attack on the war in Vietnam and U.S. foreign policy in general:

> We believe the United States government has been deceptive in its claims of concern for the freedom of the Vietnamese people, just as the government has been deceptive in claiming concern for the freedom of the colored people in such countries as the Dominican Republic, the Congo, South Africa, Rhodesia and in the United States itself....

> The murder of Samuel Younge in Tuskegee, Alabama is no differ-
> ent from the murder of people in Vietnam, for both Younge and the
> Vietnamese sought and are seeking to secure the rights guaranteed
> them by law. In each case, the United States bears a great part of the
> responsibility for these deaths. Samuel Younge was murdered be-
> cause United States law is not being enforced. Vietnamese are being
> murdered because the United States is pursuing an aggressive policy
> in violation of international law....
>
> We are in sympathy with and support the men in this country
> who are unwilling to respond to the military draft which would com-
> pel them to contribute their lives to the United States aggression in
> the name of "freedom" we find so false in this country.[40]

To say the least, SNCC's statement against the war and its expressed sympathy (in reality, a thinly disguised call) for draft resistance, while not totally unexpected, was still a bombshell. SNCC
activists were seen as heroes not only to an entire generation of
young people in the United States, but to some of the poorest of
southern Blacks for whom they sacrificed their lives. The Johnson
White House was furious and attempted to isolate SNCC from the
rest of the civil rights movement. Roy Wilkins and Clarence Mitchell
of the NAACP, along with Whitney Young of the Urban League, du-
tifully issued statements at the White House's request attacking
SNCC. The notable exception was Martin Luther King Jr., who had
long privately disagreed with American policy in Vietnam but was
still not prepared to openly break with the Johnson administration.
Julian Bond, a leading member of SNCC, who won election to the
Georgia House of Representatives in the fall of 1965, was denied his
seat because he endorsed SNCC's antiwar stance a week before his
swearing-in. He would have to win two more elections and a
Supreme Court decision before he was seated.[41]

Taking a stand against the war was bad enough, but expressing
sympathy for resistance to the draft made SNCC members crimi-
nals, if not traitors, in the eyes of the Johnson White House. The pe-

culiar structure of the Selective Service System, which was head-quartered in Washington, but essentially administered by four thousand draft boards across the United States, had always been a source of anger for civil rights activists. They were overwhelmingly dominated by politically appointed white businessmen and veterans hostile to the needs and concerns of African Americans. In the South, Jim Crow supporters dominated the local draft boards. "In fact, it seemed as if many southern draft boards were targeting people in the movement."[42] In Julian Bond's case, he was first rejected for military service by his local Atlanta draft board, but later the chairman of his draft board expressed regret to a *Newsweek* reporter: "That nigger Julian Bond, we let him slip through our fingers."[43] By the time of the 1967 spring staff meeting of SNCC, more than sixteen SNCC workers had refused induction and were facing prison terms, including Cleveland Sellers, SNCC's national program director, who believed that draft boards were trying to "wipe out" the organization.[44] "In Louisiana," according to historian James Westheider, authorities could not draft New Orleans civil rights leader Jeanette Crawford, but within a week after she refused to appear before the Louisiana HUAC, induction orders were issued for her three sons." Eventually, her youngest son refused induction and was sentenced to six concurrent five-year prison terms, "the most severe sentence given to a nonviolent draft resister during the war."[45]

The most important African-American draft resister of the entire Vietnam era was the world heavyweight boxing champion Muhammad Ali. His impact on the consciousness of Black youth worldwide toward the war in Vietnam was enormous, if not historic, in its transformative power. Born Cassius Clay, Ali was raised in Louisville, Kentucky. "The Louisville of Ali's youth," according to sportswriter David Zirin, "was a segregated horse-breeding community where being Black meant being seen as part of a servant class."[46] He quickly developed his boxing skills and at eighteen he won the gold medal at the 1960 Olympics. But winning the gold medal didn't soften the intense racism he faced back home. A week after returning home from the Olympics, he went to buy a cheeseburger at local restaurant and was refused service. In anger and despair, he tossed his medal into the Ohio River.

Ali wanted answers to the questions that troubled him. This led him to secretly join the Nation of Islam (NOI), popularly known as the "Black Muslims," which despite its conservative politics, was viewed as essentially a criminal and subversive organization by the political establishment and the police because of its extreme verbal radicalism. Ali became quite close to Malcolm X until his break with the NOI. It was only after Ali defeated Sonny Liston on February 25, 1964 that he openly proclaimed his membership in the NOI and defiantly defended his beliefs by saying, "I don't have to be what you want me to be."[47] The NOI had a strict prohibition on its members joining the U.S. military, but its members found it virtually impossible to get Conscientious Objector (CO) status on religious grounds during the war in Vietnam because the draft boards considered the NOI not to be a "real religion." "Nearly, one hundred Black Muslims served federal prison terms for draft evasion during the Vietnam War."[48]

In early 1966, as draft calls escalated to fill the troop orders to fight in the expanding war in Vietnam, the military lowered the passing percentile in the intelligence tests from 30 to 15, making Ali, who had previously failed it, eligible for military service. Ali was denied both a deferral or postponement of reclassification, and at the age of twenty-four he was reclassified 1-A—eligible for military service. He was in training in Miami and when he heard the news from a *New York Times* reporter he said, "Man, I ain't got no quarrel with them Vietcong."[49] That one sentence, according to Ali biographer Mike Marqusee, "would prove to be one of the most resonant of the sixties…. No one, least of all Ali himself, could foresee the huge impact it was to have on his future, the future of boxing and the global opposition to the war in Vietnam."[50] In 1967, he was convicted of draft evasion by an all-white jury in Houston and sentenced to five years in prison. Ali immediately appealed the decision, and he had to wait for more than three years before the Supreme Court overturned his sentence. During his time in exile from the ring, he spoke forcefully and eloquently against the war:

> Why should they ask me to put on a uniform and go 10,000 miles from home and drop bombs and bullets on Brown people in Vietnam while so-called Negro people in Louisville are treated like dogs and denied simple human rights? No I'm not going 10,000 miles from home to help murder and burn another poor nation simply to continue the domination of white slave masters of the darker people the world over. This is the day when such evils must come to an end. I have been warned that to take such a stand would cost me millions of dollars. But I have said it once and I will say it again. The real enemy of my people is here. I will not disgrace my religion, my people or myself by becoming a tool to enslave those who are fighting for their own justice, freedom and equality.... If I thought the war was going to bring freedom and equality to 22 million of my people they wouldn't have to draft me, I'd join tomorrow. I have nothing to lose by standing up for my beliefs. So I'll go to jail, so what? We've been in jail for 400 years.[51]

People around the world rallied to Ali's defense and endorsed his views. There was a mass demonstration in support of him in Cairo, pickets at the American embassy in Guyana, and a student fast in Karachi, Pakistan. Ali spoke at dozens of campuses across the United States against the war. Everywhere he went he drew large, boisterous, and enthusiastic crowds. People wanted to simply touch him, to cheer him on. It was from this worldwide support that he drew the strength to defy the most powerful government in the world. The impact of Ali's defiance had an enormous effect on Black soldiers. "When I was in the Nam, Muhammad Ali was refusing to take the oath. Our reaction was that we shouldn't have taken it either. We felt that the American Dream didn't really serve us. What we experienced was the American Nightmare," recalled Black combat veteran Robert Sanders.[52] "Muhammad Ali had an enormous impact because he was so well known and he gave up so much. By refusing to fight in Vietnam he gave up his title as Heavyweight Champion of the World," Julian Bond told Christian Appy three decades later. "And he stated his opposition to the war so simply: 'No Viet Cong never called me nigger.' I mean, that was it. You didn't have to say more than that."[53]

The growing radicalization of the Black movement of the mid-1960s found its most famous expression in the Black Panther Party for Self Defense. The BPP was a revolutionary nationalist and socialist[54] organization founded in 1966 by Huey Newton and Bobby Seale. They developed a reputation for armed but entirely legal monitoring of the police in the city of Oakland, California, notorious for its police department's brutality against the local Black community. The Panthers became world famous after they appeared armed at the Capitol building in Sacramento, California, to oppose a new gun-control law aimed at them. In their initial ten-point program, they demanded that Black men be exempt from the draft:

> We want all Black men to be exempt from military. We believe that Black people should not be forced to fight in the military service to defend a racist government that does not protect us. We will not fight and kill other people of color in the world who, like Black people, are being victimized by the white racist government of America. We will protect ourselves from the force and violence of the racist police and the racist military, by whatever means necessary.[55]

The Panthers opposed the U.S. war in Vietnam and American intervention throughout the globe. They identified with the struggle of other oppressed groups and nations, which included the North Vietnamese and the National Liberation Front (NLF) of South Vietnam. Newton declared in a letter to the NLF, "The United States is an empire which has raped the world to build its wealth here."[56] Newton even offered to raise troops to fight in Vietnam against the

United States, an offer that was declined by the NLF. The Panthers' opposition to U.S. imperialism was rooted in their belief that the defeat of American imperialism abroad was necessary for the liberation of Black people in the United States. "The Black Panther Party [members] view the United States as the 'city' of the world, while we view the nations of Africa, Asia and Latin America as the 'countryside' of the world. The developing countries are the *Sierra Maestra* in Cuba and the United States is like Cuba."[57] The Panthers saw the United States as the center of world imperialism and put themselves on the side of those fighting against it.

The BPP had an immense impact on Black youth in the big cities. J. Edgar Hoover, the longstanding and reactionary director of the FBI, in 1969 called the Panthers the "greatest threat to the internal security of the country."[58] In a top-secret report to the president in June 1970, the FBI stated that a "recent poll indicates that approximately 25 percent of the black population has a great respect for the BPP, including 43 percent of Blacks under 21 years of age."[59] The Panthers' greatest appeal was among Black youth who were the most vulnerable to the draft and combat in Vietnam. With so many radicalized Black youth entering the military, it would not be long (particularly after the assassination of King in April 1968) before a political eruption took place inside the U.S. military.

The most significant figure in Black America to oppose the war in Vietnam was Martin Luther King Jr. Despite the split in the civil rights movement, King was still seen by many Americans as the leading figure in the Black movement. After all, King was the leader of the Montgomery bus boycott, the winner of the 1964 Nobel Prize for Peace, and was personally identified with every major legislative victory of the civil rights movement. The Johnson White House expected King to follow their political lead, but King was very unsatisfied with the progress of reform. He was especially shaken by the Watts rebellion in Los Angeles in August 1965, and it made him question aspects of his nonviolent philosophy and the commitment of the Democrats to eradicate poverty in the country. After a tour of Watts, King called the rebellion "a class revolt of under-privileged against privilege."[60] King privately opposed the war in Vietnam and thought the escalation of the war would derail the Great Society programs of the Johnson administration, but he feared that openly breaking with the administration on the war would lead to political isolation.

Johnson kept the pressure on King. King spoke to Johnson about getting Congress to act quickly on legislation to help the inner city following the riots in Watts. Johnson responded, "They [Congress] all got the impression that you're against me in Vietnam.... You don't leave that impression."[61] King's eventual open opposition to the war in Vietnam had much to do with the declining benefits of his alliance with the Johnson White House. At the end of the June 1966 March against Fear in Jackson, Mississippi, King told a reporter, "The government has got to give me some victories if I'm going to keep people nonviolent."[62] None were forthcoming.

On April 4, 1967, Martin Luther King Jr. delivered his famous "Declaration of Independence from the War in Vietnam" at the Riverside Church in New York. It was one of the best antiwar speeches in American history. He began by defending his decision to speak out against the war. When asked by critics why he was speaking out against the war and mixing the issues of domestic civil rights and foreign policy he responded, "I believe that the path from Dexter Avenue Baptist Church—the church in Montgomery, Alabama, where I began my pastorage—leads clearly to this sanctuary tonight." That is, the struggle against domestic racism inevitably lead to struggling against America's racist foreign policy. King quickly went into a lengthy discussion of his reasons for opposing the war:

> A few years ago there was a shining moment...it seemed as if there was a real promise of hope for the poor—both Black and white—

through the Poverty Program. Then came the buildup in Vietnam, and I watched the program broken and eviscerated as if it were some idle plaything of a society gone mad on war.... So I was increasingly compelled to see the war as an enemy of the Poor and attack it as such.

We were taking the young Black men who had been crippled by our society and sending them 8000 miles away to guarantee liberties in Southeast Asia which they had not found in Southwest Georgia and East Harlem. So we have been repeatedly faced with the cruel irony of watching Negro and white boys on TV screens as they kill and die together for a nation that has been unable to seat them together in the same schools.

As I have walked among the desperate, rejected and angry young men, I have told them that Molotov cocktails and rifles would not solve their problems.... But, they ask, what about Vietnam...? Their questions hit home, and I knew I that I could never again raise my voice against the violence of the oppressed in the ghettos without having first spoken clearly to the greatest purveyor of violence in the world today—my own government.

King went on to discuss the United States's inglorious history in Vietnam:

They [the Vietnamese] must see Americans as strange liberators. The Vietnamese proclaimed their own independence in 1945 after a combined French and Japanese occupation and before the communist revolution in China. Even though they quoted the American Declaration of Independence in their own document of freedom, we refused to recognize them. Instead, we decided to support the French in its reconquest of her former colony.

After the French were defeated...we supported one of the most vicious of modern dictators—our chosen man, Premier Diem.... When Diem was overthrown they may have been happy, but the long line of military dictatorships seemed to offer no real change—especially in terms of the need for land and peace.

King ended his speech with a rousing call for a "revolution in values."

I am convinced that if we are to get on the right side of the world revolution, we as a nation must undergo a radical revolution of values.... A true revolution of values will soon cause us to question the fairness and justice of our past and present policies.... These are revolutionary times. All over the globe men are revolting against old systems of exploitation and oppression.... Now let us begin. Now let us re-dedicate ourselves to the long and bitter—but beautiful—struggle for a new world.[63]

This was no ordinary Sunday sermon on U.S. foreign policy. King traced not only his own evolution as a civil rights leader to an antiwar leader, but the evolution of his own thinking that allowed him to do this—by seeing the Black struggle for freedom in the United States as tied up with a worldwide revolutionary movement against oppression.

Whether he was aware of it or not, King was following a political path that Malcolm X saw many African Americans taking in the sixties. "The masses of Black people today think in terms of Black," Malcolm argued. "And this Black thinking enables them to see beyond the confines of America."[64] King's bombshell speech was roundly attacked by Johnson's supporters and the leading magazines and newspapers in the country. The *Washington Post* declared that King's Riverside speech was a "grave injury" to the civil rights movement and had "diminished his usefulness to his cause, to his country, and to his people."[65] The viciousness of the attacks reveals how deeply King's opposition to the war worried his liberal supporters, who considered rightly that King's new public stance would be a tremendous boost to the antiwar cause. This was best understood by military leaders and intellectuals.

Looking back several years after King's speech, George L. Jackson, naval commander and an instructor at the School of Naval Command and Staff, observed that "the Negro civil rights action has introduced definite constraints on the military capability of the United States."

He continued:

The most important of these constraints is that produced by the coalition of civil rights organizations and the antiwar organizations. This coalition has spearheaded the shift in public opinion away from support for the Vietnam conflict.... The identification of the civil rights movement with the antiwar enthusiasts was given its greatest impetus in April of 1967, when the late Reverend Dr. Martin Luther King took a strong public stand on the issue.[66]

CHAPTER FIVE

FROM THE BIRTH OF THE ANTIWAR MOVEMENT TO 1968

> "The United States lost the war in both the Mekong
> Valley and the Mississippi Valley."
> —Howard Zinn, *A People's History of the United States*

The war in Vietnam produced the largest and most successful antiwar movement in U.S. history. The size and militancy of the movement was extraordinary. There was no part of the country that was not scarred by the war or left untouched by the antiwar movement. As the antiwar movement spread into larger sections of the population during the course of 1969, 1970, and 1971, millions of people were drawn into protests, and participants moved further and further to the left. To be sure, the movement was not always on the upswing; it went through periods where it seemed to disappear, periods where it exploded, and periods in between.

What is all the more remarkable about this is that just a short time before, the United States was in the midst of the McCarthy era. The virulent anticommunism of the 1950s not only created a suffocating conservative conformity in the domestic political life of the United States, but widespread public support for a foreign policy that claimed to be "battling communism" around the globe.

How is it possible that an antiwar movement could arise out of these circumstances and transform the political landscape of the country in so short a time?

As already noted, the antiwar movement was itself part of a wave of radicalization that had already begun well before 1965. Many of the activists who began organizing against the war in Vietnam had been involved in, or influenced by, several other struggles: the Black struggle for civil rights in the U.S. South; the movement against the proliferation of nuclear weapons; protests against the anticommunist witch hunts of the 1950s; and the struggle for free speech centered on the University of California at Berkeley campus. Events such as Freedom Summer, and with it, the emergence of SNCC, as well as the Berkeley Free Speech movement—not to mention the growing public criticism of American foreign policy in the developing world—all contributed to the creation of a new generation of political radicals in the United States for whom the war in Vietnam would become the major focus of political activity (though this was not so obvious in the early days of the war). All these factors would create the underlying dynamic that would be the driving force of the antiwar movement and, according to historian Howard Zinn, led to "the United States [losing] the war in both the Mekong Valley and the Mississippi Valley."[1]

FORERUNNERS OF A NEW MOVEMENT

"Prior to 1962 there had been no outright discrimination against Buddhists. However, among South Vietnam's three to four million practicing Buddhists and the 80 percent of the population who were nominal Buddhists, the regime's favoritism, authoritarianism, and discrimination created a smoldering resentment."
—The Pentagon Papers

Historian of the Vietnam antiwar movement Fred Halstead is essentially correct when he says that "a peace movement of sorts existed in the United States in 1960 but it had nothing to do with the war in Vietnam…. The war was not a central issue in American life."[2] The existing peace movement was focused on nuclear disarmament and nonproliferation. However, as Kennedy's proxy war escalated and opposition to the U.S.-backed Diem government exploded on the streets of South Vietnam, the war began to edge its way into the existing peace movement.

The leadership of most existing peace organizations, however, vociferously opposed the introduction of Vietnam into the movement. The National Committee for a Sane Nuclear Policy (SANE) and Turn Toward Peace were the two best-known peace organizations in the country in the early 1960s. SANE, the better known of the two, was founded in 1957 to work for a nuclear test ban treaty and disarmament. Turn Toward Peace was founded in 1961 as a coordinating organization of more than sixty organizations, which included SANE. Both organizations, liberal to the core, embraced anticommunism.

SANE opposed any form of militant direct action and "refused to allow communists or socialists in its membership—an 'exclusionary policy.'"[3] They were certainly not going to challenge the underlying assumptions of U.S. policy in Vietnam. The organization was led by such establishment liberals such as Norman Cousins, a former editor of the *Saturday Review*, who on several occasions acted as an unofficial emissary to the Russian government for the Kennedy administration. "Some peace leaders did not want to divide an already weak 'peace community' with harsh talk about the U.S. adventure in Vietnam," according to historians Zaroulis and Sullivan. "The audience that SANE hoped to reach—John F. Kennedy's liberals—were the same people who were overseeing the Vietnam agenda, and they would not listen—so the reasoning went—to pleas for nuclear disarmament voiced by critics of their Vietnam policy."[4]

While the leadership of SANE was prevented by its devotion to the Democratic Party from taking a principled position on Vietnam, others were not. The issues of nuclear testing and disarmament produced some of the first stirrings of campus activism in the late fifties and early sixties. The major beneficiary of this new spirit of activism was the Student Peace Union (SPU) founded in Chicago in 1959. After a spurt of growth and a merger, the SPU grew to about 1,500 dues-paying members in December 1961. It doubled its membership during the next year and had campus chapters in the Midwest, Northeast, on the West Coast, and even in the South. "For several years," according to historian Maurice Isserman, "the Student Peace Union would remain the largest and most influential group of the New Left."[5] The SPU was heavily influenced by the left wing of the Young Peoples' Socialist League, which later became the International Socialists. The SPU, in many ways, was a forerunner of the New Left. Many of the socialists in the SPU argued for bringing the war in Vietnam into the broader peace movement, despite the opposition from the old guard of SANE.

Opponents of American policy in Vietnam were helped immensely by events abroad. "Shortly before Easter, Bertrand Russell, a key figure in the British Campaign for Nuclear Disarmament (CND), issued a statement declaring that the United States was conducting a war of annihilation in Vietnam."[6] Russell was an internationally well-known and revered liberal philosopher. He brought great prestige to the movement on both sides of the Atlantic. In the United States at the annual Easter Peace Walks held in solidarity with the CND's Aldermaston "Ban the Bomb" march, activists who wanted to express support for Russell's stand on Vietnam wore "I Like Bertrand Russell" buttons.

The Easter peace marches took place in various U.S. cities, including Chicago, Minneapolis, and New York City. At the largest one, at UN Plaza, veteran radical pacifist A. J. Muste spent his entire speech attacking U.S. policy in Vietnam, while members of the Student Peace Union carried signs denouncing the United States in Vietnam, much to the displeasure of SANE organizers. In fact, the UN march's chairman, Bayard Rustin, a former radical pacifist and soon-to-be supporter of the war in Vietnam, attempted to have all signs making reference to Vietnam removed from the demonstration. But he gave up after failing to win the crowd to his side.[7]

While speeches of Russell and Muste and the actions of the Student Peace Union helped push Vietnam in from the fringes of the peace movement, it would be events in Vietnam that would produce the first wave of pickets and demonstrations specifically targeting American policy there. What has gone down in the history books as the "Buddhist crisis" began in April 1963 with the Diem regime enforcing a ban on displays of religious flags in South Vietnam (which had previously never been enforced). The fanatically Catholic regime of Ngo Dinh Diem (a former seminarian) had built a political base of Catholic refugees who had fled the northern half of Vietnam in a well-orchestrated CIA operation. "Prior to 1962," according to the Pentagon Papers, "there had been no outright discrimination against Buddhists. However, among South Vietnam's three to four million practicing Buddhists and the 80 percent of the population who were nominal Buddhists, the regime's favoritism, authoritarianism, and discrimination created a smoldering resentment."[8]

On May 8, Buddhist monks protesting the Diem administration's policies were attacked in Hue and nine were killed by government troops. The following day, ten thousand people demonstrated in Hue against the killings. This was the beginning of the end of the Diem government.[9] Over the next several months, successive waves of demonstrations by Buddhist monks (and spreading to larger sections of the population furious at the Saigon government) met increased repression from Diem's security forces. The most dramatic and unforgettable event was on June 11, when Buddhist monk Thich Quang Duc committed suicide by burning himself to death at a busy intersection in Saigon in front of group of foreign newsmen. In solidarity with the persecuted Buddhists, three members of the radical Catholic Worker movement in New York picketed the UN for ten days straight with signs that read, "We demand an end to U.S.

military support of Diem's government." On the tenth day of their picket, they were joined by 250 other peace activists and their picket was broadcast on the ABC evening news.[10]

Later that fall, Madame Nhu, the wife of Ngo Dinh Nhu, Diem's brother and head of the South Vietnamese secret police, toured the United States. Sent as Diem's goodwill ambassador to the United States, she quickly revealed the ugliness of her brother-in-law's regime. Nhu was met with sporadic but boisterous protests on almost every campus she visited. She angered and dismayed many by describing the Buddhist suicides during an interview as "barbecues," and adding, "Let them burn, and we shall clap our hands."[11] She was heckled at Harvard by a group of more than one hundred students (mostly members of the Students for a Democratic Society) and upon finishing her speech where she claimed quite incredibly that there was "absolute religious freedom in Vietnam."[12] At Columbia University, where more than three hundred heckled her speech, the Student Peace Union organized many protesters. "The number of demonstrators at other campuses—several organized by SPU chapters—varied from a dozen at Chapel Hill, North Carolina, to several hundred at Madison, Wisconsin, and Ann Arbor, Michigan."[13] Nhu's tour was an absolute disaster for American policy.

The Diem regime's handling of the Buddhist crisis, along with the growing strength of the National Liberation Front, convinced the Kennedy administration that Diem and his family had to go. In early November 1963, President Diem and his brother were overthrown and assassinated in the CIA-orchestrated coup. Madame Nhu found herself stranded abroad and never returned to Vietnam. While Diem's repression of the Buddhists and Madame Nhu's goodwill tour of the United States turned out to be twin disasters for the United States, the war in Vietnam was still a proxy war involving a relatively small number of Americans in direct combat. Vietnam temporarily made its way in from the fringes of the old peace movement and onto the front page of the country's newspapers, but was soon back on the margins.

Political activism around issues of nuclear testing and disarmament peaked in 1962 and dropped off quickly after the United States and the USSR signed a treaty banning above-ground testing. The Student Peace Union, which had helped bring Vietnam into the center of the movement during 1963, would collapse by the end of the year. The year 1964 saw the U.S. war in Vietnam escalate while Johnson ran as a peace candidate in the presidential election. Johnson had pledged, "We are not about to send American boys nine or ten thousand miles away from home to do what Asian boys ought to be doing for themselves."[14] The true extent of America's involvement in Vietnam was hidden from the vast majority of the population. Soon after Johnson was sworn in for his first full term as president, the fundamental direction of the war changed—it truly became an American war—and with it was born a new movement.

1965: BIRTH OF THE NEW MOVEMENT

"What kind of system is it that justifies the United States or any country seizing the destinies of the Vietnamese people and using them callously for our purposes? We must name the system…. For it is only when that system is changed and brought under control that there can be any hope for stopping the forces that create a war in Vietnam today."
—Paul Potter, president of SDS, April 1965

From 1960 to 1965, a new generation of radicals was born in the United States; they would eventually be called, by supporters and opponents alike, the New Left. The new radicals had to wage a struggle against the increasingly anachronistic anticommunism of the "old peace movement" leaders to just get the movement off the ground.

In March 1965, the United States shifted from fighting a proxy war in Vietnam to a full-scale ground and air war, primarily to be fought by its own military forces, that would eventually number

more than half a million troops. The Saigon government, after a series of coups, was tottering on the very edge of collapse, and only a
U.S. invasion could save it. On February 7, 1965, the American air
base at Pleiku in South Vietnam was attacked by the NLF. Eight
Americans were killed and more than 126 were wounded. On
March 2, Johnson ordered the sustained bombing of North Vietnam ("Operation Rolling Thunder") that would continue for the
next four years. Six days later, the 9th Marine Expeditionary Force
landed outside Danang, the first wave of American infantry to land
in South Vietnam.[15]

Despite the boastful optimism of the White House and the overwhelming support of Congress and the media, Johnson and some of
his closest advisers were privately uneasy about how long the public
would support the war in Vietnam. The war in Korea had been highly
unpopular, with a large number of casualties (36,500 U.S. deaths; millions of Korean civilian deaths), and ended in a stalemate. Korea (and
the French defeat in Vietnam) cast a long shadow over the early days
of the war in Vietnam. William Bundy, one of Johnson's most important national security advisers, recalled that the lesson of Korea was
that public support had "a time limit on it."[16] For a significant number
of people, the time limit ran out as soon as the war began.

Antiwar organizing first took the form of "teach-ins," beginning
at the University of Michigan at Ann Arbor, and then spreading to
more than one hundred campuses across the country. At Ann Arbor
on March 24, less than two weeks after the marines landed in
Danang, more than 3,000 students participated after class in a teach-
in that lasted through most of the night. They listened to lectures
and debates on a wide variety of subjects related to the war in Vietnam, despite being picketed by right-wing, prowar students and
being threatened by a bomb scare. Ann Arbor became the model for
the rest of the country.[17]

The largest was the Vietnam Day teach-in at the University of California at Berkeley on May 21–22, 1965, where the Free Speech Movement had exploded a year earlier. It went on for thirty-six hours straight, and some thirty thousand people participated. During his speech, Second World War veteran and novelist Norman Mailer declared quite prophetically, "You [Lyndon Johnson] are a bully with an air force, and since you will not call off your air force, there are young people who will persecute you back. They will go on marches and they will make demonstrations, and they will begin a war of public protest against you, which will never cease."[18] The internationally known Marxist and biographer of Russian revolutionary Leon Trotsky, Isaac Deutscher, concluded his speech by arguing that the only solution to the world's problems "is a socialist world, one socialist world. We must give back to the class struggle its old dignity. We may and we must restore meaning to great ideas, the ideas of liberalism, democracy, and communism—yes, the idea of communism."[19] That Deutscher could make such a statement and not be driven off the stage was testament to the changes taking place in U.S. society.

The Johnson administration was contemptuous of the campus teach-ins and directed a lot of its fury at faculty members who participated in them. Secretary of State Dean Rusk, referring to the teach-ins, remarked in a speech he gave at the end of April, "I sometimes wonder at the gullibility of educated men and the stubborn disregard of plain facts by men who are supposed to be helping our young to learn—especially how to think."[20] That people were no longer gullible toward government propaganda and were learning how to think for themselves doesn't seem to have crossed Rusk's mind.

In response to the teach-ins, the State Department sent out a "truth team" to Midwest campuses to make the administration's case for war. At every stop, the team was grilled by students and put on the defensive. Thomas Conlon, of the Agency for International

Development (AID), headed the team. At the University of Wisconsin forum in Madison, Conlon and his team faced an audience of seven hundred students, most of them wearing black armbands. The students hit them hard with tough questions. To a student who condemned torture, Conlon claimed, "The Americans don't torture." In response to another student's accusation that the United States ran South Vietnam, he answered, "We don't run it," which provoked shouts of "aw, come on."[21] "At the end of its three-week expedition into the heartland, the 'truth team' went back to Washington, not to be heard of again."[22]

Teach-ins peaked on May 15–16, when 122 college campuses were connected by a special radio hookup to hear one of the most extensive discussions of the war, sponsored by the Inter-University Committee for a Public Hearing on Vietnam. In the middle of this wave of teach-ins, the Students for a Democratic (SDS) sponsored a national demonstration against the war in Washington, D.C.

SDS was "formed in 1960, when a handful of student radicals took over the Student League for Industrial Democracy (SLID), the youth league of the social-democratic League for Industrial Democracy."[23] SDS would emerge as the main radical student organization of the 1960s. By the end of the decade, it had nearly one hundred thousand members on campuses across the country.[24] At the time of its antiwar march in Washington, SDS had between two and three thousand members, and was mostly known for mobilizing northern whites for the southern civil rights struggle.[25] During the Easter recess (the weekend of April 17), a time of traditional peace demonstrations, twenty to thirty thousand people participated in the first nationwide march against the war. Of the many SDS-approved placards were: "Stop World War III Now," "Negotiate," "End the War in Vietnam," and "Escalate Freedom in Mississippi." They heard speeches by Yale professor Staughton Lynd, who drew a direct connection between France's disastrous colonial war in Algeria and the current American war in Vietnam. Senator Ernest Gruening, one of two senators who voted against the Tonkin Gulf resolution, called for a halt of U.S. bombing of North Vietnam. I. F. Stone, the radical journalist, who had pushed SDS to call the April march, tore apart the administration's rationale for war.

The most significant presence at the march, however, was the young SNCC leader Robert Moses, a hero of the civil rights movement, who "attempted to connect the war to the civil rights movement, and pointed out that the country's leaders who conducted the war for the ostensible freedom of the South Vietnamese were the same leaders who refused to guarantee the freedom of some Americans in the U.S. South."[26] Right from the very beginning of the war, the new student antiwar movement and the left wing of the civil rights movement were united in their opposition to the war in Vietnam. It was estimated that 10 percent of the antiwar demonstrators that day were Black, roughly equivalent to the percentage of Blacks in the American population at the time.

The most memorable speech of the day was given by Paul Potter, president of SDS. His speech in many ways captured the radicalization taking place among a large number of politically active young people, both Black and white—in particular, their break with the liberalism of the Democratic Party, which they saw as both hypocritical and responsible for the war in Vietnam. "The incredible war in Vietnam has provided the razor, the terrifying sharp cutting edge that has finally severed the last vestiges of illusions that morality and democracy are guiding principles of American foreign policy," Potter declared. He then went on to present a political challenge to everyone there. "What kind of system is it that justifies the United States or any country seizing the destinies of the Vietnamese people and using them callously for our purposes? We must name the system. We must name it, describe it, analyze it, understand it, and change it. For it is only when that system is changed and brought under control that there can be any hope for stopping the forces that create a war in Vietnam today."[27] While some in the crowd shouted out "capitalism" and "imperialism" to Potter's questions, he later explained why he didn't "name the system": "I refused to call it capitalism because capitalism for me and my generation is an inadequate description of the evils of America—a hollow, dead word tied to the thirties."[28] Within a few years, a significant number of Potter's generation would conclude that capitalism was indeed a very adequate explanation for the evils of American society.

The SDS demonstration was considered a major success and surprised almost everyone by its size and enthusiasm. "But the ghost of Joseph McCarthy almost destroyed the march before it began," according to historians Zaroulis and Sullivan. "At the eleventh hour, a group of older-generation people who had been helping to organize it suddenly decided that they could not, after all, go along with SDS's 'nonexclusionary' policy. Nonexclusion meant that anyone from any group could join a march or demonstration."[29] SANE, the main antinuclear testing group, didn't endorse SDS's march precisely because it wasn't virulently anticommunist. Then, on the eve of the march, radical pacifist leader A. J. Muste and Socialist Party leader Norman Thomas "seemed to disavow the participation of far left groups" in the coming SDS march.[30]

Despite the Cold War thaw and the activism that took the bite out of HUAC, anticommunism was still embraced by all the major institutions of American society. The newly emerging organizations of the New Left that sought to throw it off found themselves in bitter conflict with the older established organizations of the liberal-left and peace organizations. SANE even went so far as to fire one of its key organizers after he was called in front of HUAC and pleaded the Fifth Amendment. This kind of behavior alienated many young student activists. As 1960s veteran and author Jo Freeman wrote, "One SNCC organizer spoke for many of the New Left when, answering accusations of Communist infiltration of the civil rights movement, he declared, 'I don't care what he believes. If he's willing to put his body on the line, he's welcome.'"[31]

The success of the April 1965 national march and the campus teach-ins transformed the antiwar movement. But ironically, the success of these events produced a sense of malaise in SDS, brought on to a large degree by a sense that national protests weren't effective. For example, SDS leader Carl Davidson explained that after the national march, "I was convinced I was going to read on the front page that the war was over, that Johnson had seen all those people and would start to pull the troops out."[32] Activists were used to seeing more immediate results around civil rights struggles in the early to mid-1960s. SDS organizer Paul Booth explained, "We were completely disoriented by the phenomenon of mass protest and no reaction."[33] Booth and others developed this sentiment into a theory that the United States was "impervious to pressure placed directly on it." As Booth wrote with another activist, "If we leave Vietnam, it will be a reflection of LBJ's tactical wisdom, not of our political force."[34] Partly as a result of this development, SDS—though it would be the largest radical student organization until its breakup in 1969, and though its local chapters were very active in the antiwar movement—never again took the initiative in calling national protests.

By October 1965, there had been more than sixty protests against the war across the country involving about one hundred thousand people. SANE called for a national demonstration on November 27, 1965, to try to recapture its preeminent position among peace groups after failing to endorse the April SDS demonstration. As part of its call, SANE announced that "kooks, communists, and draft-dodgers" weren't welcome at the demonstration.[35] But they soon became worried about the turnout and invited SDS to participate. SDS President Carl Oglesby explained that the group's choice was to "sit on the sidelines and let the march fail and give Johnson and his crowd the opportunity to crow over the death of the peace movement, or else go in there and try to make it work."[36] The discussions between Oglesby and SANE organizers highlighted the debate in the antiwar movement over the question of immediate withdrawal and the right of the Vietnamese people to self-determination. Oglesby, for instance, had a "huge fight" with SANE leader Stanford Gottlieb after Oglesby offered the slogan "Vietnam for the Vietnamese." "I thought," said Oglesby, "that was a pretty normal thing for people to say, and there was no problem with it, but he saw it as…an implicit endorsement of the communist side. This was the kind of thing I was up against."[37]

At the demonstration itself, Oglesby made a pointed speech addressing the questions facing the movement. "The original commitment in Vietnam was made by President Truman, a mainstream liberal," Oglesby said. "It was seconded by President Eisenhower, a moderate liberal. It was intensified by the late President Kennedy, a flaming liberal. Think of the men who now engineer that war—those who study the maps, give the commands, push the buttons, and tally the dead: Bundy, McNamara, Rusk, Lodge, Goldberg, the president himself. They are not moral monsters. They are all honorable men. They are all liberals." Oglesby speculated about a meeting between the "dead revolutionaries" of 1776 and the modern liberals prosecuting the war in Vietnam—in which the latter complained that Vietnamese rebels couldn't be fighting a "revolution" because they used terror and got help from foreign fighters.

"What would our dead revolutionaries answer?" Oglesby said.

They might say: "What fools and bandits, sirs, you make then of us. Outside help? Do you remember Lafayette? Or the three thousand British freighters the French navy sunk for our side? Or the arms and men we got from France and Spain? And what's this about terror? Did you never hear what we did to our own Loyalists? Or about the thousands of rich American Tories who fled for their lives to Canada? And as for popular support, do you not know that we had less than one-third of our people with us? That, in fact, the colony of New York recruited more troops for the British than for the revolution? Should we give it all back?"

Revolutions do not take place in velvet boxes. They never have. It is only the poets who make them lovely. What the National Liberation Front is fighting in Vietnam is a complex and vicious war. This war is also a revolution, as honest a revolution as you can find anywhere in history. And this is a fact which all our intricate official denials will never change.[38]

As the growing movement against the war broke free of the restrictions that its early leadership tried to impose on it, activists grappled with a series of questions. One of the most important was whether the antiwar movement should stand for the immediate withdrawal of U.S. troops or a call for "negotiations now" to settle the war. SANE and Turn Toward Peace were worried about the radical direction of the new antiwar movement. Western Area Turn Toward Peace Director Robert Pickus, for example, issued a press release condemning the San Francisco march planned to coincide with the April 1965 national antiwar march. "It is time that someone within the peace movement challenged activity which is, in fact, more hostile to America than to war," Pickus declared. Getting out of Vietnam, he argued, "is not the way to end the war in Vietnam."[39]

Pickus pressed his opposition to the "out now" demand in antiwar organizing. During the lead-up to the Vietnam Day teach-in at Berkeley, for example, he "sought to impose an organizational apparatus to check the credentials of all the participants, in order to ensure that they agreed with his general views," according to participant James Petras. "His method of operation seemed to us a 'rule-or-ruin' approach." On the day of the teach-in, Pickus debated Hal Draper of the Independent Socialist Club on the question of whether the movement should call for negotiations or immediate withdrawal. "To oppose American intervention in Vietnam, as Hal Draper pointed out in his debate with Pickus, is to call for the *immediate* withdrawal of U.S. troops," Petras wrote. "To call for it 'later,' (under whatever pretense) is to legitimize violence in the here and now—since one cannot impose utopian dreams on what the U.S. Army does in fighting a war of conquest. One would not be too irreverent to refer to this type of 'peace' approach as 'War now—Peace later.'"[40]

Such views remained in the minority among the antiwar movement when Oglesby gave his speech. But by now, they spoke for a core of activists who rejected the "common sense" that dominated the early days of the movement. Eventually, as the struggle spread, such ideas became accepted in the mainstream of the movement. Efforts to stifle debate or confine the movement within political limits judged to be "acceptable" failed, because the course of events and demands of the struggle itself radicalized more and more people, leading them to look beyond the liberal orthodoxy. The protests and teach-ins had an effect on tens of thousands of people, turning them against the war.[41]

The antiwar movement spread beyond the campuses and emerged as a mass movement in 1967. Martin Luther King Jr.'s public declaration of his opposition to the war helped with this enormously (see Chapter Four). The three hundred thousand-strong April 15, 1967, march to the United Nations to protest the war, the largest protest to date against the war in Vietnam, began in New York's Central Park. "April 15 was a cold, gray day in New York. Despite light rain, demonstrators surged into Sheep Meadow in Central Park throughout the morning.... The crowd spanned a wide cross section of American society," according to Tom Wells.

> Youth predominated, some sporting long hair and jeans, others tweed coats and ties. Also present were middle-aged businessmen in dark suits, housewives in dresses and nylons, bespectacled high school science teachers, and doctors in long white coats. There were nuns and priests outfitted in robes and collars and professors adorned with tassels, mortarboards, and gowns. Hundreds of medal-

decorated war veterans with blue hats marked 'Veterans for peace' perched on their heads were gathered at the southern end of the park. Nearby stood a contingent of American Indians in native attire. Entire families dotted the crowd.[42]

Martin Luther King Jr. led the march, along with Black entertainer and activist Harry Belafonte, Dr. Benjamin Spock (the famous baby doctor), and SNCC leader Stokely Carmichael, among others. That same day, a sixty thousand-strong rally in San Francisco was addressed by Coretta Scott King, the wife of Martin Luther King Jr., and was endorsed by the Santa Clara Labor Council. According to Wells, the "participation of thousands of trade union members were marked signs of the peace movement's continuing growth."[43]

At the protest, sixty men gathered to burn their draft cards, responding to a call that had been initiated by Cornell students. Dozens of other men spontaneously joined in and burned their cards too, so that a total of 170 burned their draft cards. A new law punished draft-card burning by as much as five years in prison. "We are no longer interested in merely protesting the war," said army reservist Gary Rader, who had burned his card that day. "We are out to stop it."[44] The sentiment reflected a sense among a growing number of young activists in the movement that big rallies were not enough. Also reflected was a sense of bravado combined with a heavy dose of moralism. One of the leading spokesmen of a newly formed antidraft group, Resistance, Lennie Heller, argued that men who refused to return their draft cards "had no balls."[45] Former SDS secretary Clark Kissinger took a different approach, holding a "draft acceptance ceremony" in front of the induction center in Chicago (complete with a five-piece brass band playing). He gave a speech announcing how he would enjoy getting paid to recruit other soldiers to the antiwar cause. Kissinger was not called up.[46]

On August 28, the National Mobilization Committee (Mobe)—a coalition of various liberal, pacifist, and left organizations that was an outgrowth of the Spring Mobilization Committee that had organized the April protest in New York—announced that a national protest would be held on October 21 at the Pentagon, involving both mass protest and civil disobedience. An official press statement announced that the plan was to "shut down the Pentagon." Jerry Rubin, leader of the highly theatrical Yippies (Youth International Party), who had been invited into the Mobe leadership by veteran radical pacifist Dave Dellinger, announced, "We're going to raise the Pentagon three hundred feet in the air."[47] A flavor of the Yippie's theatrical antics can be found in the Mobe newsletter, the *Mobilizer,* where an article listed as one of the possible actions in D.C. during the October 21 protest, "A thousand children will stage Loot-ins at department stores to strike at the property fetish that underlies genocidal wars."[48] On the other end of the spectrum of the coalition were the liberals and moderates who insisted on a strict separation between the civil disobedience and possible confrontation at the Pentagon and the mass march at the Lincoln Memorial. Fred Halstead, a Mobe leader and member of the Socialist Workers Party, blocked with the moderates, because in his words, "We supported increasing the influence of the moderates in the general publicity and tone of the event because we agreed with them that this was the best approach to turn out the largest numbers."[49] Of course, the claims about shutting down the Pentagon and disrupting the war machine were pure hype; but the advocates of purely legal mass protest were equally wrong in their insistence that mass, legal protests (not to mention lobbying) were sufficient to stop the war.

On the day of the protest, more than one hundred thousand people marched on the Pentagon—with thousands prepared to engage in civil disobedience—after rallying at the Lincoln Memorial. It was the largest demonstration up until that time at the citadel of American military power, which was guarded by a tight phalanx of thousands of military policemen with bayonets drawn. "The crowd was largely students, many with banners identifying their schools and colleges," according to Zaroulis and Sullivan, "but there were also church groups, old-line peace and leftist groups, unions, a contingent from the Progressive Labor Party—more than 150 organizations in all, and a handful of celebrities, including Norman Mailer, who commemorated the event by writing *Armies of the Night*."[50] A group of a few thousand—a loose coalition involving SDS and a group calling itself the Revolutionary Contingent—made a run up the embankment toward the mall to try and make it past security into the Pentagon. Only twenty-five eventually made it through. A number of protesters faced off with the MPs; some taunted the troops; others appealed to them. Halstead describes the scene:

> After the steps had been partly filled, a unit of some thirty troops carrying rifles was sent down to block off the steps from below. They quickly found themselves surrounded, perhaps two thousand demonstrators at their backs on the steps and a huge crowd immediately in front of them on the mall. They stood there in a line, their guns pointed at the demonstrators on the mall. Those in the crowd started talking to them while one youth walked along the line putting flowers in the gun barrels. Photos of this became classics. The unit was soon withdrawn.[51]

The Pentagon was so worried about the effects of such large protests on the American war effort that it had the U.S. Air Force drop "1.75 million leaflets on North Vietnam warning the North Vietnamese not to be misled by protests in the United States into thinking that America had lost its will to fight."[52]

As the development of draft resistance shows, the antiwar movement involved more than large-scale mobilizations. The movement took on the American war machine wherever it could. This meant organizing against the most visible manifestations of the war for young people, for example, university complicity with the war, particularly, the presence of Dow Chemical on campuses.

Dow Chemical Company became a particular focus of organizing because it was one of the main producers of napalm, the infamous flammable jelly that disfigured large numbers of Vietnamese civilians during the war. "It's a terror weapon," said a veteran air force pilot who dropped napalm on a regular basis. "People have this thing about being burned to death."[53] Dow, like many other private corporations, sent recruiters to campuses around the country for years without any opposition. As the horrible effects of napalm became known, *Ramparts* magazine did an in-depth report on napalm in January 1967.

And as antiwar sentiment grew on campuses, organizing against Dow took on a special emphasis. On February 21 and 22, the first sit-ins took place against Dow at the University of Wisconsin at Madison; nineteen were arrested. That fall, protests against Dow spread to campuses across the country, most of them organized by SDS chapters. The seminal event took place at Madison on October 16, 1967, where "thirty thousand students…were met with a two-page mimeographed handout, without a date or signature. 'From Tuesday to Friday of this week,' it began, 'Dow Chemical Company will be recruiting on campus. On Tuesday, this fact will be brought to the attention of the entire campus. On Wednesday, students will block Dow from recruiting.'"[54]

On Tuesday morning (October 17), over two hundred students picketed the Commerce Building on campus, where Dow recruiters were located, chanting antiwar slogans. The next day, around one hundred students walked into the building, sat down in front of the office that Dow was using, and linked arms. The numbers of students sitting in against Dow grew to around 350, while about two thousand gathered outside. The campus police, with off-campus reinforcements, began to take positions outside the Commerce Building. The campus police chief tried to broker a deal where the students would leave if Dow left, and the students agreed to the deal. However, Chancellor Sewell would not have it, and he ordered the police to clear the building. What happened next is recounted by Zaroulis and Sullivan:

> Dressed in riot gear, the police charged the perhaps three hundred
> students barricading the recruiters' door. In a matter of minutes the

building was cleared, but several thousand students, watching and waiting outside, were horrified to see their battered, bloodied fellows who emerged. To disperse this larger crowd, the police used tear gas—the first time it had been used on a college campus. The crowd became angry; people began to throw rocks and bricks. The police sprayed mace (a nerve gas) but the crowd did not move. Dogs and a riot squad were brought in. At last the crowd melted away. Three policemen and sixty-five students were treated for injuries.[55]

The wanton brutality of the police produced a two-day student strike. Dow was temporarily banned from campus, and in retaliation the administration suspended thirteen students and fired three faculty members who joined the strike.

The events at Madison had an enormous impact on the fight against Dow as well as a major radicalizing effect on the students involved. After all, here was a university that was considered one of the great liberal institutions of higher learning using police tactics that seemed to come straight out of Latin American or Eastern bloc "Communist" countries. University complicity with the war in Vietnam became from this point onward one of the key issues of the antiwar movement.

While the battle raged over the presence of Dow Chemical at Madison, on the West Coast antiwar activists—ranging from traditional pacifist groups like the War Resisters League to SDS and the newly formed antidraft organization Resistance—initiated "Stop the Draft Week," which was to last from October 16 to 20. The week would focus on closing down the Northern California Draft Induction Center located in Oakland, California. The first day (Monday, October 16) 125 people sat in at the induction center and were arrested in a commonplace display of civil disobedience. The next day more than three thousand people gathered before dawn on what became known as "Bloody Tuesday." The police were waiting and attacked the crowd—some of whom defended themselves with garbage can lids and crash helmets—

with clubs and mace. As with the Madison protests against Dow, the police violence shocked people. On Wednesday and Thursday, more than ninety-seven people were arrested in a return to the traditional civil disobedience that started the week.

On Thursday, a 19-year-old UC student and member of the Stop the Draft Week steering committee announced that they planned on Friday to stop the buses carrying inductees from getting to the induction center. "We intend to give the cops one hell of a run for their money," he proclaimed.[56] And they did. Ten thousand turned up, and instead of massing in front of the induction center, they blocked all the streets surrounding it. When police moved in, the crowds would withdraw and block the street, dodging the police and moving forward whenever the police moved away. "For three hours they succeeded in blocking entrance to the center occasionally stopping some busloads of inductees, carrying a running street battle with police, throwing up barricades, grouping and surfacing to attack again in a constant flow."[57] Eventually the demonstrators left exhilarated, feeling at least temporarily victorious. One UC student later remembered it as "the greatest day of my life."[58] California Governor Ronald Reagan denounced the protest, blithely remarking, "There is nothing that justifies bloodshed, violence, damage to property, and harm to individuals."[59]

The fight against Dow at Madison and Stop the Draft Week in Oakland, according to Berkeley activist Frank Bardacke, produced "a more serious and more radical movement."[60] The size of the April and October mobilizations revealed the new mass character of the antiwar movement, while events at Madison and Oakland revealed a leap in the willingness of student activists to engage in more militant action. All this contributed to the radicalization of younger activists, who were increasingly drawn in larger numbers to radical politics. By the end of 1967, SDS, for example, had grown by nearly ten thousand members.[61]

1968: TET, THE DEMOCRATS,
AND THE ANTIWAR MOVEMENT

"Nineteen sixty-eight was the fulcrum year, the year the balance scales tipped
against the American war effort in Vietnam. It was a year in which events
happened so quickly, hammer blow after hammer blow."
—Nancy Zaroulis and Gerald Sullivan

Johnson had been elected in 1964 with the greatest majority since
Franklin Roosevelt's reelection triumph in 1936. Four years later, on
the eve of the 1968 election, he had become the most hated man in
America. "I feel like a hitchhiker caught in a hailstorm on a Texas
highway," he told his press secretary. "I can't run. I can't hide. And I
can't make it stop."[62]

The mass opposition to the war in Vietnam was creating a major
split in the Democratic Party, yet it seemed that no one would challenge Johnson for the party's nomination. By the end of 1967, after it
became clear that Bobby Kennedy, the repository of all the romantic
myths of the Kennedy family, would not challenge Johnson, Eugene
McCarthy, a little-known Democratic senator from Minnesota, announced on November 20, 1967, that he would seek the party's
nomination for president. This came a month after the mammoth
demonstration at the Pentagon. He had been a member of the Congress since 1949 and was elected to the Senate in the Democratic
sweep of 1958. He had an undistinguished career in both the House
and the Senate, and was considered something of an outsider from
the Senate's boys' club. Whatever his private views, he supported the
Tonkin Gulf resolution and voted for every war-appropriation bill.

McCarthy was very straightforward about his political goals—re-
habilitating the American political system and getting the antiwar
protests off the streets:

There is growing evidence of a deepening moral crisis in America—
discontent and frustration and a disposition to take extralegal if not
illegal actions to manifest protest.

I am hopeful that this challenge...may alleviate at least in some
degree this sense of political hopelessness and restore to many people
a belief in the process of American politics and of American government...[and] that it may counter the growing sense of alienation
from politics, which I think is currently reflected in a tendency to
withdraw from political action, to talk of nonparticipation, to become cynical and to make threats of support for third parties or
fourth parties or other irregular political movements.[63]

Though he had little chance of winning, McCarthy's campaign
excited many college-age activists still in the process of a political
evolution toward the left and who thought the McCarthy campaign
an opportunity to send the hated Texan back to his ranch. Many
went "Clean for Gene"—cutting their hair and wearing suits and
ties. "His mere announcement brought in a flood of money and
thousands of volunteers, a few with considerable competence. Even
more important, ten thousand students from as far away as Michigan and Virginia came to the state to lick envelopes, draw up lists,
and, critically, talk to voters in house-to-house canvassing."[64]

McCarthy's campaign would have likely become a footnote in history, however, if it weren't for the Tet Offensive. For months the administration had been proclaiming that the end of the war was in
sight; Tet destroyed all these PR efforts. The domestic political effect
of Tet was devastating for Johnson. In the New Hampshire primary,
McCarthy got 40 percent of the vote, making it clear to Johnson that
he could not be reelected. Soon after, Bobby Kennedy announced that
he would also seek the Democratic nomination for president. Faced
with two popular rivals, Johnson announced at the end of March that
he would neither seek nor accept the nomination of his party for
President. The presidency was now up for grabs. Hubert Humphrey,
Johnson's vice president, would also join the race at the end of April.

Could the party that was responsible for the war in Vietnam sell itself as the party that would end it? The original U.S. commitment in

Vietnam was made by Harry Truman, who supported and financed French recolonization after WWII. John Kennedy escalated the U.S. military presence in South Vietnam and turned it into laboratory for counterinsurgency theories and programs. And Lyndon Johnson, of course, invaded South Vietnam with an army that would grow to half a million soldiers on the ground, destroying large areas of that nation with heavy bombing, killing and wounding hundreds of thousands of Vietnamese. The Democratic Party–controlled Congress funded the war year in and year out, which included the votes of such well-known critics of war policies as Bobby Kennedy and Eugene McCarthy. How could the war party capture the antiwar vote? This may have been a difficult game to play but it was nothing new for the Democrats, who had been since the turn of the century the "graveyard of social movements,"[65] that is, the party that would attempt through reforms, cooptation (jobs, money, corruption), and repression to absorb and dissipate movements that sought greater social reform or radical restructuring of American society. McCarthy was quite clear about this in the speech announcing his candidacy.

With Johnson out of the race, the preferred candidate for much of the party establishment, typified by Chicago's reactionary Mayor Richard J. Daley, became Bobby Kennedy, who had been a staffer for Senator Joseph McCarthy and would later become a U.S. senator from New York since leaving the Johnson cabinet. The Kennedy family had a long and corrupt relationship with people like Daley for years. The Kennedy brothers were also identified with some of the worst aspects of American foreign policy in the early sixties.

They inherited and authorized the CIA's disastrous "Bay of Pigs" invasion of Cuba in early 1961, the most spectacular of the U.S. government's failed attempts to crush the Cuban Revolution.

But it didn't stop there. Bobby Kennedy led a special White House committee that presided over "Operation Mongoose," a wide-ranging covert program of sabotage, assassination, blackmail, and other activities to destroy the Castro government. Bobby declared that it was "top priority" to get rid of Castro and that "no time, money, effort—or manpower…be spared."[66] It ultimately failed, but resulted in untold death and destruction across Cuba. The Kennedys' frustrations with Cuba led to certain "innovations" in U.S. foreign policy that would prove disastrous to the people of many developing countries in years to come. They created "special forces" (U.S. Army Green Berets) to fight revolutionary guerrilla movements, they "modernized" the training of foreign military and police forces (that resulted in military coups and widespread use of torture) and they escalated U.S. involvement in Vietnam. Bobby Kennedy argued to his brother, after they toppled and assassinated the corrupt, long-standing South Vietnamese dictator and U.S. ally Ngo Dinh Diem from power in early November 1963, "It's better if you don't have him but you have to have somebody that can win the war, and who is that?"[67] While the "who" never emerged, it didn't stop the United States from destroying large parts of Vietnam in order to win the war against the NLF and the North Vietnamese.

While Bobby became the inheritor of the halo surrounding his brother, the slain former president, JFK, he still needed a major image makeover.[68] It has largely been forgotten how hated a figure he was as attorney general. Bobby spent a lot of time trying to change his public face in order to be a viable candidate, sometimes going to embarrassing and maudlin lengths. He would confide to Senate colleagues or reporters such things as, "I wish I'd been born an Indian" or "I'm jealous of the fact that you grew up in a ghetto, I wish I'd had that experience," and, even more ridiculous, "If I hadn't been born rich, I'd probably be a revolutionary."[69] But he did touch a chord with many Black and white working-class people. Wherever he campaigned, frantic crowds gathered and tried desperately to touch him. Sometimes he was a terrible public speaker and, at other times, he could be very effective. Following Martin Luther King Jr.'s assassination, he spoke to a predominately Black crowd in Indianapolis, and told them he could identify with their anger because "his brother was killed by a white man."[70]

Yet this revolutionary wannabe was not known as an opponent of Johnson's war policies. Despite his personal hatred for Johnson, Kennedy supported his policies in Vietnam. Bobby Kennedy never voted against any of the appropriation bills that funded the war. I. F. Stone, the great left-wing journalist, wrote an article in October 1966 entitled, "While Others Dodge the Draft, Bobby Dodges the War."[71] Even Bobby Kennedy's slavishly loyal biographer Arthur Schlesinger was forced to admit, "Kennedy brooded about Vietnam but said less in public."[72] What were Bobby and other Senate liberals "brooding" about? Two things: the prospect of the United States losing the war and the growing dissent in the country that threatened the Democratic Party's domination of national politics since the early 1930s. After Johnson announced that he would not run for re-election, many people believed that Bobby could have won both the Democratic nomination and the presidency. He never advocated the unilateral withdrawal of American forces from Southeast Asia. He peppered most of his speeches in 1968 about the need for "peace" in Vietnam, but offered little more than talk of a "negotiated settlement" to end the war, a position not very different from what Johnson or Nixon proposed while both continued the war against the Vietnamese people. On June 4, after winning the California primary, Bobby's career was cut short by an assassin's bullet in Los Angeles.

As delegates headed to Chicago for the Democratic Party National Convention in August 1968, the atmosphere was incredibly tense. At Fort Hood, Texas, soldiers who had already been sent to Chicago in April to put down a rebellion in the city following the assassination of Martin Luther King Jr. were once again put on alert for possible duty at the Democratic convention. On the night of August 23, more than one hundred Black GIs from the First Armored Cavalry Division began protesting being sent to Chicago. They continued to meet well into the morning hours of the next day, when forty-three of them were arrested. They received widespread support from antiwar activists and the Black community. This set the tone for all that followed.

Back in Chicago, Daley turned the city into an armed camp in preparation for the protests. "The convention site itself, the Amphitheater," according to Todd Gitlin,

> was sealed off with barbed wire. All twelve thousand Chicago police were placed on twelve-hour shifts. Five to six thousand National Guardsmen were mobilized and put through special training with simulated longhair rioters. A thousand FBI agents were said to be deployed within the city limits, along with innumerable employees of the military intelligence and who knew which other local and federal agencies. Six thousand U.S. Army troops, including units of the crack 101st Airborne, equipped with flamethrowers, bazookas, and bayonets, were stationed in the suburbs.[73]

With Bobby dead, the party establishment swung its support to Vice President Hubert Humphrey. Closely identified with Johnson's war policies, he had done miserably in the primaries. "Although too late to enter many primaries, in those where he did compete against the two antiwar candidates he was soundly trounced."[74] In the remaining primaries, Humphrey won a meager 2.2 percent of the vote. Yet, by the time he got to the convention in Chicago, he had a majority of the delegates. Despite strong showings in several primaries, McCarthy garnered only 23 percent of the delegates at the convention, largely due to the control of state party organizations over the delegate selection process.

After the assassination, many delegates for Kennedy chose to support George McGovern rather than McCarthy. The eventual nominee, Vice President Hubert Humphrey, was not an antiwar candidate. Humphrey made it clear on CBS's *Face the Nation* the weekend before the Democratic convention that he supported

President Johnson's Vietnam policies. John Gilligan, running for the U.S. Senate, proposed to the Democratic convention that a "peace plank" be included in its platform, calling for an unconditional stop to all bombing in North Vietnam and a "swift conclusion" to the war. Humphrey rejected the peace plank, and it was defeated 1,567 to 1,041. Hundreds of delegates tied black ribbons around their arms in protest. [75]

The Chicago convention is best remembered for the police violence against antiwar demonstrators by Daley's beefy police and for the assault on reporters and critics inside the convention center.

The antiwar movement was greatly divided over whether there should have been demonstrations at the Democratic convention at all, which reflected a sometimes open, other times hidden, division over the movement's relationship to "antiwar" Democrats. A small group of well-known antiwar activists led by Yippies (Youth International Party) Jerry Rubin and Abbie Hoffman, and the National Mobilization to End the War in Vietnam, led by radical pacifist Dave Dellinger, and former SDS leader Tom Hayden, called for a demonstration in Chicago.

Johnson's decision to not seek a second term meant that the antiwar movement lacked a strong target on which to focus a protest in Chicago. The fear of violence—deliberately stoked by Daley—also acted as a deterrent to people showing up to protest. As a result, only about ten thousand people (five thousand from outside Chicago and five thousand Chicagoans) came to demonstrate. The Yippies, in particular, played into the hands of opponents of the antiwar movement with their amateurish and insulting behavior toward everyone who wasn't a Yippie. They called for a "Festival of Life," which included plans for "hundreds fornicating in the city's parks and on Lake Michigan's beaches; releasing greased pigs all over; slashing tires along the freeways."[76] The Yippies, who extravagantly attacked American culture, were obsessed with orienting toward the media, hoping desperately that the wilder their plans, the more coverage they would get. What was needed was a well-organized and disciplined demonstration calling for the Democrats to end the war, but what people got when they arrived was chaos and confusion (caused, it should be added, chiefly by Daley's thugs).

In one of the most memorable scenes in American history, several hundred antiwar demonstrators marched down Michigan Avenue and sat down in front of the Hilton Hotel, hoping to hear from Eugene McCarthy. Douglas Dowd, a veteran socialist and professor from Cornell University, was on the scene, and he recalled to Wells:

> Waves of helmeted cops, 'big guts' sticking out, meaty red faces contorted with rage, filed out of buses. They lined up, platoon-style, began jogging in place. Arms raised upward chanting, 'Kill, Kill, Kill,' the police wheeled to face the demonstrators. They went to work.... Heads cracked, knees buckled, arms were jerked "until they had almost left their sockets." The plate glass window of the Hilton's Haymarket Lounge shattered with a 'sickening' crash; shrieking protesters and onlookers spilled though, some sliced horribly by the glass. The cops pursued them inside, clubbing wildly, "like mad dogs"; when they departed, seven writhing bodies adorned the floor. For twenty packed minutes, the bloodletting ran its course. "It was one of the most awful experiences of my life."[77]

Chicago police attacked demonstrators in front of the international press corps, while the demonstrators chanted, "The whole world is watching."[78] It was broadcast live on national television. Police violence got worse as they went on a rampage all over the city against anyone who was young and wearing long hair. One demonstrator made an impromptu sign that read "Welcome to Czechago,"[79] making a direct analogy between the events in the world's greatest democracy and the crushing of the democracy movement in Czechoslovakia by Russian tanks earlier that month. The hopes of antiwar activists to have the Democrats nominate an antiwar candidate were literally smashed by the billy clubs of the Chicago police and the rigged nominating process of the party. These events helped turn a large number of activists into revolutionaries.

The police riot in Chicago was perhaps the most extreme case of police repression against the antiwar movement, but infiltration, intimidation, and repression were widespread throughout the country. As the war went on, these activities mushroomed to the point where thousands of agents were involved. In addition to the FBI and the local Red Squads[80]—special police units set up to harass and repress radicals—the U.S. Army and the CIA also got in on the act. "Army surveillance alone," write Zaroulis and Sullivan, "covered 18,000 civilians in a two-year period ending in the fall of 1969."[81] The CIA created a special unit, later known as Operation CHAOS, whose job was to ferret out links between domestic protest and foreign enemies (they found none).

The purpose of these activities was primarily to intimidate and repress the social movements rather than enforce laws or gather information. One FBI paper confirmed that its counterintelligence program (COINTELPRO) aimed to "enhance the paranoia endemic in these circles—and get the point across that there is an FBI agent behind every mailbox."[82]

The local police Red Squads engaged in activities as far-ranging as surveillance of church groups to assassination of Black Panther activists. Historian Ellen Schrecker summarizes their activities:

> During the 1960s and early 1970s, maintaining order meant repressing dissent through the intertwined techniques of surveillance and disruption. Although much of the surveillance was undercover, much—like the ubiquitous police photographers at demonstrations—was overt and expressly designed to intimidate. Red Squad activists enjoyed discomfiting their targets by addressing them by name at demonstrations. Pretext arrests combined harassment with information gathering and, at least in Philadelphia, may well have been devised to trigger violence. Wiretaps, burglaries, and other

covert operations were routine, though illegal. Even in a city with a liberal administration, like New Haven in the 1960s, the police wire-tapped over a thousand people.

Informers were ubiquitous, by far the most widely used method of surveillance and disruption. Not only did they provide material for the files, but as agents provocateurs they encouraged the groups they infiltrated to undertake exactly those illegal and provocative activities that would justify the continuing police attention to them. Under-cover agents found that their supervisors expected them to turn in lurid reports and the more compliant informers often produced them, even if they had to propose the operations themselves. This was the case, for example, in New York, where eager police agents within the Black Panther Party planned bombings and then supplied mate-rial for them. Equally important were the activities of undercover agents in sabotaging their organizations' legitimate work.

All of these police activities—overt and concealed—were clearly designed to destroy the targeted organizations.[83]

In the month following the convention, "Humphrey struggled with his Vietnam albatross. In early September, he suggested that some American troops might be brought home in late 1968 or early 1969; he was promptly corrected by President Johnson, who said that no such plan was in progress."[84] The antiwar movement itself fell into a lull following the Democratic convention; it came out of Chicago tarred by the violence directed against it on the streets of America's Second City. "The antiwar movement in any and all of its manifestations was fragmented," according to Zaroulis and Sullivan, "and, as usual, in an election year, sapped of its energy."[85]

But some of the events that fall, despite their relative small size, foreshadowed many things to come. On October 12, the largest demonstration that fall, fifteen thousand people marched against the war in San Francisco, with a contingent of five hundred mem-bers of the military. Also in October, McGeorge Bundy, a close ad-viser to John Kennedy and Lyndon Johnson and one of the architects of the war in Vietnam, announced publicly that he had changed his mind on the war. He said that the American people would not tolerate "annual costs of $30 billion and an annual rate of sacrifice of more than 10,000 American lives."[86] During the first two years of the Nixon administration, large numbers of former liberal supporters of the war would change their minds, further deepening opposition to the war across the country and in the military.

In the waning days of the campaign, Humphrey began to catch up to Nixon in the polls. At the last possible minute, Johnson announced on October 31 that the bombing of North Vietnam had stopped and peace negotiations would begin. It wasn't enough to save Humphrey, but it was an extremely close election, with 43.3 percent of the popular vote for Nixon and 43 percent for Humphrey. The Republicans portrayed themselves simultaneously as the party of "law and order" and "peace with honor" and won the presidency.

CHAPTER SIX

THE U.S. WORKING CLASS AND THE WAR

In the late 1960s, the U.S. media and political establishment "rediscovered" the working class, though not the real working class—which was white, Black, Latino, and increasingly made up of women. They did not rediscover the working class that was in transition from the clutches of the Cold War anticommunism (which had mauled and paralyzed the American union movement) to one being shaken, and in important cases, remade by the popular movements of the 1960s. The working class that they claim to have discovered was really a middle-class stereotype that portrayed the working class as white men who were in rebellion against the civil rights and antiwar movements and liberalism in general.

The media, in particular, latched on to some very real and very ugly events to promote this image. Five days after the Kent State killings, three hundred construction workers, armed with lead pipes and crowbars, rampaged through New York's financial district attacking antiwar protesters as well as bystanders while the police stood watching. Witnesses reported seeing men in suits directing the attacks. Soon after, New York Building Trades Council president Peter Brennan organized a one hundred thousand strong pro-war rally in Manhattan.

Brennan claimed that the May 9, 1970, attack was spontaneous. But as historian Philip Foner notes:

It had emerged clearly from investigations by reporters that union officials and construction firms had joined in promoting and encouraging the hard-hat demonstrations, and the employers closed down their jobs and paid the hard hats for marching....

The [New York] *Post* did an excellent job, too, in exposing how the rampages against the antiwar protesters, and the mass pro-war union rally on May 20, were organized by joint action of the ultraright in New York, especially the right-wing sheet, the *New York Graphic*, and union officials, and that the union leadership told its members that if they did not sign the roll call at the mass rally, they would lose their pay for the day.[1]

These events seemed to confirm that workers (called "hardhats" by the media) were pro-war and open to supporting reactionary politicians. The most notorious figure appealing to racist sentiments was former Alabama governor and presidential candidate George Wallace. "Some members of the traditionally Democratic, white working class in some parts of the country," according to Barbara Ehrenreich, "were suddenly rallying to racist figures who appealed to racist sentiments."[2] The Nixon administration, which was delighted by the pro-war mob action, was actively involved in using the "hard hat" actions to make his case for the idea that a "silent majority" of God-fearing, hardworking Americans backed his policies. Nixon was soon to appoint Brennan as his secretary of labor.

While the events of those days produced some of the most enduring and disturbing images of the Vietnam era, they also disguised a greater reality, one that the media consciously avoided and reactionary politicians opposed. According to historian Peter Levy, "Contrary to the stereotype of 'hard hats' as hawks, virtually every survey demonstrated that at any given time manual workers were just as likely to oppose the war as were youths, the archetypal doves."[3] As the war dragged on, many unions went on record as opponents of the war; and union members marched in significant numbers in antiwar protests, though unions never took the lead in organizing against the war. In the latter years of the war, American workers—Black, white, men and women—also went on strike against the economic costs (mostly inflation) of the war. None of this should surprise anyone; working-class and poor communities suffered the most from the economic costs, in terms of U.S. casualties, and in terms of physical and mental disabilities of returning soldiers.

A WORKING-CLASS WAR

"Where were the sons of all the big shots who supported the war? Not in my platoon. Our guys' people were workers. If the war was so important, why didn't our leaders put everyone's sons in there, why only us?"
—Steve Harper, 1971

All wars in modern times are fought by armies whose rank and file is composed largely of working-class people. It has been long recognized that during the war in Vietnam, the overwhelmingly working-class character of the military forces was carried to an extreme. As Colin Powell, the former chairman of the Joint Chiefs of Staff and secretary of state, eloquently puts it in his 1995 autobiography:

> I particularly condemn the way our political leaders supplied the manpower for that war. The policies—of determining who would be drafted and who would be deferred, who would serve and who would escape, who would die and who would live—were an antidemocratic disgrace. I can never forgive a leadership that said, in effect: These young men poorer, less educated, less privileged—are expendable (someone described them as "economic cannon fodder"), but the rest are too good to risk. I am angry that so many of the sons of the powerful and well placed and so many professional athletes (who were probably healthier than any of us) managed to wangle slots in Reserve and National Guard units. Of the many tragedies of Vietnam, this raw class discrimination strikes me as the most damaging.[4]

But never say never. Powell published these words several years before he agreed to become secretary of state in the administration of

George W. Bush, one of the "sons of the powerful," who escaped combat in Vietnam because his father's influence got him into the safe confines of the Texas Air National Guard. Yet, Powell's points are correct, if nearly a generation late. The antiwar movement was well aware of the class and racial biases of the Selective Service Administration (SSA).

"Most Americans who fought in Vietnam were powerless, working-class teenagers sent to fight an undeclared war by presidents for whom they were not even eligible to vote," declares historian Christian Appy in his underappreciated book *Working-Class War*.[5] The Selective Service Administration under General Lewis B. Hershey, which administered military conscription, or the "draft," evolved in the two decades following the Second World War and the postwar economic boom. It created a myriad of opportunities for the middle- and upper-class, celebrities, and the politically connected to avoid military service and possible combat with a variety of deferments.

The best known of these were deferments for full-time college and graduate students during the first half of the war in Vietnam. This, of course, disproportionately benefited middle- and upper-class youth, who could afford to be full-time students. Working-class students usually worked and went to school part time. "A Harvard *Crimson* editor from the class of 1970 tallied his twelve hundred classmates and counted only fifty-six who entered the military, just two of whom went to Vietnam. By contrast, thirty-five men from the Harvard class of 1941 died in World War II, and hundreds more saw combat duty," according to Baskir and Strauss in their classic study *Chance and Circumstance*.[6]

Joining the National Guard or reserve forces was another way for middle-class and well-to-do people to avoid the draft. During the war over one million men served in the reserves or National Guard, with about fifteen thousand of them mobilized for combat in Vietnam. You had little or no chance of seeing combat if you could get into the National Guard or army reserves at that time. They became the preserve of white, middle-class draft dodgers. "In the army reserves, for example, the percentage of college graduates among the enlisted men was three times higher than the regular army."[7] It was virtually impossible for Blacks to get into the National Guard. In 1964, the Army National Guard was 1.45 percent Black, and this decreased to 1.26 percent by 1968. In Mississippi, a state that in the 1960s was 42 percent African American, there was only one Black man in the National Guard, and it was little better in the North, where the Michigan National Guard was only 1.34 percent Black.[8]

Local draft boards were dominated by politically appointed white, older, conservative businessmen and veterans. "A 1966 study of the 16,638 draft board members around the nation found that only 9 percent had blue-collar occupations, while more than 70 percent were professionals, managers, proprietors, public officials, or white-collar workers over the age of fifty. Only 1.3 percent were Black."[9] Until 1967, women were not legally allowed to sit on draft boards. As a consequence these boards were oblivious, or outrightly hostile to, the difficult economic circumstances of powerless working-class kids.

On the other hand, they were quite open and accommodating to the needs of the politically connected or famous. George Hamilton, who made a career out of being a bad actor, was able to win a "hardship" draft deferment because he successfully argued that his mother, who lived in a Hollywood mansion, was dependent on his $200,000 salary for support.[10] In sharp contrast, Edward Neal, who was Black, and worked two jobs to support his mother, disabled father, and eight brothers and sisters, was denied a hardship deferment by local draft board in Mississippi.[11] Professional athletes also got easy access to the National Guard. "We have an arrangement with the [Baltimore] Colts," admitted Major General George Gelson of the Maryland National Guard in 1966. "When they have a player with a military problem, they send him to us." Similar arrangements existed all across the country.[12]

To meet the insatiable manpower demands of the war in Vietnam, the Defense Department lowered the mental aptitude tests and other requirements of draftees, while creating special programs to draw "disadvantaged youth" into military service—the best known of these was Project 100,000. This was the liberal version of the old and cherished right-wing myth that military discipline will "straighten out troubled youth." They were derisively referred to as "McNamara's boys." Most of the youth brought into the military under Project 100,000 were semiliterate, from troubled homes, many of them unemployed or underemployed. According to Baskir and Strauss, "Instead of reducing the effect of social and economic inequities, they had the opposite effect. The burden of the war shifted even more to society's less privileged. While these men were volunteering and filling draft quotas, their more favored peers were staying in college, joining the reserves, or figuring out other ways to stay away from Vietnam."[13]

Ultimately, about two and a half times that number were brought into the military under Project 100,000, half of whom eventually saw some of the worst combat of the war, with a death rate twice the rate of American combat forces as a whole.[14] The upside of Project 100,000 for the Johnson administration (besides filling its manpower quotas) was that the "war did not have to disrupt the daily lives of more affluent and politically vocal citizens."[15]

The effect of all this was catastrophic on working-class neighborhoods and communities across the country, whether they were in urban or semirural settings. Appy memorably describes them as areas of "concentrated pain."[16] In 1970, Australian journalist John Pilger visited one of these areas—Beallsville, Ohio, near the West Virginia border. It is located in Monroe County, where at the time of the war 40 percent of the residents lived below the official government poverty line of $3,000. Pilger vividly captures the pall of death that hung over Beallsville:

Beyond the junkyard is the high school from which fewer than 3 percent of the pupils go on to college; the rest go to the mines or to the service industries of Cincinnati or are idle. In 1970 they went to the military draft, and when seventeen young men of the "senior class of '70" received their diplomas, they strode ritually across the football field and then up, to where many of the classes of '65, '66, '67 and '68 were enshrined: the graveyard.[17]

Thirty-five young men from Beallsville were drafted between 1965 and 1970, and many were sent Vietnam where they were wounded or killed. "We've already lost the goddamn war," Beallsville mayor, Ben Gramlich, declared to Pilger. "I'm not against it, but we're running outta young 'uns to give." The town undertaker lamented, "I just felt it was one helluva toll to take out of a little place." By 1971, Beallsville with a population of 475 had lost six young men to the war in Vietnam—the highest per capita loss of life in the entire country.[18] But Beallsville was only the most extreme version of what was happening in many places and gained some notoriety because of media coverage; most places suffered in horrible silence.

West Virginia, a state famous for the dangerous work of mining coal and suffering high unemployment from the mechanization of those very mines, had the highest casualty rate in the nation—711 casualties or 39.9 deaths per 100,000 people. Oklahoma, a state with one of the largest Native American populations had the second-highest casualty rate in the country. Thomas Edison High School in Philadelphia, a predominately Black, working-class public high school, sustained the largest number of Vietnam war casualties of any high school in the nation with fifty-four. A memorial exists at the school to commemorate the dead. Puerto Rico, America's colony in the Caribbean where residents are not allowed to vote for the president of the United States, had 48,000 of its men serve in Vietnam with 345 of them killed, slightly less than Utah (365) and just ahead of Maine (342).[19] "Postwar army records," according to Baskir and Strauss, "show that an enlisted man who was a college graduate had a 42 percent chance of going to Vietnam, versus a 64 percent chance for a high-school graduate and 70 percent chance for a high-school dropout."[20] Chicago, seen and promoted as the quintessential "American city," according to a study by Gilbert Badilo and Dave Curry, found that "youths from low-income neighborhoods were three times as likely to die in Vietnam as youths from high-income neighborhoods. They also found youths from neighborhoods with low educational levels to be four times as likely to die in Vietnam as youths from better-educated neighborhoods."[21] Every state, city, small town, or farming community has it own story of "concentrated pain" to tell.

THE MYTH OF THE REACTIONARY WORKING CLASS

If working-class communities were so hard hit by the war, why would they be the most avid hawks? Was there, in fact, a reactionary political backlash occurring in the United States in the late 1960s, spearheaded by the white working class? *New York Times* labor reporter A. H. Raskin thought so, "The typical worker—from construction craftsman to shoe clerk—has become probably the most reactionary political force in the country." [22] This image of "the typical worker" (whom Raskin identifies as white) was epitomized by the premiere in 1971 of the long-running sitcom *All in the Family,* starring Carroll O'Connor as Archie Bunker, produced by Hollywood super-liberal Norman Lear. O'Connor played the buffoonish bigot Bunker, whose malaprop-laced speech came to symbolize the white working class on television for more than a decade.[23] Along with network television, the American news media played a major role in creating the "hardhat" myth, particularly during and after the 1968 election. As Barbara Ehrenreich puts it,

"They discovered a working class more suited to their mood: dumb, reactionary, and bigoted."[24]

In order to be "rediscovered," workers had to be lost or, at least, lost in the minds of the opinion makers of the country. The American working class was, of course, anything but lost in the 1930s and 1940s, as it battled and defeated many of the most powerful corporations in the world. The labor movement was responsible for most of the social welfare legislation of that era; it was the great wellspring of radical politics that was embraced by millions.

In the two decades following the Second World War, the United States experienced unprecedented economic growth, the growth of a relatively large middle class, the suburbanization of the population, and talk of endless prosperity as it seemed that the "business cycle" had been overcome. In this chirpy fantasyland of postwar delusion, it was argued that the end product of all this was that the blue-collar worker had become "irrelevant" or simply "disappeared." Well-respected sociologists and political scientists trained a generation of college students that the mass of the Americans were backward, superstitious—even a threat to democracy.

The worst of these was ex-"socialist" Seymour Martin Lipset[25] whose 1959 book *Political Man* has a chapter called "Working-Class Authoritarianism," which blamed the working class for the twin plagues of fascist and communist "totalitarianism" around the world.[26] Lipset was an avowed elitist with nothing but contempt for working-class people. "Acceptance of the norms of democracy requires a high level of sophistication and ego security. The less sophisticated and stable an individual, the more likely he is to favor a simplified view of politics, to fail to understand the rationale underlying tolerance of those with whom he disagrees, and find difficulty in grasping or tolerating a gradualist image of political change," Lipset wrote.[27] Sophistication and secure "egos" were apparently missing in working-class people, but found in abundance in the middle and upper class—the pillars of democracy in Lipset's world. According to Barbara Ehrenreich, "Lipset's study is still valuable, however, as a summary of middle-class prejudices."[28]

These middle-class prejudices, however, were considered the common sense of the time. "Working-class intolerance and authoritarianism" was the "conventional wisdom" of American sociology in the 1950s and 1960s, notes Richard F. Hamilton in *Class and Politics in the United States*. As a result of years of training, "many social scientists have come to expect tolerance to vary directly with class level"[29]—that is, for tolerance to increase as we move down the economic ladder. For Hamilton, American sociologists (and we should add political scientists and journalists) simply ignored evidence that contradicted the image of the backward white worker.

A 1966 study, for example, revealed that "the higher one's class of origin or class destination the more likely that one prefers to exclude Negroes from one's neighborhood."[30] When confronted with this, the authors of the study couldn't believe their eyes and responded by saying, "This curiosity has no obvious explanation and makes us suspicious of these data."[31] This in part reflects the middle-class character of most academics (and journalists and political scientists), but also the deeply ingrained bigotry that exists against working-class people in this country, producing what Hamilton calls a "perceptual distortion." True enough, but there is also a deeper issue. This perceptual distortion (challenged by a relatively small number of left-wing academics) applied to the entire practice of their profession. Karl Marx long ago called bourgeois economists the "hired prizefighters of capital."[32] The same term can applied to their academic cousins in sociology and political science, whose job is to obscure the true nature of the social structure of capitalism and to continually provide reasons why the lower classes were unfit to rule. For the bulk of American academic history, the working class was portrayed as a dangerous class, particularly as it became more multiethnic and multiracial, through the late part of the nineteenth and twentieth centuries.[33] In the aftermath of the Second World War, some of the worst aspects of this overt racial and ethnic bigotry receded, but was replaced by a more allegedly "scientific" analysis mixed with psychobabble—what Ehrenreich calls "snobbery disguised as sociology."[34]

The media "rediscovered" the blue-collar working class during the 1968 election. "Like the poor before it, the working class as discovered was the imaginative product of middle class anxiety and prejudice."[35] The "anxiety" and "prejudice" was caused by what the media reported was working-class support for the independent candidacy of George Wallace for president. The former governor of Alabama was infamous for his opposition to the civil rights movement, particularly school integration. His running mate was retired Air Force General Curtis LeMay, the former head of the Strategic Air Command, who advocated using nuclear weapons in Vietnam to win the war. Wallace's 1968 campaign on the American Independent Party ticket was, in many ways, a rallying point for the old segregationist Democrats, who would soon defect en masse to the Republican Party.

But Wallace proved himself to be a clever bigot, who portrayed himself as an "outsider," and played on white working-class fears and resentments. Wallace got on the ballot in fifty states and toured the country, specifically campaigning in white working-class communities. He emphasized their economic insecurity, while mixing patriotism and attacks on Washington bureaucrats. In the end, he got ten million votes (winning the Deep South states of Alabama, Georgia, Mississippi, Louisiana, and Arkansas), with slightly less than half of them from outside the South.[36] Wallace's political fortunes peaked four years later, after returning to the Democratic Party in his third effort to win the presidency in 1972. He won the Democratic primaries in Michigan (a state with a large blue-collar and union constituency) and Maryland before a near-fatal assassination attempt left him disabled, ending his campaign.

Was Wallace's campaign a sign that blue-collar workers were prowar and a bastion of reaction? Kevin Phillips, then a Republican Party strategist, says no. He concluded that "there was no reliable Wallace backing among blue-collar workers and poor whites as a class."[37] Richard Hamilton also insists that "the widespread focus on class, on the working-class support for Wallace, has seriously misrepresented the actual realities."[38] For example, in Wisconsin, "Wallace's percentages were lowest in Milwaukee's South Side [a white working-class neighborhood]. His percentages were high in the affluent North Side districts and highest in the very affluent north shore suburbs. In Madison, the Wallace percentage was greatest in the very affluent suburb of Maple Bluff."[39]

Wallace's electoral support was still primarily concentrated in the rural South and border states. It's also important to keep in mind that some of Wallace's supporters in the summer of 1968 had been supporting the "liberal" Bobby Kennedy's run for the presidency following his victory in the California primary, before his assassination in June. For Barbara Ehrenreich, the idea of a white working-class groundswell for Wallace was largely a media-created myth, "In their voting habits, too, blue-collar Americans were not, at the time of their discovery, shifting to the right. Nor was much of anybody, except perhaps for the media people who were now so anxious to document a surge of right-wing populism."[40] This didn't mean there wasn't bigotry in the working class or even large pools of racism in the country, but to argue that it was working-class people who were "the most reactionary force in the country" was a consciously manufactured myth.

It is also important to remember that there were people trying to organize a backlash and they weren't working-class people. They were, most notably, the Republican Party, the premiere party of big

business, which was in the process of, among of other things, incor-
porating the old segregationist wing of the Democrats into their
party under Nixon's "southern strategy" to roll back the gains of the
civil rights movement along with continuing an unpopular war in
Southeast Asia.

What was the attitude of working-class people toward the war?
One of the earliest and most telling expressions of antiwar sentiment among working-class people took place in Dearborn, Michigan, where the residents in the then predominately mixed-income,
white suburb of Detroit, participated in a referendum on the war
initiated by UAW member and long-time revolutionary socialist
John Anderson.[41] The referendum read: "Are you in favor of an immediate ceasefire and withdrawal of United States troops from Vietnam so that the Vietnamese people can settle their own problems?"
Forty-one percent voted yes; a study of the vote revealed that blue-
collar workers voted against the war in much larger proportions
than managers or professionals.[42] In November 1968, a virtually
identical resolution once again was put before Dearborn residents,
and this time the resolution passed with 57 percent of the vote.[43] In
1970, the same year as the "hard-hat riots," one survey "found that
48 percent of the northern white working class was in favor of immediate withdrawal of American troops from Vietnam, while only
40 percent of the white middle class took this position."[44] Antiwar
sentiment increased further among working-class people during
1971 and 1972. According to Peter Levy, "By the fall of 1971 Gallup
polls showed that 61 percent of all respondents favored pulling out
of Vietnam by the end of the year, with union households adopting
this view more than any other group except racial minorities."[45]

Yet, at the same time, nearly half of those who favored immediate
withdrawal also expressed negative views of antiwar demonstrators.
How do we explain this seemingly strange contradiction? In two
ways. One is that it was an expression of misdirected class anger and

resentment. After all, the bulk of antiwar activists and demonstrators were still primarily drawn from the middle class and still evaded military service even after the abolition of college deferments. They were the children of the bosses and supervisors, and of the lawyers and politicians, whom most workers hated or, at best, treated with great cynicism. In sharp contrast, their children were in the military and had already died or were coming home with a variety of physical and mental disabilities. Richard Nixon, George Wallace, Spiro Agnew, and others artfully played on this class division, fanning the flames of resentment in a failed effort to try prevent the antiwar movement from spreading deeper into the population. Nevertheless, these campaigns did have an effect. The left that emerged during the antiwar movement was drawn to Third-Worldist and Maoist politics that tended to see American workers as "bought off" and therefore part of the problem; that is, their views of the working class mirrored those of the sociologists. This unfortunately precluded them from playing a role in connecting the class concerns of the working class with issues related to the war in a way that could have bridged the gap that the right wing was so eager to widen.

The second reason for the separation of the labor movement from the antiwar movement is that the bulk of America's trade union leaders, led by AFL-CIO president George Meany, supported the war to the very end, attacking without restraint the antiwar movement as "kookies" and "Communist dupes." Even Meany's slavishly devotional biographer Joseph Goulden had to admit that Meany supported Vietnam long after "much of the country went elsewhere."[46] A month after the May 20, 1970, pro-war rally by New York's building trades unions, an antiwar demonstration was called by District 37 of AFSCME (which represented tens of thousands of New York City's municipal employees), District 65 of the UAW, and other New York local unions. While it drew nearly twenty-five thousand union members, or about half the number of the pro-war labor rally, it was significant in that it was the first trade union rally against the war. But it was also significant that it came nearly five years after the U.S. invasion of South Vietnam, and five years after large-scale protests and a huge shift by a large section of the population against the war. As Sharon Smith puts it, "The opportunity for significant working-class participation in 1960s social movements had passed."[47]

CLASS STRUGGLE DURING THE WAR

"The mailmen…represent something close to a national minority. They are, by and large, good family men, steady wage earners. [If they] begin thumbing their nose at the government, then the comfortable American bourgeoisie has real reasons to worry, and worry hard."
—*Newsweek*, April 6, 1970, on the postal wildcat strike.

While American workers may not have been able to put their particular stamp—as a class—on the antiwar movement in the United States, it is sometimes forgotten that the last great upsurge in struggle by American workers took place during the war in Vietnam, at a time when the notions of "patriotism," "loyalty," "sacrifice," and "supporting the troops" were powerful weapons to prevent workers from battling their bosses over their working conditions. "A seismic rebellion was brewing among rank-and-file workers as the 1960s decade grew to a close," according to Sharon Smith. "Wages stagnated in the late 1960s as the postwar economic boom began to falter. Anger at stagnating wages, combined with growing frustration at production speedups and the disinterested union bureaucracy, exploded into a series of working-class revolts beginning in 1968. These revolts were influenced by the antiwar or Black Power movements and by the radicalization of the period."[48] While American workers may not have gone on strike against the war (i.e., calling for immediate withdrawal or a halt to bombing or troop deployments), they certainly went on strike against the economic costs of the war, creating a more polarized situation and the biggest opening for radicals and revolutionaries in a generation to build an organized socialist presence among U.S. workers.

Despite rising incomes and benefits (and homeownership) during the 1950s and 1960s, American workers were frustrated. In the mid-1950s, Harvey Swados, a radical writer, set out on the task of exposing "The Myth of the Happy Worker." Unlike his contemporaries, who were writing about the end of class society, Swados, based on his experiences, wrote, "The worker's attitude toward his work is generally compounded of hatred, shame, and resignation."[49] Not a pretty picture. Most of the union contracts of the time, which gave management complete control of production and grievance procedures to rectify problems, were, by and large, cumbersome and ineffective. While the pace and conditions of work would be the source of many battles in the next decade, the actual fruits of the post-Second World War economic boom were not shared by all workers. Women earned less than men, the Black unemployment rate was twice as high as the white, and, as the old saying goes: They were the last hired and the first fired. Large sections of the U.S. working class were unorganized, particularly in the massively expanding public sector, health-care industries, higher education, and the South, where many manufacturers were relocating because of the region's intense anti-union business climate. By the early to mid-1960s, like the first raindrops of a coming storm, the "seismic rebellion" was beginning to stir, and it is no accident that it took place after nearly a decade of civil rights activism.

Veteran union activist and socialist Stan Weir was one of the first to document and appreciate the political significance of this new development in his "A New Era of Labor Revolt," which pointed out that five major unions experienced wildcats in 1964.[50] The wildcat strike was the weapon of the rank and file after all official union channels for solving grievances had become closed. They were called "wildcats" because they were not officially recognized or led by local or national union officers and were in violation of "no-strike" provisions of union contracts. In many ways, wildcat strikes were directed as much against union officials (who were seen as complacent or collaborating with management) as they were against the employers.

"Over the course of the 1960s," according to labor historian Kim Moody, "the frequency of wildcat strikes grew: the number of strikes that occurred during the life of contract went from about one thousand in 1960 to two thousand in 1969. Contract rejections, which had been rare before the 1960s, soared to over one thousand in 1967."[51] While battles over the conditions of work and the authority of management continued to be a major source of struggle at America's workplaces during the 1960s, another factor that had the potential to draw in larger number of workers into struggle emerged: inflation. The immediate economic effect of the war was the great inflation that began in 1966 (and would last for the next seventeen years), eating away at workers' wages and producing a strike wave against the employers and a revolt of the rank and file inside the unions. *Life* magazine's August 22, 1966, cover story "Strike Fever," decried what it called the "rampant new militancy" and the "dilemma of labor leaders."[52] That summer, aircraft mechanics belonging to the International Association of Machinists (IAM) struck several major airlines, grinding 60 percent of the country's air traffic to a halt. Defying their leaders as well as Johnson's calls to return to work, they remained on strike for five weeks. The slogan of the striking machinists revealed the obvious influence of the civil rights movement on the overwhelmingly white striking workforce: "We're working under chain-gang conditions for cotton-picking wages."[53]

From 1968 onward, the two axles that the rank-and-file rebellion rode on were the great inflation and the impact of the Black Power movement in the workplace, particularly in the auto plants in the greater Detroit area. It's not surprising that Martin Luther King Jr.'s last struggle was helping to organize striking sanitation workers in Memphis in 1968. "Strike activity of all kinds rose dramatically in the second half of the 1960s, exceeding by most measures the level of strike activity of the 1930s and, with the exception of 1946, the 1940s. This strike wave climaxed in 1970 when over 66 million days were lost due to strikes, a record exceeded only by 1946 and 1959 in the postwar era," writes Moody.[54]

This was no mere blip in strike activity; it represented a whole new generation of workers who wanted to reconfigure the union movement. "Black workers often led the most radical struggles," notes Smith. "Black autoworkers in Detroit, for example, raised demands against what they called 'niggermation'—the combination of speedup and racial discrimination."[55] The League of Revolutionary Black Workers became the umbrella organization for the various Revolutionary Union Movements (RUMs) that formed throughout the various companies and plants in the auto industry.[56] The post-Reuther leadership of the UAW, led by Leonard Woodcock, was forced to deal with this new militancy by both attacking Black revolutionaries and calling a strike in 1970 against General Motors. The strike was later chronicled in William Serrin's *The Company and the Union*. The strike lasted sixty-seven days and was the most expensive strike in U.S. history. Other unions, such as SEIU Local 1199, the hospital workers' union based primarily in New York City, saw the opportunities to merge "Soul Power with Union Power" by expanding the union movement into low-wage areas of the economy, including into the hostile territory of the South.[57]

Though the rank-and-file rebellion began when a majority of Americans still supported the war in Vietnam, strikes increased dramatically after the Tet Offensive in early 1968, a time when a majority of Americans shifted their opinions and wanted the war brought to a quick end. As inflation picked up in 1969 and many expected the war to end soon, the strike figures began to go through the roof. "The government recorded 5,600 work stoppages in 1969, the most in over fifteen years, while union wage settlements continued a 'dizzying climb,'" according to labor reporter Lee Sustar. "The Nixon administration, trying to hold the line on inflation, prepared for the worst, moving to strengthen emergency strike legislation."[58]

At General Electric, one of the largest defense contractors in the country and then the fourth-largest corporation in the world, with four hundred thousand employees, a coalition of unions (IUE, UE, and IBEW) overcame the traditional company policy of divide and conquer called "Boulwarism," and launched a one-hundred-day strike beginning in October 1969.[59] Even such a pro-war hawk as AFL-CIO President George Meany called on GE to abandon its "19th century approach" and declared, "I want General Electric management, stockholders, and customers to know this. The GE strikers will have every bit of support they need from the entire AFL-CIO until the hour of victory."[60] What was also notable about the GE strike and a strike by oil refinery workers (earlier in 1969 outside of San Francisco) was the participation of campus-based radicals who offered support to the strike and were, in turn, welcomed by rank-and-file workers.[61] The previous May in France the largest general strike in history had convinced a new generation of revolutionaries (who had previously believed that workers were bought off by postwar prosperity) that they were once again the class that could transform society. The resurgence of working-class struggle in the Unites States, while not on the same scale as Europe, gave concrete expression to the same ideas here, though these developments were more limited.

As 1970 approached, Nixon's secretary of labor, George Shultz, predicted "stormy weather" on the contract front, with nearly five million workers affected by contracts due to be negotiated, about twice the 1969 total, and more than in any other year in the previous decade. "But," according to Sustar, "it was the unexpected postal strike that epitomized the militancy of the period."[62] U.S. postal workers were barred from collective bargaining and striking under federal law. Congress set pay rates and other terms of employment. Postal workers were already frustrated with their situation when the incoming Nixon administration threatened to remove the civil-service status of employees with proposals to reorganize the postal service.

Congress dragged its feet on pay and benefit increases during 1969 and 1970, while the leaders of the two major postal unions— the National Association of Letter Carriers and the American Postal Workers Union—provided no leadership. On the night of March 18, 1970, postal workers in New York City defied the federal government, their union leaders, and federal law by walking off the job. Within days, the strike spread to over two hundred cities, eventually involving 210,000 workers. It was the largest walkout against the federal government in its history. Workers waved signs that read, "We Have Them by the Throat—It's Now or Never," "Watch Out for Tricky Dick," and "Dump the Rat—We Have No National Leader."[63]

A March 19 *New York Times* editorial, entitled "Postal Anarchy," revealed how uneasily ruling circles viewed the strike. The editorial decried the strike, lamenting how the no-strike policy for federal employees had hitherto "prevailed with almost perfect effectiveness," and noted with alarm the connection between the postal walkout and other forms of social unrest:

> Even more dismaying is the encouragement the postal workers' defiance gives to the lawlessness already so rampant in many sectors of society that it is beginning to undermine national stability. What hope can there be for fostering respect for law and democratic processes among all the disaffected elements in the ghetto, on campus and elsewhere if Federal employees disregard their oath to stay on the job or if public administrators fail to invoke the full legal penalties?[64]

Nixon mobilized the National Guard to deliver the mail, which created chaos. Guardsmen, some of whom fraternized with the strikers, openly mocked Nixon. One guardsmen told the *New York Times*, "You've heard of the Boston massacre and the My Lai massacre. Tomorrow you're going to see the New York mail massacre. It's going to be a farce. I'm a medic. I don't know a thing about the Post Office Department. Nobody knows what they are supposed to do."[65] The strike lasted two weeks, with postal workers winning an immediate 14 percent wage increase, and led directly to passage of the Postal Reorganization Act of 1970, which modernized the postal service and provided for collective bargaining for postal workers. *Newsweek* believed that the strike foretold something much deeper going on among American workers, "The mailmen...represent something close to a national minority. They are, by and large, good family men, steady wage earners. (If they) begin thumbing their nose at the government, then the comfortable American bourgeoisie has real reasons to worry, and worry hard."[66]

It should be kept in mind that these major strikes by important unions in key areas of the economy all took place during wartime, when the media were portraying American workers as a bastion of reaction. What did American workers think of the war in Vietnam? They voted with their feet by walking the picket line in the waning days of the war. Barbara Ehrenreich sums up the era well: America's blue-collar workers were in revolt in the late sixties and early seventies, but not along the right-wing, traditionalist lines sketched by the media. "The late sixties saw the most severe strike wave since shortly after WWII.... For all the talk of racial backlash, black and white workers were marching, picketing, and organizing together in a spirit of class solidarity that had not been seen since the thirties. Nixon's 'silent majority' was yelling as loud as it could—not racial epithets but the historic strikers' chant: 'Don't cross the line.'"[67]

CHAPTER SEVEN

FROM QUAGMIRE TO DEFEAT

The year following the Tet Offensive of 1968 was the bloodiest year of the American war in Vietnam. As revenge for the humiliation suffered during the Tet Offensive, the United States unleashed a frightening wave of destruction. Despite the huge military cost to the National Liberation Front (NLF), it was clear that the Tet Offensive had destroyed the ability of the United States to effectively prosecute its war in Vietnam. In response, President Lyndon Johnson announced that he would not seek reelection. In a close race against Vice President Hubert Humphrey, Richard Nixon was elected president, in part because he implied that he had a "secret plan" to end the war in Vietnam. "The greatest honor history can bestow is the title of peacemaker," he said in his inaugural speech.[1] It is a testament to the political quandary that the American ruling class found itself in that an anticommunist militarist could package himself as a "peace" candidate.

Despite all the talk of peace, the war would continue for another four years. Almost as many Americans died in Vietnam during Nixon's presidency as in the Johnson years. How does one explain this? The incoming Nixon administration set itself the goal of bringing the American war in Vietnam to an end without it being seen as a defeat for U.S. imperialism. In attempting to achieve this, Nixon would not only raise to new heights the destruction the United States would inflict on Vietnam, but would widen the war into neighboring countries.

These war policies revived and deepened the antiwar movement in the United States. The antiwar movement would surge to the zenith of its strength, while soldiers, sailors, and air force personnel began to rebel in larger numbers. A special commission appointed by Nixon to assess unrest on the campuses following the invasion of Cambodia, led by William Scranton, the former Republican governor of Pennsylvania, argued that the country was "so polarized" that the division in the country over the war was "as deep as any since the Civil War." Scranton declared that "nothing is more important than an end to the war" in Vietnam.[2] It was the strength of this opposition that not only led to the final withdrawal of U.S. troops from Vietnam, but also to the adoption of repressive measures by an increasingly paranoid Nixon administration that would lead to its downfall.

THE SECRET BOMBING OF CAMBODIA

> "I refuse to believe that a little fourth-rate power like North Vietnam does not have a breaking point."
> —Henry Kissinger

While Nixon hoped that history would bestow the title of "peace-maker" on him, in private he was adamant that he would "not be the first president of the United States to lose a war."[3] Nixon was just as committed to maintaining an anticommunist state in South Vietnam as his predecessors. To maintain this state, the NLF and the North Vietnamese would have to be crippled beyond any ability to threaten the Saigon government. This was the "peace with honor" that Nixon talked about—in essence a peace on the terms of the United States. "Nixon's secret peace plan was turning out to be just another way to continue fighting the war."[4] He justified military escalation by arguing that acting like a "madman" was the best way to end the war. "I call it the madman theory," he said. "I want the North Vietnamese to believe I've reached a point where I might do anything to stop the war."[5]

The co-architect of the Nixon administration's policies in Indochina was national security adviser Henry A. Kissinger. Nixon and Kissinger were both acutely aware that the political ground had shifted since the Tet Offensive. Kissinger, writing in *Foreign Affairs* in January 1969, described the Tet Offensive as the "watershed of the American effort. Henceforth, no matter how effective our actions the prevalent [American] strategy could no longer achieve its objectives within a period or with force levels politically acceptable to the American people."[6] One part of the strategy ultimately settled on was called "Vietnamization"—U.S. ground forces would be slowly withdrawn and the ground war would be turned over to the South Vietnamese, backed by massive U.S. airpower and logistics. The second part would be to spread the war and intensify the air war. Indeed, officials told the *New York Times* that Cambodia was a laboratory to "test public acceptance" of the plan to substitute "attack planes for foot soldiers."[7]

Since its independence and declared neutrality in the 1950s, Cambodia was ruled by Prince Norodom Sihanouk, who kept the Americans at arms length. The eastern fringe of Cambodia, along the South Vietnamese border, had become a refuge for NLF soldiers, as the U.S. bombing of the Vietnamese countryside made life increasingly unbearable. North Vietnamese soldiers were also forced deeper into Cambodia from the Ho Chi Minh trail, which snaked through southern Laos, to escape around-the-clock U.S. bombing. The stated goal of the invasion was to destroy what the American military believed to be the military headquarters of the entire NLF/NVA (North Vietnamese Army) operation in South Vietnam, what they called the Central Office of South Vietnam (COSVN).

The COSVN was portrayed as the equivalent of a giant jungle version of the Pentagon. In fact, no such thing existed.

The secret bombing of Cambodia ran from March 1969 until August 1973. Nixon set up an elaborate system of deception to hide the bombing campaign from the public, the media, and Congress.[8] Revealing what can only be described as a cannibalistic mindset, the first raids were called "Breakfast," followed by "Dinner," "Snacks," and "Dessert," while the entire operation was known as "Menu." During the first fourteen months of the campaign, the United States conducted more than 3,630 B-52 raids, dropping over one hundred ten thousand tons of bombs on Cambodia. When the bombing ended, the United States had dropped a total of 257,465 tons of explosives.[9] A single B-52 squadron in 1971 dropped in one year half the tonnage that U.S. planes dropped in the entire Pacific theater during World War II.[10] "The effect on the war in Vietnam was nil," according to Marilyn Young, "the effect on Cambodia was devastating."[11] The Cambodian Ministry of Health reported that by the end of 1971, two million of the country's seven million people were displaced and 20 percent of the country's property had been destroyed.[12] Cambodia had begun its descent into a hell that would culminate with the triumph of the genocidal Khmer Rouge in 1975.

Despite the bombing of Cambodia, the NLF and the North Vietnamese didn't come "begging for peace." Destructive as the bombing was, there was never any evidence that it had any impact on the Vietnamese nationalists' capacity to fight. In their frustration with the failure of the bombing campaign in Cambodia, Nixon and Kissinger decided to turn their sights directly on North Vietnam with an intensity that would exceed all previous levels of destruction. "I refuse to believe," Kissinger remarked, "that a little fourth-rate power like North Vietnam does not have a breaking point."[13] In September 1969, he gave the following instructions to his staff: "It shall be the assignment of this group to examine the option of a *savage, decisive blow against North Vietnam.* You start with no preconceptions at all. You are to sit down and map out what would be a *savage blow.*"[14] (Italics in original.)

The name of Kissinger's plan—for whatever bizarre reason—was "Duck Hook." It was a wide-ranging plan that included "a land invasion of the North, the systematic bombing of its dikes so as to destroy the food supply, and the saturation bombing of Hanoi and Haiphong."[15]

CAMBODIA AND THE RESURGENCE
OF ANTIWAR ACTIVITY

"I would rather be a one-term president and do what I believe is right than be a
two-term president at the cost of seeing America becoming a second-rate power
and to see this nation accept the first defeat in its proud 190-year history."
—President Richard Nixon, 1970

The antiwar movement had no illusions about Richard Nixon, but the first half of 1969 saw a continuation in the lull of antiwar activity that followed the Democratic convention the year before. While Nixon was escalating the war with the secret bombing of Cambodia and developing plans for an intensified air war against North Vietnam, his administration was engaging in a "peace offensive," which included the beginnings of negotiations with the North Vietnamese. This was essentially a public-relations campaign to convince the American public that the war was coming to an end. Nixon was helped greatly in this effort by U.S. television and print media. One commentator, writing in the *New York Times* on the eve on Nixon's first inauguration in January 1969, wrote that Vietnam would "fade from the national agenda" because Nixon pledged to end the war.[16] British journalist Godfrey Hodgson, who covered U.S. politics, argued that many people believed that "the war was over, because you didn't see it on the tube anymore."[17] Nixon's efforts succeeded for a short time. "In fact, by providing no targets of opportunity, nothing to react to, Nixon had muffled one of the movement's strongest weapons."[18]

However, the illusion of peace soon faded. To placate antiwar sentiment at home and restlessness among the troops, Nixon announced the withdrawal of twenty-five thousand soldiers in June 1969. Despite this token gesture, the antiwar movement, which had been on hiatus for nearly a year, planned nationwide demonstrations on October 15, the first Vietnam Moratorium Day. On that day, more than one hundred thousand rallied in Boston, and Coretta Scott King led a march of thirty thousand past the White House in a silent candlelight procession. In an unprecedented outpouring of public dissent, marches and demonstrations involving more than two million people took place in communities across the country.[19] This was followed on November 15 by the largest demonstrations in U.S. history, when more than a million people marched against the war in Washington, D.C. and San Francisco.

Though the AFL-CIO executive board, steeped in anticommunism, never wavered in its support for the war, some unions now began to criticize it. A full-page ad against the war that appeared on the day of the October 15, 1969, moratorium marches included the signatures of César Chávez and Paul Shrade, Western director of the UAW. Another series of ads asking the government "to face up to the reality that there is nothing to be won in Vietnam that is worth one more drop of American blood" was signed by Walter Reuther for the UAW, Frank E. Fitzsimmons and Thomas E. Flynn for the Teamsters, and Thomas E. Boyle and Marshall Shafer for the Chemical Workers.[20]

Forty unions endorsed the moratorium march in New York, labor leaders spoke at many of the protests, some antiwar protests were held in union shops, hospitals and nursing homes, and thousands of union members attended the various protests that day.[21] On February 25, 1970, the *Washington Post* carried a full-page ad signed by 123 unionists, including the leaders of 22 unions, who declared, "We urge all trade unionists to join with their fellow Americans to demand an immediate withdrawal of troops and cessation of hostilities in Vietnam, and to begin putting our money where it counts—at home." The ad was dominated by a picture of a GI with the slogan, "War is hell," written across his helmet. A banner headline read, "A rich man's war and a poor man's fight." The statement insisted, "We cannot and will not have both guns and butter."[22] Yet it must be said that protests from union heads were mostly verbal; by and large, the leaders failed to mobilize large union contingents at antiwar protests, and they certainly were not willing to initiate official action at the workplace against the war.

Despite repeated denials to the contrary, the Nixon White House was shaken by these demonstrations. Already, in July 1969, Melvin Laird, the secretary of defense, announced the Nixon Doctrine, a policy of limited involvement of American ground forces in foreign wars. Laird explained that under the new doctrine, "indigenous manpower [would be] organized into properly equipped and well-trained armed forces with the help of materiel, training, technology, and specialized military skills furnished by the United States."[23]

Nixon announced a further withdrawal of thirty-five thousand troops in September. On November 3, on the eve of another round of mass demonstrations, the president announced that Vietnamization would be speeded up. As Christmas approached, he declared another fifty thousand troops were to be withdrawn. In Seymour Hersh's biography of Henry Kissinger, *The Price of Power*, he puts forward a convincing case that the mass demonstrations of October and November 1969 prevented Nixon and Kissinger from implementing Operation Duck Hook. The troop withdrawals, however, were so agonizingly slow that they satisfied no one—neither the antiwar movement nor the restless American troops in Vietnam.

These moratorium events had certainly shaken the Nixon administration and forestalled some of their worst plans for the Vietnamese, at least for the moment. However, the devastation of Vietnam continued.

The CIA, for example, implemented a new "pacification" program called "Operation Phoenix" in the aftermath of Tet, whose goal was to destroy the NLF "infrastructure." While the program murdered many NLF activists, it also targeted anyone who was sympathetic to the NLF or critical of the regime in the South. Organized under CIA director William Colby, Phoenix agents assassinated at least twenty thousand, twenty-eight thousand more were captured, and seventeen thousand allegedly "defected."[24] U.S. forces involved in the program reported that they would lead teams of mercenaries into villages not only to kill or kidnap "suspects" for torture, but also to collect loot.[25] Colby boasted that Phoenix killed sixty thousand NLF activists.[26] This secret torture and assassination program had a devastating impact on local NLF activity.

Torture was used systematically by U.S. forces. Military intelligence officer K. Barton Osborne described the use of torture he witnessed in Vietnam:

> The use of the insertion of the 6-inch dowel into the canal of one of my detainee's ears, and the tapping through the brain until dead. The starvation to death (in a cage) of a Vietnamese woman who was suspected of being part of the local political education cadre in one of the local villages.... The use of electronic gear such as sealed telephones attached to...both the women's vaginas and the men's testicles [to] shock them into submission.[27]

One soldier recounted to journalist Mark Baker what happened to three Vietnamese detainees taken for a ride in a helicopter with a U.S. intelligence officer:

> The first gook wouldn't talk. Intelligence gives you a signal, thumb towards the door, and you push the guy out.... If the second guy didn't look like he wants to say something, or he's lying, the intelligence officer says, "This guy's out the door." You kick him out.... The last prisoner is crying and he's...talking Vietnamese like crazy.... Before

we get back to the base camp, after this guy do [sic] all the talking, and
the intelligence officer documents everything, they kick him out the
door anyway.[28]

It appeared that Nixon, once again, as in the spring of 1970, was finally turning the war over to the South Vietnamese and the television
news helped create this illusion. Av Westin, an executive producer with
ABC News, sent a telex to his Saigon bureau chief that read, "I think
the time has come to shift some of our focus from the battlefield…to
themes and stories under the general heading: We Are on Our Way
Out of Vietnam."[29] In mid-April, 1970, Nixon announced that one
hundred thousand more combat troops were leaving Vietnam.

However, behind the scenes, Nixon and Kissinger were once again
planning another dramatic escalation of the war. In March 1970,
Prince Sihanouk was toppled in a coup by his prime minister, the pro-
American General Lon Nol. Cambodia now had a government that
would do Nixon's bidding. On April 30, 1970, Nixon appeared on national television and announced that U.S. forces were invading Cambodia, though in his speech he referred to the invasion as an
"incursion" to "guarantee the continued success of our withdrawal
and Vietnamization programs," by wiping out enemy "sanctuaries."[30]
In his speech, Nixon warned of increasing "anarchy both abroad and
at home," decrying "mindless attacks on all the great institutions,
which have been created by free civilizations in the last five hundred
years. Even here in the United States, great universities are being systematically destroyed." He warned, "If, when the chips are down, the
world's most powerful nation, the United States of America, acts like
a pitiful, helpless giant, the forces of totalitarianism and anarchy will
threaten free nations and free institutions throughout the world."[31]

The campuses literally exploded in rage. Within four days of the
announced invasion, strikes were in progress at more than a hundred campuses. Symbols of the military were under attack everywhere, especially ROTC buildings on campuses. "It was something

I'd never seen before," remembered one activist in New York. "I could feel the polarization. You could cut that with a knife in society, it was so incredible.... On that day or two after the Cambodian invasion, this whole city was filled with thousands of people all over the street debating. You could just go from group to group arguing.[32]

Tom Wells describes how the anger went beyond peaceful protests:

Maryland students launched a "hit and run" attack on their school's ROTC headquarters and skirmished with state police. At Princeton, students firebombed an armory. Students battled police for more than three hours at Kent State, inciting a dusk-to-dawn curfew. Shortly afterward, "a fire of undetermined origin" roared through the school's wooden ROTC building; firemen were impeded by students slicing fire hoses and throwing rocks. Ohio's governor called in the National Guard. Students at Stanford went on a rampage, breaking into shops and smashing windows; among the rampagers was Robert McNamara's son.[33]

Nixon was at first exuberant, calling the protesters "bums."[34]

Then on May 4, exhausted National Guardsmen, who had spent the previous days attempting to break a wildcat Teamsters strike, shot and killed four students at Kent State University in Ohio, wounding nine others.

The country was stunned, and student strikes and protests spread to more than thirteen hundred colleges and universities and involving by some estimates half of the entire nation's student body.[35] Ten days later, two Black students were killed and twelve wounded by police at Jackson State College in Mississippi. More than five hundred campuses were shut down. National Guard troops were sent to 21 campuses, and in the week of the Kent State killings "thirty ROTC buildings were destroyed by fire or bombs."[36] Many of the leading newspapers wrote that the country was coming apart.

A nervous Nixon appeared at a press conference on May 8 and announced that the United States would be out of a Cambodia by June 30. Vice President Spiro Agnew fanned the flames. In a speech the evening of May 4, he called the Kent State killings "predictable," and he condemned "elitists" who encouraged the campus protests and used the Bill of Rights to protect "psychotic and criminal elements in our society."[37]

If there was a high point reached by the antiwar movement, it was the massive response to the invasion of Cambodia. "Those two weeks [around May 9]," says veteran antiwar activist Norma Becker, "were the high point of activism. I'm talking about the spontaneous upsurge all over. The schools closed down, junior highs, highs, colleges—everyone was in the streets protesting."[38] Every form of protest was involved. In addition to the strikes and the fire-bombings, there were also sit-ins and blockades, marches and rallies, teach-ins, workshops, and anti-draft protests where students turned in their draft cards.

The protests were not limited to the campuses or to students. There were mass rallies in many towns, as well as GI protests at a dozen military bases. "Former Peace Corps volunteers," writes Wells, "occupied six offices of the Peace Corps building in Washington, D.C.; they named them 'Ho Chi Minh Sanctuary' and flew the NLF flag out a window, readily visible from the White House."[39] Though George Meany and several other AFL-CIO leaders defended Nixon's invasion of Cambodia, several union leaders, executive boards, and conventions issued a flurry of statements condemning the invasion of Cambodia and the war as a whole. Walter Reuther, in his last public statement, proclaimed, "We cannot successfully preach nonviolence at home while we escalate mass violence abroad."[40] These statements, which in many cases reflected a change of tune by unions that had previously expressed support for the war, were virtually ignored by the media. Meany's statement, on the other hand—"In this crucial hour, he [Nixon] should have the full support of the American people"—was trumpeted everywhere.[41] This was part of Nixon's propaganda campaign aimed at showing there was a "silent majority" of ordinary Americans that still supported him. Some of this new union opposition reflected the fact that union leaders felt more comfortable criticizing the war now that a Republican was in office; but it also reflected growing rank-and-file frustration over the war.

In response to this incredible outburst of anger over Nixon's action, liberal Democratic Senator George McGovern and liberal Republican Senator Mark Hatfield, with the support of fifteen other senators, introduced an amendment to the upcoming defense appropriation bill that would have cut off all funding for American military operations and the withdrawal of all U.S. troops by December 31, 1971, unless both Houses of Congress declared war. On May 12, both senators "bought a half hour of time on NBC television to make a nationwide appeal for support of their amendment. During the program they asked viewers to send contributions to help defray that cost of the airtime ($70,000). They received $480,000. After paying the program's expenses and buying radio, TV, and newspaper advertisements they had $110,000, left over, which they gave to charity."[42]

The McGovern-Hatfield amendment was defeated 55–39 on September 1, by a Democratic Party-controlled Senate, after a long debate that lasted most of the summer. Another bill was defeated in the Senate in the same session, by a vote of 71–22, that would have stopped the U.S. Army from sending draftees who didn't want to go to fight in Vietnam.[43] Despite the fact that more than 71 percent of Americans were telling pollsters that Vietnam was a "mistake," while 58 percent regarded the war as "immoral," and a clear majority believed that all U.S. troops should be removed by the year's end, Hatfield pronounced the vote on his and McGovern's amendment a "moral victory." But a moral victory wasn't going to end the war. The real story was not of "moral victories" over Nixon, but the futility of looking to the U.S. Senate to end the war. "In fact, no Congress ever turned down a request for funds to prosecute the war until 1973, after the Paris Peace treaty was signed."[44]

OPPOSITION TO THE WAR DEEPENS

Nixon may have weathered the domestic storm of protest, but he was far from being in a secure political position. It became clear to him that any further efforts to expand the war with U.S. ground troops would risk another potential domestic upsurge. His Cambodia adventure lifted the lid on protest in communities that had seen little antiwar activity beforehand. This was particularly true among Mexican Americans.

One of the most important events of the antiwar movement that took place in the wake of the Cambodia bombings was the Chicano moratorium.[45] "The war in Vietnam politicized the Chicano community," according to historian Rudy Acuña. "Although the Chicano population officially numbered 10 to 12 percent of the total population of the Southwest, Chicanos comprised 19.4 percent of those from that area who were killed in Vietnam. From December 1967 to March 1969 Chicanos suffered 19 percent of all casualties from the Southwest. Chicanos from Texas sustained 25.2 percent of all casualties of that state."[46] This slow burn of casualty rates combined with a rising movement against racial discrimination and oppression made the war in Vietnam a particular flash-point of anger.

The Brown Berets, a revolutionary nationalist group of young Mexican-American activists predominately from the Los Angeles area, formed the first National Chicano Moratorium Committee in 1969. They called their first demonstration against the war, in solidarity with the nationwide moratorium movement, on December 20, 1969, with two thousand participants. They staged another protest two months later on February 28, 1970, with about six thousand Mexican Americans in attendance. In March 1970, at the Second Annual Chicano Youth conference in Denver, it was decided to organize hundreds of local moratorium actions against the war that would culminate with a national event to be held in Los Angeles on

July 29. In between the conference and the planned national moratorium, were the invasion of Cambodia and the ensuing explosion of nationwide protest and the state murders of protesters at Kent State and Jackson State.

Los Angeles was infamous for the racism and violence of its police and sheriff's departments toward Mexicans. The violence of the virtually all-white Los Angeles County Sheriff's Department against the Mexican Americans grew ominously as the moratorium approached. Acuña captures both the confidence of the antiwar marchers and the quiet hatred of sheriff's deputies as the march began:

> On the morning of the 29th contingents from all over the United States arrived in East Los Angeles. By noon participants numbered between 20,000 and 30,000. *Conjuntos* (musical groups) blared out *corridos*; *vivas* and yells filled the air; placards read: *"Raza si, guerra no!" "Aztlan: Love it or Leave it!"* as sheriff's deputies lined the parade route. They stood helmeted, making no attempt to establish contact with the marchers: no smiles, no small talk. The march ended peaceably and the parade turned into Laguna Park. Marchers settled down to enjoy the program; many had brought picnic lunches. Mexican music and Chicano children entertained those assembled."[47]

Soon after the park filled, a small incident at a nearby liquor store gave the police what Acuña calls "an excuse to break up the demonstration."[48] Five hundred helmeted, club-wielding deputies attacked the peaceful crowd in the park. Their number eventually grew to fifteen hundred as they occupied the park. Acuña again: "They moved in military formation, sweeping the park. Wreckage could be seen everywhere: baby strollers [were] trampled into the ground; Victor Mendoza, walking with a cane, frantically looked for his grandmother; four deputies beat a man in his sixties; tear gas filled the air."[49]

There are many horror stories of racist violence from that day. "A Chicano when he allegedly ran a blockade; his car hit a telephone pole and he was electrocuted. A tear-gas canister exploded in a trash can, killing a 15-year-old boy."[50] But the worst was the murder of

Ruben Salazar, a popular reporter for KMEX-TV, the Spanish language station. He and two coworkers stopped at a local bar after covering the events at Laguna Park. Sheriff's deputies surrounded the bar and shot a ten-inch tear-gas canister into the building that hit Salazar in the head, killing him. Salazar was popular in the Mexican community, making a name for himself by exposing police racism. He had told coworkers that he received complaints and threats about his reporting from L.A. Police Chief Ed Davis. Salazar's killers were indicted by a federal grand jury for violating his civil rights, but they were acquitted in federal court.[51] The events at the Chicano moratorium demonstrated not only the depth of anger toward the war but also the willingness of government to use violence against antiwar activists, particularly those who were people of color.

The invasion of Cambodia also accelerated opposition to the war in the military. Vietnam veterans would now assume a leading position in the antiwar movement, changing the face of the movement. Years later, H. R. Haldeman, Nixon's chief of staff, lamented, "If the troops are going to mutiny, you can't pursue an aggressive policy."[52] Discontent was so high and the cost of the war was cutting so deeply into the country that support was collapsing even in military towns previously known for their strident pro-war stances. Jon Huntsman, a special assistant to the president, complained of the growing "antiwar sentiment in once hawkish San Diego," home of the Pacific fleet.[53]

The war was no longer politically sustainable for Nixon, who was soon facing reelection. By April 1971, a Lou Harris poll revealed that by a margin of 60 percent to 26 percent, Americans favored continued U.S. troop withdrawals "even if the government of South Vietnam collapsed."[54] There was a "rapidly growing feeling that the United States should get out of Vietnam as quickly as possible."[55] On April 7, 1971, Nixon announced that another one hundred thousand U.S. troops would be withdrawn from Vietnam by the beginning of December, leaving roughly 184,000 still there. Though

Nixon was reluctant to offer any deadlines for complete withdrawal, it seems clear in retrospect that the deadline he had in mind was the November 1972 election.

How deeply antiwar sentiment cut into the country was revealed in late April beginning with the Vietnam Veterans Against the War (VVAW) actions in Washington between April 19 and 23, followed on April 24, 1971 by a day of national demonstrations against the war. According to Tom Wells:

> Throughout the morning of April 24, demonstrators flooded the El-lipse in Washington, the staging area for the day's march to the Capi-tol. Most were young. Rank-and-file unionists, GIs, and veterans were present in greater numbers than in past peace demonstrations. According to a survey by the Washington Post, more than a third of the protesters were attending such a demonstration for the first time. 'I'm a member of the silent majority who isn't silent anymore,' a 54-year-old-furniture storeowner from Michigan remarked. The survey found that fewer than a quarter of the protesters considered them-selves radicals; most were liberals. At least thirty-nine members of Congress endorsed the demonstration. So large was the turnout for it that cars and buses carrying protesters were backed up for three miles at the Baltimore Harbor Tunnel by 11 A.M. Many of the occu-pants never made it to the demonstration.[56]

The demonstration in Washington was estimated to have grown to about half a million by the end of the day, making it up to that date the largest single demonstration in American history.[57] That same day in San Francisco, more than two hundred thousand people marched against the war.

The April 24 national demonstrations were followed by nearly a week of actions, culminating in an effort to shut down the federal government on May 3. Nixon declared Washington, D.C. "open for business," but upwards of seventy five thousand antiwar protesters scattered through out the city on May 3, blocking traffic, sitting in at various government buildings, and harassing political figures. The

D.C. police, backed by the federal government, began mass arrests of demonstrators early in the morning. By 8:00 a.m., more than seven thousand had already been arrested, and more arrests were to come. It was open season on anybody the police didn't like. "Martial law might not have been declared, but it was in effect."[58]

The city jails couldn't handle the numbers arrested so a makeshift outdoor detention camp was built near RFK Stadium, surrounded by an eight-foot-high fence. People were held without food, water, or sanitary facilities. "Calling this a concentration camp would be a very apt description," declared Dr. Benjamin Spock, who was also held in detention.[59] The Black residents of Washington responded sympathetically to the protesters, giving them food, water, and other necessities. Federal Employees for Peace held a rally in Lafayette Park across the street from the White House in the middle of the police crackdown.

While the May Day protests were chaotic and didn't achieve their objective of shutting down the government, they did, in the words of a *Ramparts* article, send "shivers down its spine."[60] The backlash against the federal government's martial law–like tactics proved to be a disaster for Nixon. Even such cynical insiders as CIA Director Richard Helms later admitted, "It was obviously viewed by everybody in the administration, particularly with all the arrests and the howling about civil rights and human rights and all the rest of it…as a very damaging kind of event. I don't think there was any doubt about that."[61]

From the first Vietnam moratorium events in November 1969, to the explosion of rage following the following the Cambodian invasion, to the spring events of 1971, millions of Americans were drawn into political action against the war. The actions were become more militant, more working class, more multiracial, and more left wing. In mid-November 1972, Nixon announced that another forty-five thousand U.S. troops would be withdrawn from Vietnam leaving roughly 139,000 there in early 1972.

The American ground war in Vietnam was grinding to an end, but the bloody American air war continued to inflict unfathomable destruction on the people of Southeast Asia. While antiwar activity continued into 1972, it was much smaller; the movement too had already reached its zenith.

DID THE LARGE DEMONSTRATIONS MAKE A DIFFERENCE?

"We had an agenda we wanted to implement, and the principal impediment to that objective in Vietnam was the mass demonstrations, given aid and comfort and support by the liberal media, which was attacking the president constantly."
—Pat Buchanan, Nixon White House aide and speechwriter

One of the lingering debates concerning the antiwar movement of the 1960s was the effectiveness of the many national demonstrations in stopping or not stopping the war in Vietnam. This debate existed from the very beginning to the very end of the antiwar movement. Soon after the first national demonstration against the war organized by SDS, leading SDS members concluded that national demonstrations were a waste of time. Every time proposals were advanced for a national protest, arguments would surface about the efficacy of mass demonstrations. Many student activists felt a vague sense that something more was needed. For example, before the October 1967 Pentagon March, the SDS national office declared, "We feel that these large demonstrations—which are just public expressions of belief—can have no significant effect on American policy in Vietnam. Further, they delude many participants into thinking that the 'democratic' process in America functions in a meaningful way."[62]

It wasn't just SDSers who drew these conclusions; radical pacifist Dave Dellinger in 1971 noticed "a fatigue, a quasi-disillusionment" with legal, mass demonstrations, a view that they were "yesterday's mashed potatoes."[63]

Part of the reason that many activists thought that mass demonstrations were ineffective was because both Johnson and Nixon claimed they weren't swayed by them, and simply because the war continued, year in and year out, no matter how big the protests got—at least until 1970, when large-scale pullouts began.

But there was also a more political aspect to the debate. As the movement radicalized, there were those in the movement who elevated the tactic of street fighting to the level of principle. On the other side, there were those who made a fetish of legal, mass demonstrations, to the point of actively discouraging more confrontational tactics on the grounds that they would deter mass participation in the movement.

The mass demonstrations were undoubtedly insufficient by themselves to force the United States out of Vietnam, but they played an important role in drawing in and educating new antiwar forces, as well as raising activists' confidence that the movement was widening its base and gaining overwhelming public support. Halstead offers the example of 13-year-old Raul Gonzales, who describes the impact of running across the April 15, 1967, mobilization against the war in Kezar Stadium on San Francisco:

> I didn't know what was going on. So I asked someone. They said it was a demonstration to get the troops out of Vietnam," Raul recalled later. "Personally, I was against the war, but I didn't really know why. I thought maybe I was the only one against it. The rally impressed me.... I had no arguments against the war. From talking to people at the demonstration, and listening to the speeches, I got arguments. It strengthened my feelings. I took the arguments I learned there and the literature that was being passed out and used that with my friends. Those who were wavering tended to side with me now that I had the facts and figures and the stuff I'd gotten at the demonstration.[64]

Yet, at the same time, many activists were right in their conclusions that more than large, set-piece protests were necessary to end the war. Ultimately, it was a combination of protest at home (including mass demonstrations, sit-ins, civil disobedience, student strikes, etc.), rebellion among GIs, and the armed struggle of the Vietnamese people that forced the United States to get out of Vietnam. In all this, there was no Chinese wall between different forms of protest or tactics—from mass peaceful demonstrations to blockades, sit-ins, strikes, and so on. These different manifestations of protest flowed in and out of one another and often one led to the other. The role of mass protests was to mobilize the maximum public manifestation of antiwar sentiment—a kind of movement rollcall—used to feed the movement's further growth in all its different manifestations.

The mass demonstrations also had an impact on soldiers, as well as on the movement's attitude to soldiers. Fred Halstead recalls how all this began at the October 1967 March on the Pentagon:

> The army brought in several thousand troops—in addition to federal marshals and police—to defend the Pentagon. Most of the troops were ordinary soldiers acting as military police for the weekend. Of those who confronted the crowd a few were angry, even brutal. But many were visibly embarrassed by the situation, and some became friendly in the course of contact with the demonstration. Word of this spread among the demonstrators, and afterward throughout the movement as a whole…. Before the Pentagon action, the idea of reaching GIs was pressed by a minority. After the October 21, 1967 march, the movement as a whole began to embrace the idea with some enthusiasm.[65]

The impact of mass demonstrations on American GIs around the world only grew as the war went on. It would be hard to see how soldiers, sailors, and airmen would have moved against the war in such large numbers without the impact of millions marching against the war at home.

CHAPTER EIGHT

FROM WATERGATE TO THE FALL OF SAIGON

THE GI REBELLION

> All the foregoing facts—and many more dire indicators of the worst kind of military trouble—point to widespread conditions among American forces in Vietnam that have only been exceeded in this century by the French Army's Nivelle mutiny of 1917 and the collapse of the Tzarist armies in 1916 and 1917.
> —Colonel Robert D. Heinl Jr., *Armed Forces Journal*, June 1971

The United States entered the war in Vietnam with the most powerful military in the world but within a few years this very same military was in a state of disarray, disintegration, and rebellion. This GI rebellion progressively undermined the ability of the United States to defeat the NLF and the North Vietnamese, and was an important factor in Nixon's decision to draw down troop levels and eventually pull the troops out completely. How could an army break down so quickly? "From the very beginning of the military escalation in Vietnam, soldiers began to question the wisdom of the conflict and acted to oppose it. They learned from the bitter experience of war itself," writes historian Richard Moser.[1] Soldiers were increasingly angered, according to historian Christian Appy, by the "contradictory ground" dividing "the official justifications of the war expressed by American policymakers and the war as it was actually lived by the soldiers."[2]

For the soldiers of the overwhelmingly working-class army, the war was a huge shock. They were trained to believe that the United

States was a moral, democratic nation, a "liberator of oppressed people" confronting a worldwide communist conspiracy, and that struggles for national liberation like that in Vietnam were part of this
grand communist conspiracy emanating from Moscow and Beijing.

Soldiers expected a war between professional armies in set-piece
battles, like those their fathers fought in the Second World War (a
war, moreover, that had been systematically romanticized). What
they found themselves doing was fighting a peasant army of men
and women—a total war against an entire population motivated by
hatred of the U.S. occupation and of its puppet regime. American
soldiers burned down villages, destroyed large areas of the countryside, killed large numbers of NLF soldiers, and engaged in wanton
brutality against civilians. As one soldier put it, "I wondered how
people would feel in Pittsburgh if the Vietnamese came over in B-
52s and bombed them."[3] American soldiers were trained to believe
that only America's enemies committed atrocities, but now they
were doing those same horrible things in the name of America.

According to Appy, "In the earlier years, the central thrust of dis-
enchantment concerned the strategic aims of the war and the lack of
convincing signs of progress. Among those who fought in latter
years…there was a more widespread sense of the war's pointless-
ness."[4] Before the Tet Offensive, opposition to the war inside the military rested on the shoulders of courageous individuals who in every
case were severely punished. In June 1965, Richard Steinke, a West
Point graduate stationed in Vietnam refused to board an aircraft
taking him to a remote Vietnamese village. "The Vietnamese war,"
Steinke said "is not worth a single American life."[5] He was court-
martialed and dismissed from the army. In February 1966, a decorated ex–Green Beret, Master Sergeant Donald Duncan, who left
Vietnam the previous September, published a powerful indictment
of the war in *Ramparts* magazine. Duncan was a militant anticommunist when he arrived in Vietnam, but his experience there trans-

formed him. Duncan wrote, "I had to accept that…the vast majority of people were pro–Viet Cong and anti-Saigon. I had to accept also that the position, 'We are in Vietnam because we are in sympathy with the aspirations and desires of the Vietnamese people,' was a lie. If this is a lie, how many others are there?"[6]

The Fort Hood Three, a trio of U.S. Army privates—James Johnson, Dennis Mora, and David Samas—refused to serve in Vietnam. They were signalers with the 2nd Armored Division stationed at Fort Hood, Texas. One was Black, one Puerto Rican, and one Lithuanian-Italian, all from poor, working-class families. Denouncing the war as "immoral, illegal, and unjust," they were arrested, court-martialed, and imprisoned.[7] In 1967, Dr. Howard Levy, who came from a left-wing family in New York and who had attended socialist meetings before being drafted into the army, refused to train the Green Berets at Fort Jackson, South Carolina. Levy argued that the Green Berets were "murderers of women and children" and "killers of peasants." He was court-martialed and sentenced to twenty-seven months in a military prison. The colonel who presided at Levy's court-martial said, "The truth of the statements is not an issue in this case."[8]

"The individual acts multiplied," according to radical historian Howard Zinn,

> a black private in Oakland refused to board a troop plane to Vietnam, although he faced eleven years at hard labor. A navy nurse, Lieutenant Susan Schnall, was court-martialed for marching in a peace demonstration while in uniform, and for dropping antiwar leaflets from a plane on navy installations…. Two black marines, George Daniels and William Harvey, were given long prison sentences (Daniels, six years, Harvey, ten years, both later reduced) for talking to other black marines against the war.[9]

Combat experience had an even greater impact on others. Declared Bill Ehrhart, a marine in Vietnam who later became a writer:

"In grade school we learned about the redcoats, the nasty British soldiers that tried to stifle our freedom.... Subconsciously, but not very subconsciously, I began increasingly to have the feeling that I was a redcoat. I think it was one of the most staggering realizations of my life."[10]

When combat experience was combined with the influence of the civil rights and Black power movements opposed to the war, the effect was even more explosive. As one Black soldier recounted, "Most of the people like me were naive...but at the same time, the Black Panther organization, the Muslims, the Kings didn't feel that we should be out there participating [in the war]...we didn't feel we were fighting for our country; half the brothers felt it wasn't even our war and were sympathetic to Ho Chi Minh.[11] Such sentiments grew in tandem with the escalation of struggles of Blacks on the home front.

After the Tet Offensive, individual resistance evolved into an outright rebellion that crippled the American military machine. In particular, the assassination of Martin Luther King Jr. on April 4, 1968, according to author Michael Herr, "intruded on the war in a way no other outside event had ever done."[12] One Black veteran remembers thinking: "If they kill a preacher, what are they going to do to us, even though we're over here fighting for them."[13]

Antiwar activity among soldiers took many forms—participating in antiwar marches, putting out antiwar newspapers on bases, organizing GI coffeehouses, desertion, sabotage, avoiding combat, acts of mutiny, and the killing of unpopular officers. GI newspapers, according to historian David Cortright, were "the fundamental expression of the political opposition within the armed forces."[14] Cortright believes that there were more than three hundred GI newspapers produced during the war with varying levels of duration, from one issue to many years. They were an irritant to the military high command, since many took the title *FTA* or "Fuck the

Army." This was a play on the recruitment motto of the U.S. army in the 1960s—"Fun Travel Adventure." The best known was the Chicago-based *Vietnam GI,* produced by Vietnam veteran Jeff Sharlet (who later died from cancer caused by his exposure to the dioxin-laced herbicide Agent Orange). It had a print run of over fifteen thousand and was distributed across military bases in the United States and Vietnam.[15] GI coffeehouses were another major irritant to the military high command. Often initiated by civilians attempting to reach soldiers with an antiwar message, civilian and GI activists fought a running battle with the military to keep them open outside some of the biggest bases in the country. The most famous of these was the Oleo Strut (named after a part of a helicopter), which was set up outside Fort Hood near Killeen, Texas.[16] The coffeehouses were places that GIs could talk about the war and racism, listen to rock music, and socialize outside the confines of military controlled or authorized facilities.

The first GIs to organize were Vietnam veterans who returned to the United States. Vietnam Veterans Against the War (VVAW) was founded in 1967 by Jan Barry, who had been stationed in Vietnam in 1963. He was disturbed by what he called America's "colonial military policy" in Vietnam, and later dropped out of West Point to pursue a writing career. Barry first participated in antiwar activity when he marched in the 1967 Spring Mobilization to End War in Vietnam. During 1967 and 1968, hundreds of veterans joined VVAW, but the organization all but collapsed into Eugene McCarthy's failed campaign for the Democratic Party's nomination for president in 1968. The group revived in 1969 and 1970 as a result of a political awakening of Vietnam veterans around such issues as their ill treatment at Veterans Administration (VA) hospitals, the public exposure of war crimes committed at My Lai, and the killing of antiwar demonstrators at Kent State and Jackson State following Nixon's invasion of Cambodia in 1970.[17] VVAW moved from being a single-issue organization—to end the war—to a multi-issue movement around the class issues of Vietnam veterans.

This revival also brought in new members who came from mostly working-class families and who had experienced some of the most intense combat of the war. The most famous were Ron Kovic, whose life was depicted in the book and film *Born on the Fourth of July*, and Al Hubbard, a Black veteran who brought the need to address the racist treatment of Black soldiers and veterans to VVAW. John Kerry, the U.S. senator from Massachusetts and 2004 Democratic candidate for president, also joined during this time, but what made him so different from most other members was that he was from a wealthy background and had connections to the upper levels of the Democratic Party through family and friends. Vietnam Veterans Against the War would organize two historic events in 1971 that catapulted the organization into the leadership of the antiwar movement—the Winter Soldier Investigation into war crimes in Vietnam and the march on Washington called Dewey Canyon III.

While VVAW was growing at home, it also had active duty members in Vietnam—combat soldiers, for whom resisting the war was literally a life-and-death issue—and they started taking action to save their lives. Some walked away by simply deserting. That was the biggest problem that the U.S. military faced after the Tet Offensive—merely holding their forces together. "The number of draft evaders and resisters was dwarfed by the number of deserters from the active duty armed forces," according to historian H. Bruce Franklin.[18] The Defense Department recorded 503,926 "incidents of desertion" from July 1, 1966, to December 31, 1973, while in 1971 alone 98,324 servicemen deserted. This means that during the course of the war in Vietnam, nearly the same number of men deserted the armed forces as the total number of American soldiers stationed in Vietnam at the war's height. In 1970, the army experienced 65,643 desertions, the equivalent of four infantry divisions. Admiral Elmo R. Zumwalt Jr., chief of naval operations dramatically proclaimed, "We have a personnel crisis that borders on a disaster."[19]

"During 1969–1972 commanders who continued to pressure their men for high body counts were almost universally detested," writes Appy.[20] Those who could not walk away from the war began to mutiny, or to kill or injure officers who sent them into dangerous combat missions. In August and September 1969, two infantry units mutinied after suffering heavy casualties in previous actions.[21] "During the next two years, the press published numerous reports of entire units refusing direct combat orders, and the public actually got to see two incidents of rebellion on network television," writes Franklin.[22]

The killing of officers, known as "fragging," skyrocketed in the last three years of the war. The term "fragging" originally came from the use of fragmentation grenades, but then was applied generally to the warning sent to or killing of officers and non-commissioned officers (NCOs). The army reported 126 fraggings in 1969, 271 in 1970, and 333 in 1971. Fraggings actually increased during the time that the number of U.S. troops dropped from 500,000 to 200,000. More than 80 percent of fragging victims were officers or NCOs. "By mid-1972, the Pentagon was officially acknowledging 551 incidents of fragging with explosive devices, which left more than 86 dead and more than 700 wounded."[23] These Pentagon-provided figures are probably an underestimation of the number of officers killed by their own troops.[24]

African-American soldiers faced racism in the military not only from the officer corps, but also from racist white soldiers. On the night of King's assassination, for example, some white GIs at Cam Ranh Bay celebrated by donning KKK outfits and parading around the base. That same night there were rebellions by Black soldiers at

U.S. military bases around the world. In 1970, Wallace Terry conducted a survey of 392 African-American enlisted men for *Time* and the *Washington Post*. The survey revealed that 64 percent believed that their "fight was in the U.S.," not Vietnam. Eighty-three percent believed that America "is in for more racial violence," and 50 percent said they would use weapons "in the struggle for their rights in the U.S."[25] Even more ominously for the American ruling class, "A significantly high percentage promised to carry home the lessons that they learned in self-defense and Black unity to…the Black Panther Party."[26] Vietnam had created sympathy for revolutionary politics among a large layer of Black soldiers.

While the U.S. ground troops were being rapidly withdrawn in 1971–1972, the Vietnam vets were moving into the leadership of the antiwar movement at home. Winter Soldier, the name given to the VVAW's war crimes investigation, was the term Tom Paine used for soldiers who stayed the course during the darkest days of the American Revolution. The "new winter soldiers," as they saw themselves, would end the war by exposing U.S. war crimes in Vietnam. Al Hubbard said that the purpose of the Winter Soldier Investigation was to show that "My Lai was not an isolated incident," but "only a minor step beyond the standard official United States policy in Indochina."[27] The Winter Soldier Investigation took place in Detroit from January 31 through February 2, 1971. During that weekend more than one hundred American veterans of the war in Vietnam testified to war crimes that they had participated in or witnessed. Another five hundred to seven hundred veterans came from all across the country to listen to the testimony.[28]

The painful, gut-wrenching, tear-filled testimony riveted and shocked everyone present. Veterans testified to committing or witnessing rape, the routine killing of civilians, and mass murder. Sergeant Jamie Henry, who testified to witnessing the murder of nineteen women and children during his tour of duty, explained,

"You are trained 'gook, gook, gook' and once the military has got the idea implanted in you that these people are not humans…it makes it a little bit easier to kill 'em."[29] Hundreds of veterans joined VVAW after the hearings, and Winter Soldier Investigations modeled on Detroit were held in many other cities around the country. Senators and congressmen publicly called for official investigations into the charges raised.

Then came Dewey Canyon III. Named after two failed invasions of Laos by the United States and South Vietnamese armies, it was described by VVAW as a "limited incursion into the country of Congress." It would be five days of demonstrations, from April 19 to 23, 1971, to protest the war and the treatment of veterans. As many as two thousand Vietnam veterans spent five days harassing the political establishment in Washington. They sat in at the Supreme Court to protest the illegality of the war. They humiliated pro-war senators, such as the late racist bigot Strom Thurmond. Veterans and Gold Star mothers—as those who'd lost children are called—made their way into Arlington National Cemetery to lay a wreath for the American dead in Vietnam.

Jan Barry presented a list of sixteen demands from VVAW to a Congressional delegation which included: "immediate, unilateral, unconditional withdrawal" of all U.S. forces from Indochina; amnesty for all Americans who refused to fight in Vietnam; a formal inquiry into war crimes; and improved veterans' benefits.[30] There were two high points to Dewey Canyon III. One was John Kerry's powerful speech before the Senate Foreign Relations Committee, which he ended by asking, "How can you ask a man to be the last man to die in Vietnam? How can you ask a man to die for a mistake?"[31]

The second, and far more important event was the ceremony on Capital Hill where vets returned their medals to the U.S. government in great anger and eloquence. Jack Smith, a highly decorated ex-marine sergeant, was the first to go. He said his medals were a "symbol of dishonor, shame, and inhumanity." He offered an apology to the Vietnamese people, "whose hearts were broken, not won" because of "genocide, racism, and atrocity."[32] Hundreds followed him.

> A fifty-six-year-old WWII vet, Gail Olson, too overcome to speak, played a faltering taps on his bugle; then explained he wished to honor all who died in Vietnam, including his son William. He tried to say something on behalf of the children of Vietnam, but could not continue, and ended by saying he prayed for peace. He had put tears in the eyes of some of the fiercest-looking vets. Two Gold Star mothers came up next. "I am here to join all of these men," said one of them. "In each one of them I see my son."[33]

One vet threw his Purple Heart toward the Capitol building and said, "I hope I get another one fighting these fuckers."[34]

Dewey Canyon III was the lead story every night on the television news and on the front page of newspapers across the country. The face of the antiwar movement had completely changed for millions of people.

By 1971, the ruinous state of the American army in Vietnam was clear for all to see. The senior commanding officer of U.S. forces in Vietnam, General Creighton Abrams declared, in a state of mad frustration, "Is this a god-damned army or a mental hospital? Officers are afraid to lead their men into battle, and the men won't follow. Jesus Christ! What happened?"[35] The June 1971 issue of the *Armed Forces Journal* published an article by Colonel Robert Heinl called "The Collapse of the Armed Forces," where he declared that:

> The morale, discipline and battle worthiness of the U.S. Armed Forces are, with few salient exceptions, lower and worse than at any time in this century and possibly in the history of the United States. By every conceivable indicator, our army that now remains in Vietnam is in a state *approaching collapse*, with individual units avoiding or having refused combat, murdering their officers and noncommissioned officers, drug-ridden, and dispirited where not *mutinous*.[36]

REVOLUTION IN THE AIR

"The invasion of Cambodia and the senseless shooting of four students at Kent
State University in Ohio have consolidated the academic community against the
war, against business and against government. This is a dangerous situation. It
threatens the whole economic and social structure of the nation."
—*BusinessWeek*, May 16, 1970[37]

Q. *Mr. President, some Americans believe this country is heading
for revolution.*

A. *(Nixon) That would require a rather extended answer. Briefly,
this country is not headed for revolution.* [38]

By the end of 1970, the United States had experienced more than
a decade of rising political struggles that radicalized a generation of
Americans and transformed the political landscape of the country.
Activists who had begun with a moral revulsion against U.S. atrocities in Vietnam became by 1968 staunch opponents of American
imperialism. A poll conducted among college students in April
1970, for example, found 41 percent agreeing with the statement,
"The war in Vietnam is pure imperialism."[39] Many who had begun
with illusions in the Democratic Party became disillusioned with
the liberals' support for the war, and moved toward finding a politics
independent of the two-party system. Many who hoped at first only
to "stop the war" became critical of the entire economic, political,
and social system. Inspired by the Vietnamese national struggle and
various other anti-imperialist struggles in the "Third World," they
became anticapitalist revolutionaries searching for answers to how
the United States could be fundamentally transformed.

The signs of serious political crisis for the American ruling class
were everywhere. The United States was the only major industrial
capitalist country to have witnessed uprisings in all its major cities.
Its military forces, once considered to be the most powerful in modern history, was losing a war to one of the poorest nations in the
world, while increasingly larger numbers of soldiers were refusing to

fight. Tens of millions of Americans had participated in one way or another in the massive protests against the war in Vietnam and for civil rights. The sleeping giant of the American working class was beginning to stir, influenced by a combination of these movements and its declining working and living conditions. The first signs of economic crisis were returning after nearly a generation of prosperity.

The barbarity of the war, the rebellions in the cities, and the growth of the Black liberation struggle played an important role in radicalizing both soldiers in Vietnam and radical student activists in the United States. But also important were international developments. In particular, the 1968 explosion of struggles around the world, from Paris to Prague to Mexico City, had a profound effect on radicals in the United States. The May events in Paris, which began with student protests and spilled over into a general strike involving ten million French workers, not only convinced a new layer of radicals that revolution was possible, but also began for the first time in many years to reintroduce the central role of workers in changing society—although in the United States the idea that workers were "bought off" died hard on the left.

"For a growing number, the struggle against the Vietnam War, and the struggle for Black liberation, exposed the nature of the American capitalist state, and led to the understanding that it must be overthrown," wrote independent socialist Jack Weinberg (of Berkeley Free Speech Movement fame) and Jack Gerson in 1969. "All this time, a growing restlessness and rebelliousness was developing among students in particular and young people in general."[40] This was a reaction to the intense crisis gripping American society and the failures of liberalism. For Weinberg and Gerson this had its biggest impact inside SDS:

> Propelled both by an escalating crisis in American society and the manifest bankruptcy of its early liberal, reform-oriented approach, SDS politics went through a very rapid evolution to the left, from

left-liberal protest in 1964 ("Part of the Way with LBJ") to anti-imperialist resistance in 1967 to varieties of anticapitalist revolutionism
today. What began as a movement in many ways resembling a super-
idealistic children's crusade to save the world was becoming increasingly grim and serious.[41]

This new "grim and serious" attitude meant that by the fall of
1968, according to one public opinion survey, more than one million college students considered themselves to be revolutionaries,
of which over 360,000 supported the need for a "mass revolutionary party."[42]

Another aspect of the growing radicalization was the development of a women's movement as women activists began to challenge their traditional roles as the "makers of coffee" and began to
link issues of women's oppression with that of racial and national
oppression. Women had been entering the workforce in larger
numbers, and it was boosting their confidence to challenge sexist
attitudes and discrimination. Women in SNCC, SDS, and other organizations who first raised the issue of women's equality within
the movement were ridiculed, and women had to organize and
fight to assert their place as leaders in the overall struggle and in the
fight for their own rights. The movement during the Vietnam War
era peaked in August 1970, when fifty thousand protesters marched
in a nationwide protest for free abortion on demand, no forced
sterilization, 24-hour community-controlled day care, and equal
pay for equal work.[43]

If one were to compare the state of the United States in the mid-
1950s with that of the early 1970s, it would be unrecognizable. These
historic struggles had an even more profound impact on a large section of the population that was convinced that a radical restructuring or a revolutionary transformation of American society was
possible. In 1970, for example, the New York Times reported that,
"four out of ten college students—nearly three million people—

thought a revolution was necessary in the U.S."[44] The politics that came to overwhelmingly dominate this new generation of American revolutionaries was "Third Worldism"—identification with the national struggles of the Vietnamese, the Cuban revolutionaries Fidel Castro and Che Guevara, and with Mao's China.

Before the late sixties, there was only one small socialist group in the United States influenced by China, the Progressive Labor Party (PL), which was formed in the early 1960s by expelled members of the CPUSA who had sided with China in the Sino-Soviet Dispute. PL during the course of the next decade would grow into a force on the left and had its biggest impact inside SDS, the main organizational expression of the student left.[45] But this was all still to come.

The turning point for the influence of Maoism internationally was Mao's initiation of the "Great Proletarian Cultural Revolution" beginning in 1966. Simon Leys, an expert on Chinese politics and culture, sums up the "Cultural Revolution":

> The "Cultural Revolution" had nothing revolutionary about it except the name, and nothing cultural about it except the initial tactical pretext. It was a power struggle waged at the top between a handful of men and behind the smokescreen of a fictitious mass movement. As it turned out, the disorder unleashed by this power struggle created a genuinely revolutionary mass current, which developed spontaneously at the grass roots in the form of army mutinies and workers' strikes on a vast scale. These had not been proscribed in the program, and they were crushed pitilessly.[46]

But this is not how the Cultural Revolution was viewed internationally. The Cultural Revolution appeared as a movement from below to storm the bureaucracy. "Mao," according to author Chris Harman, "it seemed, had mobilized the youth against the old structures and turned spontaneity against the party apparatus. He had shown there were no limits to what could be achieved if people threw off old habits of deference and obedience. He had insisted that the world could be overturned tomorrow, if only individuals made the effort—that 'one spark could start a prairie fire.'"[47] This was the great appeal of Maoism to radicalizing activists in the United States.

The international impact of the Cultural Revolution coincided with a historic political opening for revolutionary politics in the mid-1960s in the United States. However, Maoism opened a back door for the rehabilitation of Stalinism because, according to Beijing's line, Russia had been socialist under Stalin, but had become capitalist after 1956. "Stalin is the bridge between Lenin and Mao," *Red Papers 1* declared.[48] The *Red Papers* were a series of theoretical publications of the Bay Area Revolutionary Union, one of the first non-PL Maoist organizations, founded in 1968 in the San Francisco/Oakland region, that attempted to project a Maoist political perspective in the United States.[49] The *Red Papers 1* went on to say, "Stalin was a great Marxist-Leninist who made some errors; some could have been avoided, others were scarcely avoidable."[50] Quickly flowing from this rehabilitation of Stalin was all the worst aspects of Stalinist politics in the 1930s and 1940s, such as the "cult of personality." Mao was portrayed as an infallible demigod whose little red book had all the answers for revolutionaries.

In 1969, SDS, the largest radical student organization to emerge during the previous decade, collapsed as two large factions—one led by PL and the other by Bernardine Dohrn and Bill Ayers (soon to call themselves the Weather Underground) and other non-PL Maoists led by Mike Klonsky—battled for control of the organization. The controversy primarily revolved around a series of political positions that PL took, specifically that all forms of nationalism were "reactionary." Dohrn, Ayers, and Klonsky marshaled their supporters and unilaterally expelled PL and its supporters (who made up a large number of delegates at the convention) from SDS for being "counterrevolutionary." While two SDSs were declared—one led by PL and the other led by Dohrn, Ayers, and Klonsky—the organization was effectively dead.

Dohrn and Ayers formed the Weather Underground (WU), which was in many ways a caricature of guerrilla politics, and involved a lot of ultraradical posturing. The other non-PL faction went on to participate in the formation of several Maoist parties. A number of local SDS chapters, turned off by the pumped-up rhetoric and posturing of the split, denounced both sides.

The WU, which never numbered more than two hundred or three hundred active members, made its name in October 1969 during its "Days of Rage" in Chicago, where eight hundred people showed up in combat boots and goggles armed with sticks to do battle with the police and "to tear the motherfucker apart."[51]

Kirkpatrick Sale offers a picture of Weathermen politics: "The primary attachment to Third World revolutionaries, the sense of imminent collapse of the American state, the unwillingness to depend on other sources in the society (either liberal or working-class), and the allegiance to violence. If the job of the revolutionary is to make the revolution, that's what the Weathermen, in their own particular way, were trying to do."[52] The Weathermen saw themselves as outlaws in a society ripe for revolution but where no social force existed to make the revolution. Weinberg and Gerson argue that, "The central driving force behind the Weatherman is desperation.... The response of Weatherman comes from its combined feelings of outrage and impotence. It generates such a great sense of urgency, that suddenly in its mind the urgency itself is translated into a material force capable of decisively tipping the balance in favor of its deep desires."[53]

Holding to a concept of "white skin privilege," WU saw American workers as beneficiaries of American imperialism. "Your television set, car and wardrobe," read one of its statements, "already belong, to a large degree, to the people of the rest of the world."[54] During the November 1969 General Electric strike, one witness reported Weathermen activists showing up at a picket line with a poster "stating something along the lines of 'Ho, Ho, Ho Chi Minh, the NLF are gonna kill GE workers.'"[55]

The Weathermen would carry out a minor bombing campaign over the next decade. Mark Rudd, a leader of the 1968 Columbia University student uprising and WU cofounder, calls the Weather Underground "a huge fuck-up! We did the work of the FBI by destroying SDS. We accidentally killed three of our own people. We split and undermined the larger antiwar movement...the importance of the Weather Underground was that it was a total disaster."[56]

Out of the breakup of SDS also emerged the "New Communist movement"—consisting of several Maoist organizations that would together eventually number in the thousands of activists. Based on the merger of many smaller local organizations and collectives into national groups, organizations such as the Revolutionary Union (later the Revolutionary Communist Party) and the October League were for a time the largest groups on the left. Though these groups considered the "primary" contradiction to be between oppressed and oppressor nations, many of them nevertheless began to develop a more serious orientation to the American working class, although their hyped-up Maoist rhetoric made it difficult for them to relate to workers.[57] These parties, modeled on the top-down CPs of China and Russia, were essentially Stalinist caricatures of Lenin's Bolshevik Party—dogmatic, undemocratic, and each claiming to be the "vanguard" of the working class even though they were clearly not. Their tendency toward increasing sectarianism increased as the social movements went into decline. Thus, the rise of Maoism was short-lived. After Nixon's visit to China in 1972 and the creation of a U.S.-Chinese alliance against the former Soviet Union, Maoism began to go into crisis and then into an irreversible decline in the United States.

Why was it that other longstanding revolutionary socialist currents like Trotskyism, represented by the American Socialist Workers Party (SWP), proved unable to provide a credible alternative?

The SWP was one of the longstanding organizations of the "old left." Founded in 1938, it had its origins in the Trotskyist opposition to Stalin. When the U.S. war in Vietnam escalated during the course of the 1965, the SWP threw itself into the movement. One of their leading members, Fred Halstead, who later chronicled the role of the SWP in the antiwar movement in his voluminous book *Out Now!*, played a prominent national role and the Young Socialists of America (YSA), the youth group of the U.S. Socialist Workers Party, worked tirelessly against the war inside a network of student antiwar groups called the Student Mobilization Committee. Why didn't this translate into a bigger influence of Trotskyist politics?

The SWP had the virtue of being staunchly for immediate withdrawal, unlike, for example, the Communist Party, which tailed the Democratic Party and supported "negotiations now." But the SWP single-mindedly insisted that the movement must focus on the demand "Out Now!" to the practical exclusion of all other issues.

The SWP argued that the key to the antiwar movement was mobilizing ever-larger antiwar protests. To be able to mobilize these demonstrations, nothing should be done to antagonize liberal public opinion by engaging in either more militant tactics or associating with any other movements like Black liberation or labor or the women's movement.

For many antiwar activists who were politicized and inspired by the militant tactics of the civil rights movement, as well as by the struggle of the Vietnamese, this emphasis on strictly legal protest was a turnoff. Perhaps even more important, the SWP failed to orient its youth group on SDS (considering it too "multi-issue"), effectively turning its back on tens of thousands of radicalizing students.

But perhaps the most important factors in the decline of the revolutionary politics that emerged out of the 1960s is that it came up against extreme repression on the one hand, and the decline of the most important social movements from which they emerged on the other. The Black movement and the Vietnam antiwar movement both peaked in 1970 and began afterwards to go into retreat. Working-class struggle began to spark up in the late 1960s—though it never reached the strike levels in France or Italy—only to die down by the mid-1970s. Indeed, 1975–1977 were watershed years, in the sense that the ruling class, having been in retreat for the previous several years, regrouped, and began a process of ideological and economic offensives against the gains of the civil rights movement and the labor movement. At the same time that thousands of people became open to creating revolutionary organizations, based on the idea that the times were ripe for revolution, the conditions that created the radicalization were beginning to recede. Nevertheless, what is so remarkable about this period is that it shows how rapidly a society that had been steeped in conservatism could become transformed, and how literally millions of people could develop a sense of their own power and of the need to effect a fundamental change in American society.

ENDGAME: FROM WATERGATE TO THE FALL OF SAIGON

> "You know they could hang people for what's in here."
> —former Defense Secretary Robert McNamara on the *Pentagon Papers*

"Vietnamization" was a strategy that was doomed to fail. Why? It had already been tried. The war was "Americanized" in 1965 precisely because the first attempt at Vietnamization—the notion of creating a stable, pro-U.S. puppet regime in South Vietnam after the

1954 Geneva peace agreement—had failed so miserably. Its failure was rooted in the corrupt, pro-landlord (and pro-U.S.) nature of the Saigon regime. It had no mass social base and its demoralized troops were no match for the highly motivated nationalist forces. By falling back on a policy that had been discarded, the United States was already admitting defeat.

The United States was now losing a war before the eyes of the world. According to liberal historian Stanley Karnow, "Nixon and Kissinger desperately needed a drastic new initiative"[58] to detract from their failures. This "new initiative" turned out to be the invasion of another neighboring country—Laos—to sever the Ho Chi Minh trail. The United States was going to rely on South Vietnamese troops with heavy U.S. air, artillery, and logistical support—a major test of Vietnamization. In February 1971, fifteen thousand South Vietnamese troops invaded Laos in an operation called Lam Son 719. The U.S. Air Force flew eight thousand aerial sorties in support of the invasion. The South Vietnamese troops advanced about a dozen miles into Laos without much opposition, and then they were hit with a major counteroffensive by five divisions of the North Vietnamese Army. It immediately became a major rout, with the South Vietnamese Army fleeing back to South Vietnam, losing 71 tanks and 127 armored personnel carriers on the way. More than two thousand five hundred South Vietnamese troops were killed and several thousand wounded, and the United Stated lost 107 helicopters.

Because no U.S. ground troops were involved in the invasion, it didn't provoke anything close to the domestic explosion around Cambodia. But militarily it was a complete failure. The Laos debacle proved that even with U.S. air and logistical support, the South Vietnamese Army was a useless fighting force. There was a rapid disintegration of the U.S. position in Vietnam during the remaining two years of the war. By the end of 1971, there were one hundred eighty five thousand U.S. troops in Indochina, down from three hundred thirty five thousand in 1970. The United States did, however, still have its B-52s, which killed many people but had little impact on the fighting capacity of the Vietnamese people.[59]

Increasingly, mainstream commentators began to use the term "quagmire" in reference to the war, describing the war as a mistake and a disaster. Whole sections of the established ruling class began jumping ship.[60]

The summer of 1971 also witnessed an important political event that would eventually destroy the Nixon presidency. In June 1971, the *New York Times* started publishing a secret government history of the war in Vietnam that has come to be known as the Pentagon Papers. Originally commissioned by former Defense Secretary Robert McNamara to chronicle the history of presidential decision-making involving Vietnam, the study documented three decades of deceptions and lies that made up the history of U.S. policy toward Southeast Asia.

McNamara declared the study classified and allowed only a limited print run. Daniel Ellsberg was a former Defense Department analyst and McNamara "whiz kid" in the Johnson administration, who now worked for the semi-governmental think tank, the Rand Corporation.[61] He turned hard against the war and leaked the study to the *New York Times* after Senator William Fulbright refused to hold hearings on it. Nixon exploded and tried to prevent the *Times* and other newspapers from publishing the history. The Supreme Court ruled against Nixon and the papers were published.

In response, Nixon would take the first steps down the road to self-destruction. He ordered his staff to put together a secret intelligence unit, only answerable to him, to plug "leaks" in the government. Known as the "plumbers," they were to carry out a criminal spree against the political enemies of Richard Nixon. "Without the Vietnam War there would have been no Watergate," according to Robert Haldeman, the former chief of staff to Nixon.[62]

The Nixon White House was already well suited to persecute their political enemies. "If you can't lie," Nixon once told a friend, "you'll never get anywhere."[63] Egil Krogh, a White House staffer, summed up well the Nixon White House mindset, "Anyone who opposes us, we'll destroy. As a matter of fact, anyone who doesn't support us, we'll destroy."[64] Nixon was frightened that Ellsberg had information on his policies, particularly the ongoing secret bombing of Cambodia. Neil Sheehan, the *Times* reporter to whom Ellsberg turned the Pentagon Papers over, wrote in his introduction to them, "The leaders of the United States for the past six years at least, including the incumbent president, Richard Milhous Nixon, may well be guilty of war crimes."[65] The break-in at the Democratic Party headquarters at the Watergate office complex a year later—the event that triggered Nixon's downfall—was part of a vast operation by Nixon to suppress dissent.

While Vietnamization was failing and the Pentagon Papers shook the country, Nixon was planning a series of foreign policy initiatives that he hoped would shift the global balance of power in favor of the United States and, specifically, weaken North Vietnam in future negotiations. He held high-profile summits in Beijing and Moscow. In February 1972 he made his famous trip to China, and then went to Moscow several months later, where he signed an arms-control agreement with the Russians. These initiatives were brilliant public-relations ploys by the Nixon administration packaged as "peace efforts." In fact, what Nixon really wanted was to promote greater international rivalry by making an alliance with China against Russia. Nixon also wanted to get Russia and China to pressure North Vietnam to settle on terms more favorable to the Americans. Secret negotiations to end the war between the United States and North Vietnam had taken place at various times with little progress since Nixon came into office.

Nixon's "opening" to China was greeted enthusiastically by the majority of Americans, who believed that it would make the world a safer place to live in. It was these initiatives, along with the continued decline of U.S. troops in Vietnam, that were major contributing factors to Nixon's landslide election win in November 1972.

Sensing that Nixon's initiatives could weaken the support of their Russian and Chinese allies, and seeing the weakening position of the United States on the ground in Vietnam (by June 1972, only forty seven thousand U.S. troops remained), the North Vietnamese leadership planned a major offensive for the spring of 1972. On March 30, 1972, a combined force of two hundred thousand NVA and NLF troops rolled across the demilitarized zone and swept the Army of the Republic of Vietnam (ARVN) aside, destroying what little faith there was left in Vietnamization. The goal of the Spring Offensive was to force the United States back to the negotiating table.

Despite American air support, the ARVN retreated, and by early April, Saigon lost control of Quang Tri province. By May 1, the NLF flag flew over the capital city and the road to Hue was open. The offensive was so effective that the commander of all U.S. forces in Vietnam, General Creighton Abrams, believed that "the whole thing may well be lost."[66] The NLF recaptured territory in Quang Ngai province and the Mekong Delta. It was only the most vicious application of American air power that prevented the collapse of the Saigon government. At the Battle of Kontum in the central highlands, in one three-week period, more than three hundred B-52 strikes took place. Quang Tri province got the same treatment, with U.S. air power reducing cities to rubble. U.S forces hit the North with seven hundred B-52 raids in April, including a sustained forty-eight-hour attack on Hanoi and Haiphong.

The United States and North Vietnam went back in secret to the negotiating table in May 1972 and continued to meet throughout the summer. Kissinger led the American team and Le Duc Tho the North Vietnamese team. In the past, negotiations stalled on two key issues—the "mutual withdrawal" of American and North Vietnamese troops from South Vietnam, and the status of the Thieu government in Saigon. The breakthrough came when the United States dropped its demand for the North Vietnamese to withdraw its troops from South Vietnam, and the North Vietnamese dropped their demand for the removal of Thieu and called for recognition of two political entities: Saigon and the Provisional Revolutionary Government of the NLF. Kissinger accepted the draft and set up a timetable for the formal signing in Hanoi. But Nixon believed that he could get a better deal after the coming election and wanted to forestall signing the treaty.

Following Nixon's landslide election, Kissinger met with Le and demanded further concessions. The North Vietnamese said no and began to evacuate children and the elderly from Hanoi and readied their air raid shelters.[67] Nixon then began what has gone down in history as the "Christmas bombings." Beginning on December 18, 1972, with a day off for Christmas, Nixon unleashed ten days of B-52 strikes on Hanoi and Haiphong. The United States dropped 36,000 tons of bombs on factories, railroad yards, and bus stations; Hanoi's largest hospital was bombed, as well as the residential neighborhood of Kheim Thien.[68]

While half the population of Hanoi was evacuated, more than two thousand civilians died. John Negroponte, the current U.S. ambassador to Iraq and then a member of the National Security Council, wryly commented, "We bombed the North Vietnamese into accepting our concessions."[69] But the peace treaty signed by the United States, North Vietnam, South Vietnam, and the NLF's Provisional Revolutionary Government was essentially the same one that Nixon had already agreed to *before* the Christmas bombing. The United States was inflicting maximum military damage before it accepted a political defeat it already knew it was going to accept—as if to say, "You may have won, but we'll make sure you inherit rubble."

On January 23, 1973, the treaty ending the American war in Vietnam was signed in Paris. The last U.S. troops were withdrawn from

Vietnam in March 1973. Historian Marilyn Young sums up Nixon's war in Vietnam:

> Between 1969 and 1972, as Nixon made war in the name of peace, 15,315 Americans, 107,504 Saigon government troops, and an estimated four hundred thousand-plus DRV and NLF soldiers died in combat. There are no reliable statistics on civilian dead and wounded, though one source estimated 165,000 civilian casualties in South Vietnam for each year of Nixon's presidency.[70]

Facing impeachment for his involvement in Watergate, Nixon resigned the presidency in August 1974. American allies in the Saigon government would survive only a little longer. In April 1975, the remnants of the Saigon government surrendered to the invading forces of the NVA. Thirty years of war was over. The United States had suffered a humiliating defeat before the eyes of the world. One of the poorest countries on earth had defeated the greatest military power in modern history.

CONCLUSION

THE LEGACY OF VIETNAM

> "A large percentage of Americans have traditionally regarded wars of colonialism or economic expansion as unjust. To the extent that an American soldier perceives a war to be motivated by these factors, he will also perceive hierarchical demands to be illegitimate."
> —Major Stephen D. Wesbrook

> "Our national life has been a running argument about, and with, the sixties."
> —George F. Will, conservative columnist

> "There are so many cartoons where people, oppressed people are saying, 'Is it Vietnam yet?'—hoping it is and wondering if it is. And it isn't. It's a different time. It's a different era. It's a different place."
> —Secretary of Defense Donald Rumsfeld

For thirty years, from 1945 to 1975, the United States attempted to prevent the nationalist forces in Vietnam from coming to power. When the French were defeated at Dien Bien Phu in 1954 after a nine-year war, the United States engineered the partitioning of Vietnam into a "communist" North and an "anticommunist" puppet regime in the South. For ten years, the United States tried to stabilize a government in Saigon that was intensely unpopular with the mass of the people. In 1965, the United States invaded to prevent the NLF from coming to power and reuniting the country that the United States had divided and conquered.

U.S. officials did not anticipate the scale and scope of the war on which they were embarking. Another decade of escalating war followed, involving as many as half a million troops at its height and involving two million troops total.

The devastation wreaked by the United States on Vietnam should have put to rest once and for all the myth of the United States as a nation committed to upholding freedom and democracy throughout the world. Like the colonial powers that preceded it, the U.S. government used this sugary rhetoric to obscure a brutal reality of violent conquest. The United States dropped three times as many bombs on Vietnam than dropped by all the armies of the Second World War. More than three million Vietnamese were killed, and at least as many were wounded, along with 58,000 U.S. soldiers.[1] According to Marilyn Young:

> 9,000 out of 15,000 hamlets, 25 million acres of farmland, 12 million acres of forest were destroyed, and 1.5 million farm animals had been killed; there were an estimated 200,000 prostitutes, 879,000 orphans, 181,000 disabled people, and one million widows; all six of the industrial cities in the North had been badly damaged, as were provincial district towns, and 4,000 out of 5,800 agricultural communes. North and South the land was cratered and planted with tons of unexploded ordnance, so that long after the war farmers and their families suffered serious injury as they attempted to bring the fields back into cultivation. Nineteen million gallons of herbicide had been sprayed on the South during the war, and while the longer-term effects were unknown in 1975... severe birth defects and multiple miscarriages were apparent early on.[2]

When the United States invaded South Vietnam, it was seen as a virtually invincible power that could impose its will on most of the world through direct military intervention or through the use of its vast economic leverage. Its humiliating retreat from Vietnam demonstrated that even as mighty a power as the United States could be defeated. The Vietnamese forces won independence not because they defeated the United States militarily, but because they were able to drain the will of the United States to continue fighting. Though the United States won every major military engagement in Vietnam, it was forced to retreat because the political cost of victory became too high, as millions of Americans (workers, citizens, and soldiers alike) turned against the war. The United States was defeated in Vietnam because it lost the war in the Mekong Delta *and* at home. This defeat, in turn, created the "Vietnam Syndrome"—a reticence on the part of the United States to engage in direct military intervention around the world. The United States spent years attempting to erase the Vietnam Syndrome. Rumsfeld's fumbling comments, and the statements of Bush and other politicians, indicate that the ghosts of Vietnam have not been buried after all.

In the first days of the 2003 invasion of Iraq, the Vietnamese government issued this statement, "With a huge war machine, the United States will gain victory in military terms. However, they cannot avoid political failure."[3] The Vietnamese know from firsthand experience the truth of this statement—the course of the Iraq occupation has so far confirmed every word of it.

Often, the student movement alone is given credit for ending the war. It is true that the student movement played an important role in radicalizing millions against the war and the American trade-union leadership, led by George Meany, supported the war. But working-class Americans from the very beginning of the war were extremely uneasy about the war, and later polls showed that workers opposed the war in larger numbers than any other group. Moreover, when working-class opposition to the war found another expression—through the GI rebellion—the U.S. ruling class was forced to withdraw its ground forces and bring the war to an end.

In the end, it was these three elements that combined to defeat the United States in Vietnam: a strong national resistance movement in Vietnam; the development of a mass antiwar movement at home; and the almost complete breakdown of the fighting capacity of the American soldier as a result of the experience of combat combined with GI rebellion.

• • •

The war in Iraq now approaches its fifth anniversary and we face a historically unprecedented situation. A majority of Americans believe that the war was a mistake and want the United States to withdraw. Yet at the same time the antiwar movement in the United States remains small compared to the Vietnam antiwar movement, especially when we consider that the movement began on February 15, 2003, with the protest of millions around the world against the pending invasion. The U.S. military is stretched, demoralized, and bogged down, with no end to the fighting in sight. It faces an Iraqi opposition that, though it is responsible for frustrating U.S. war plans in Iraq, has yet been unable to form the type of united national military and political organization that the United States confronted in Vietnam.

The administration of President George W. Bush is losing a war in the Euphrates Valley and the Katrina-ravaged Gulf Coast without yet facing anything like the militant movements of the 1960s that Lyndon Johnson and Richard Nixon faced. How do we explain this? In many ways, it tells us about the continued impact of the war in Vietnam on American society. The widespread distrust of political leaders, the belief that corruption pervades the top levels of government, that the poor are sacrificed for the benefit of the rich, and that foreign wars are fought in the interest of a tiny fraction of the population, are legacies of the Vietnam era, whether one is conscious of that or not.

In May 1967, assistant secretary of defense John McNaughton wrote a memo to his boss Robert McNamara, which, in part, said, "A feeling is widely held that 'the Establishment' is out of its mind. The feeling is that we are trying to impose some U.S. image on a distant people we cannot understand (anymore than we can the younger generation here at home), and that we are carrying the thing to absurd lengths. Related to this feeling is the increased polarization that is taking place in the United States with the seeds of the worst split in our people in more than a century."[4]

Similar feelings exist among broad swaths of the American population today, particularly, the sense that the president and vice president are out of their minds. Yet, the war continues, and a consensus exists among the top leaders of the Republican and Democratic parties that the United States must remain in Iraq until the "job" is done. The job in this case is a Middle East (with its vast oil resources) dominated by the United States.

It is with this in mind that the three most important lessons of the Vietnam war must be remembered. The first lesson is that U.S. imperialism can be defeated. In 1965, when the United States invaded South Vietnam, it was seen as a virtually invincible power that could impose its will on most of world through direct military intervention or by using its vast economic might. The Tet Offensive of 1968 and the humiliating retreat from Vietnam demonstrate that even as mighty a power as the United States can be defeated.

But while the U.S. military may be in a very battered state today compared to its image on the eve of the invasion of Iraq in March 2003, it is still far from defeated. The war in Vietnam teaches us that the United States must be put under tremendous pressure to turn away from its vital interests. There was a decade between the full-scale entry of U.S. troops into Vietnam and the fall of Saigon in April 1975. Iraq is far more strategically important to the United States than Vietnam because it sits in the region of the world's most important oil reserves. Moreover, as already mentioned, the resistance in Iraq is far less united than was the NLF in Vietnam, and the anti-war movement is not only weaker in the streets, but it has yet to penetrate into the military institutions, as it did with devastating effect on morale and the ability of American soldiers to continue fighting in Vietnam. The GI movement today, centered almost exclusively on Iraq vets, is still in its infancy.

Another lesson of the war in Vietnam is that millions of Americans who had previously supported or been paralyzed by anticommunism and who had supported U.S. intervention around the world could be radicalized against these very same policies. In fact, some of the most militant antiwar veterans and GI activists had joined the military with strong anticommunist beliefs, only to have them collapse after their experience in Vietnam.[5] Bush and others have attempted to fill the void left by the collapse of anticommunism with the "war on terror" to support its policies in Iraq and Afghanistan. Many GI activists and Iraq veterans are some of the most articulate spokespersons in exposing the Bush administration's phony "war on terror," while graphically describing the terror that the United States has inflicted on the people of Iraq. The final lesson is the importance of having a vibrant, militant antiwar movement at home. It transformed politics during the war in Vietnam and provided both the inspiration in other countries to fight American imperialism and opposition within the U.S. military itself.

Now the big question: "Is Iraq the next Vietnam?" The answer is that it could be. That will be determined by two forces: the Iraqi people and the American working class. Can the Iraqi people build a movement that can defeat the American military machine? Will American workers bear the cost of the war in Iraq with their lives and a declining standard of living at home? These questions can only be resolved through mass struggle in Iraq and in the United States. The greatest lesson from the war in Vietnam is that this *can* happen, but only through the determined struggle of millions of people to stop American imperialism.

NOTES

INTRODUCTION: THE GHOSTS OF VIETNAM

1. Quoted in Eric Schmitt, "After the War: Detainees; U.S. Releases 5 Syrians Hurt in Convoy Attack," *New York Times*, July 1, 2003.
2. Quoted in Christian Appy, *Working-Class War: American Combat Soldiers in Vietnam* (Chapel Hill, NC: University of North Carolina Press, 1993), 146.
3. Some of the films that didn't illuminate the war: *The Green Berets* (1968), *The Deer Hunter* (1978), *First Blood* (the first in the "Rambo" series) (1982). Some of the better films on the war: *Apocalypse Now Redux* (2001), *Casualties of War* (1989), *Coming Home* (1978), *Born on the Fourth of July* (1989).

CHAPTER ONE: FROM THE FRENCH CONQUEST TO THE OVERTHROW OF DIEM

1. While this chapter concentrates on U.S. involvement in Vietnam, it should be kept in mind that the United States carried out equally if not more devastating policies in Laos and Cambodia. For readings on the U.S. role in those countries, see Alfred McCoy, *Laos: War and Revolution* (New York: Harper and Row, 1970); William Shawcross, *Sideshow: Kissinger, Nixon and the Destruction of Cambodia* (New York: Simon & Schuster, 1979); and Noam Chomsky and Edward S. Herman, *The Political Economy of Human Rights,* two volumes (Boston, MA: South End Press, 1979).
2. Ngo Vinh Long, "Vietnam's Revolutionary Tradition in Vietnam and America," in Marvin Gettleman et al., eds., *Vietnam and America: A Documented History* (New York: Grove Press, 1995), 5–8.
3. James William Gibson, *The Perfect War: Technowar in Vietnam* (Boston, MA: Atlantic Monthly Press, 1986), 33.

4.   Quoted in Stanley Karnow, *Vietnam: A History* (New York: Viking Press, 1983), 116.

5.   Ngo, "Vietnam's Revolutionary Tradition," 9.

6.   Karnow, *Vietnam: A History*, 118.

7.   Ibid.

8.   Ngo, "Vietnam's Revolutionary Tradition," 11.

9.   Quoted in Karnow, *Vietnam: A History*, 79.

10.   Ibid., 115.

11.   Ibid., 115.

12.   Gibson, *Perfect War*, 33.

13.   Ibid., 37–38. For a complete account of the nationalist response to French colonialism see David Marr, *Vietnamese Anticolonialism 1885–1925* (Berkeley and Los Angeles: University of California Press, 1971) and *Vietnamese Tradition on Trial, 1920–1945* (Berkeley and Los Angeles: University of California Press, 1981).

14.   Marr, *Vietnamese Tradition on Trial*, 2.

15.   Gibson, *Perfect War*, 39–40.

16.   Ho Chi Minh, "The Path Which Led Me to Leninism" in Gettleman et al., eds. *Vietnam and America*, 22. For a complete account of Ho Chi Minh's life, see William Duiker's, *Ho Chi Minh: A Life* (New York: Hyperion, 2000).

17.   V. I. Lenin, "Preliminary Draft Thesis on the National and Colonial Questions," *Collected Works*, vol. 31, (Moscow: Progress Publishers, 1966), 144–51.

18.   For an excellent overview of these events, see Nigel Harris, *The Mandate of Heaven: Marx, Mao and Modern China* (London: Quartet, 1978), 1–15; the entire text can also be found online at http://www.marxists.de/china/harris/index.htm.

19.   To understand the deterioration of the Communist International during this period, see Duncan Hallas, *Trotsky's Marxism* (London: Pluto Press, 1979) and *The Comintern* (London: Bookmarks, 1985).

20.   According to military historian Cecil Currey, they adopted the name Indochinese Communist Party "on instructions from the Comintern in Moscow because Soviet leaders believed Vietnamese revolutionaries were too weak to defeat the French colonial regime on their own. They should join with Communists in Laos and Cambodia to form a joint party representing all Indochina." Cecil Currey, *Victory at Any Cost: The Genius of Viet Nam's General Vo Nguyen Giap* (Washington and London: Brassey's, 1997), 37.

21.   Gibson, *Perfect War*, 41–43; Ngo, "Vietnam's Revolutionary Tradition," 12–15. See also Gabriel Kolko, *Anatomy of a War* (New York: New Press, 1985), 28–31.

22.   For a more in-depth discussion of the clash between U.S. and Japanese imperialism, see Walter LaFeber, *The Clash: U.S.-Japanese Relations Throughout History* (New York: W.W. Norton, 1997). To understand the divisions between and goals of the British and Americans during the war in the Pacific,

see Christopher Thorne, *Allies of a Kind: The United States, Britain and the War against Japan, 1941–1945* (New York: Oxford University Press, 1978).

23. Quoted in Gibson, *Perfect War*, 42.

24. To understand the wartime policies of Stalin's Russia and the Comintern, see Hallas, *The Comintern*, 155–159.

25. Marilyn Young, *The Vietnam Wars* (New York: Harper Perennial, 1991), 9. For a complete account of the OSS's relationship with the Vietminh, see Archimedes Patti, *Why Vietnam?: Prelude to America's Albatross* (Berkeley and Los Angeles: University of California Press, 1980).

26. Quoted in Ngo, "Vietnam's Revolutionary Tradition," 17. For the complete text of Bao Dai's abdication speech, see Gettleman et al., eds., *Vietnam and America*, 24–25.

27. Ho Chi Minh, "Vietnam Declaration of Independence," in Gettleman et al., eds., *Vietnam and America*, 26–28.

28. For a complete overview of that momentous year in Vietnam's history, see David Marr, *Vietnam 1945: The Quest for Power* (Berkeley and Los Angeles: University of California Press, 1995).

29. Quoted in Karnow, *Vietnam: A History*, 139.

30. Quoted in George McTurnan Kahin, *Intervention: How America Became Involved in Vietnam* (Garden City, NY: Anchor Press, 1987), 15–19.

31. Ibid., 6.

32. For further reading on the Vietnamese Trotskyists, see "Vietnamese Trotskyism," in *International Trotskyism 1929–1985*, ed. Robert J. Alexander (Durham, NC: Duke University Press, 1991). Also see Milton Sacks, "Marxism in Vietnam," in *Marxism in Southeast Asia: A Study of Four Countries*, ed. Frank N. Trager (Stanford, CA: Stanford University Press, 1959).

33. Quoted in Karnow, *Vietnam: A History*, 153. It should also be noted that Ho's success in selling this strategy to his supporters was based on a real fear of Chinese domination. China occupied Vietnam for one thousand years and Vietnamese nationalism has its origins in resisting this domination.

34. Kahin, *Intervention: How America*, 37.

35. Ibid., 42.

36. Ibid., 44.

37. Quoted in Howard Zinn, *A People's History of the United States, 1492–Present* (New York: Harper Perennial, 1995), 461.

38. Kahin, *Intervention: How America*, 39.

39. Ibid., 40.

40. Karnow, *Vietnam: A History*, 199.

41. Quoted in Kahin, *Intervention: How America*, 48.

42. Kahin, *Intervention: How America*, 52–65.

43. Karnow, *Vietnam: A History*, 217.

44. Quoted in Gibson, *Perfect War*, 172.

45. Gibson, *Perfect War*, 72.

46. Kahin, *Intervention: How America*, 96.

47. Young, *Vietnam Wars*, 4–46.

48. Kahin, *Intervention: How America*, 97–98.

49. Young, *Vietnam Wars*, 82.

50. Ibid., 82–83.

51. Young, *Vietnam Wars*, 60–88; Kahin, *Intervention: How America*, 122–181.

CHAPTER TWO: FROM THE OVERTHROW OF DIEM TO THE TET OFFENSIVE

1. Young, *Vietnam Wars*, 104.

2. It is a popular myth that John F. Kennedy would not have escalated U.S. military involvement in Vietnam had he lived, an argument put forth most notably in Oliver Stone's film *JFK*. A superficial knowledge of Kennedy's policies would show that this is wishful thinking without any sound basis in fact. The Kennedy administration committed itself to escalating funding and military training to maintain the puppet regime's army in South Vietnam, and committed an increasing number of U.S. military advisers, military technicians, as well as U.S-piloted planes and helicopters and maintenance personnel. Under Kennedy, the number of U.S. military advisers in Vietnam grew from 800 to more than 16,000. There is no reason to believe that, had he lived, Kennedy would not have continued these efforts and felt the same pressures as Johnson to resort to full-scale invasion to prop up a client state it had done so much to create and bolster over the previous years. Indeed, the same people who ran the war under Kennedy became Johnson's foreign policy advisers.

3. Kahin, *Intervention: How America*, 182–200.

4. Ibid., 203–35.

5. Young, *Vietnam Wars*, 138.

6. Quoted in Kolko, *Anatomy of War*, 133.

7. Gibson, *Perfect War*, 88.

8. Michael Bilton and Kevin Sim, *Four Hours in My Lai* (New York: Penguin Books, 1992), 29.

9. Quoted in Peter Davis, *Hearts and Minds* (Janus Films, 1974). *Hearts and Minds* won the Academy Award for Best Documentary in 1975.

10. Quoted in Karnow, *Vietnam: A History*, 395.

11. Ibid., 326.

12. See Irving Bernstein, *Guns or Butter: The Presidency of Lyndon Johnson* (New York: Oxford University Press, 1996) for an overview of the 1964 election and Great Society programs of the Johnson administration.

13. Gibson, *Perfect War*, 89.

14. Incidents real, imagined, or manufactured have played a major role in shifting American public opinion behind various administrations' war drives. Among the most famous were the sinking of the USS *Maine* in 1898, the sinking of the *Lusitania* in 1915, the bombing of Pearl Harbor in 1941, and the September 11, 2001, attacks on the Pentagon and the World Trade Center.

15. Gibson, *Perfect War*, 89.

16. Quoted in Daniel Ellsberg, *Secrets: A Memoir of Vietnam and the Pentagon Papers* (New York: Viking Press, 2002), 10.

17. Quoted in Bob Richter, "Tonkin Incident Might Not Have Occurred," *San Antonio Express News*, August 3, 2002.

18. Gibson, *Perfect War*, 89.

19. For the complete text of the Gulf of Tonkin Resolution, see Gettleman et al., eds., *Vietnam and America*, 252.

20. Quoted in Michael Sherry, *In the Shadow of War: The United States Since the 1930s* (New Haven, CT: Yale University Press, 1995), 252.

21. For an overview of the superpower rivalry between the United States and the former USSR and its effect on emerging Third World countries, see Walter LaFeber, *America, Russia and the Cold War 1945–1990* (New York: McGraw-Hill, 1991).

22. Quoted in Karnow, *Vietnam: A History*, 249.

23. Ibid., 248.

24. Sherry, *Shadow of War*, 250.

25. Quoted in Young, *Vietnam Wars*, 135.

26. Quoted in Kolko, *Anatomy of War*, 113.

27. Quoted in Sherry, *Shadow of War*, 251.

28. Sherry, *Shadow of War*, 252.

29. Quoted in Davis, *Hearts and Minds*.

30. Bilton and Sim, *Four Hours in My Lai*, 32.

31. Kolko, *Anatomy of War*, 180.

32. Young, *Vietnam Wars*, 161.

33. Quoted in Kolko, *Anatomy of War*, 178.

34. Kolko, *Anatomy of War*, 180.

35. Quoted in Don Oberdorfer, *Tet!* (New York: Avon Books, 1971), 123.

36. Oberdorfer, *Tet!*, 117–18.

37. Quoted in Oberdorfer, *Tet!*, 123.

38. Quoted in Jonathan Neale, *The American War: Vietnam 1960–1975* (London: Bookmarks, 2001), 92.

39. Noam Chomsky, *The Washington Connection and Third World Fascism* (Boston, MA: South End Press, 1979), 304.

40. Michael Sherry, *The Rise of American Air Power: The Race for Armageddon* (New Haven, CT: Yale University Press, 1987).

41. Chomsky, *Washington Connection*, 312.

42. Quoted in Davis, *Hearts and Minds*. After making the remark, according to

Davis, Westmoreland asked for another take to rephrase what he had said. On the second take, Davis ran out of film. On the third take, which is the one Davis used, Westmoreland made essentially the same remark. See Derrick Z. Jackson, "The Westmoreland Mindset," *Boston Globe*, July 20, 2005.

43. Seymour Hersh, *My Lai 4: A Report on the Massacre and its Aftermath* (New York: Vintage Books, 1970), 9.

44. Quoted in Appy, *Working-Class War*, 107.

45. Appy, *Working-Class War*, 153.

46. Ibid., 156.

47. Ibid., 166.

48. Quoted in Bilton and Sim, *Four Hours in My Lai*, 336.

49. Quoted in Winter Soldier Investigation, testimony given in Detroit, Michigan, on January 31, 1971, February 1–2, 1971. Testimony of the 1st Air Cavalry Division, part II. The full text of the investigation is available at http://lists.village.virginia.edu/sixties/HTML_docs/Resources/Primary/_Winter_Soldier/WS_entry.html.

50. Young, *Vietnam Wars*, 173–74.

51. Chomsky, *Washington Connection*, 314.

52. Quoted in Davis, *Hearts and Minds*.

53. Ibid.

54. Young, *Vietnam Wars*, 71.

55. Quoted in ibid.

56. Truong Nhu Tang, *A Viet Cong Memoir* (New York: Vintage Books, 1986), 68.

57. Young, *Vietnam Wars*, 184.

58. Quoted in Neale, *American War*, 34.

59. Quoted in Young, *Vietnam Wars*, 73.

60. Young, *Vietnam Wars*, 73.

61. Quoted in ibid.

62. Quoted in Kolko, *Anatomy of War*, 178.

63. Jonathan Schell, "The Military Half: An Account of the Destruction of Quang Ngai and Quang Tin," in *The Real War* (New York: Da Capo Press, 1988).

64. Quoted in Don Luce and John Sommer, *Vietnam: The Unheard Voices* (Ithaca and London: Cornell University Press, 1969), 267.

65. Quoted in Karnow, *Vietnam: A History*, 514.

66. Quoted in David Hunt, "Remembering the Tet Offensive," in Gettleman et. al., eds., *Vietnam and America*, 364.

67. Quoted in Karnow, *Vietnam: A History*, 541.

68. Quoted in Hunt, "Remembering the Tet Offensive," 365.

69. Oberdorfer, *Tet!*, 137.

70. Ibid., 138.

71. Hunt, "Remembering the Tet Offensive," 366.

72. Karnow, *Vietnam: A History*, 525.

73. Oberdorfer, *Tet!*, 51.
74. Quoted in Young, *Vietnam Wars*, 219.
75. Quoted in Hunt, "Remembering the Tet Offensive," 368.
76. Quoted in Young, *Vietnam Wars*, 217.
77. Ibid., 219.
78. Hunt, "Remembering the Tet Offensive," 368.
79. Quoted in ibid., 371.
80. Young, *Vietnam Wars*, 223.
81. Karnow, *Vietnam: A History*, 546.
82. Walter Isaacson and Evan Thomas, *The Wise Men* (New York: Touchstone, 1986), 676–713.
83. Walter Cronkite, *A Reporter's Life* (New York: Alfred A. Knopf, 1996), 257–58.
84. For the full text of Johnson's speech, see "Peace in Vietnam and Southeast Asia," in Gettleman et al., eds., *Vietnam and America*, 401.

CHAPTER THREE: COLD WAR LIBERALISM
AND THE ROOTS OF THE ANTIWAR MOVEMENT

1. H. Bruce Franklin, "The Antiwar Movement We Are Supposed to Forget," in *Vietnam and Other American Fantasies* (Amherst, MA: University of Massachusetts Press, 2000), 49.
2. Ibid., 50.
3. Ibid. For a complete discussion of the opposition of American merchant marines to the transporting of French troops to recolonize Vietnam after the Second World War, see Michael Gillen, *Roots of Opposition: The Critical Response to U.S. Indochina Policy, 1945–1954*, (New York University Dissertation, 1991).
4. Gillen, *Roots of Opposition*, 122.
5. Franklin, "Antiwar Movement We," 50.
6. Ibid.
7. Quoted in ibid., 51.
8. Ibid.
9. Ibid.
10. Quoted in Eric Foner and John A. Garraty, eds., *The Reader's Companion to American History* (Boston, MA: Houghton Mifflin, 1991), 1,087.
11. Quoted in David Ransom, "Ford Country: Building an Elite for Indonesia," http://www.cia-on-campus.org/internat/indo.html.
12. Robert Scheer, *How the United States Got Involved in Vietnam* (Santa Barbara, CA: Center for the Study of Democratic Institutions, 1965), 32.
13. John Cooney, *The American Pope: The Life and Times of Francis Cardinal Spellman* (New York: Times Books, 1984).
14. "State Department Socialist" is a disparaging term describing a self-pro-

claimed socialist who supported U.S. imperialist foreign policy during the Cold War era.

15. Franklin, "Antiwar Movement We," 53.

16. Quoted in Walter Goodman, *The Committee: The Extraordinary Career of the House Committee on Un-American Activities* (Baltimore, MD: Penguin Books, 1968), 416.

17. Shirley A. Weigand and Wayne A. Weigand, *Books on Trial: Red Scare in the Heartland*, (Norman, OK: Oklahoma University Press, 2007), 60.

18. For a complete account of the SWP's 1941 Smith Act trial, see James Cannon, *Socialism on Trial* (New York: Pathfinder, 1970).

19. There are many histories of the postwar Red Scare. One of the most easily accessible is David Caute, *The Great Fear: The Anti-Communist Purge Under Truman and Eisenhower* (New York: Simon & Schuster, 1978).

20. This period culminated in the executions of Julius and Ethel Rosenberg, former members of the Communist Party and trade union activists, falsely accused and convicted being of "atomic spies" in 1953.

21. Goodman, *Committee: Extraordinary Career*, 399.

22. Ibid., 419.

23. Quoted in ibid., 423.

24. Ibid.

25. Clayborne Carson, *In Struggle: SNCC and the Black Awakening of the 1960s* (Cambridge, MA: Harvard University Press, 1981), 11. Though they didn't capture the national imagination in the same way, there had already been sit-ins in Wichita, Kansas, and Oklahoma City in 1958. The first sit-ins to protest segregation were organized by NAACP youth in the summer of 1958 at a Dockum Drug Store in downtown Wichita. Weeks later, inspired by the Wichita events, Black youth in Oklahoma City staged a sit-in at Katz Drug Store. See Gretchen Cassell Eick, *Dissent in Wichita: The Civil Rights Movement in the Midwest, 1954–72* (Champaign, IL: University of Illinois Press, 2007).

26. Seth Cagin and Philip Dray, *We Are Not Afraid* (New York: Macmillan, 1988), 97.

27. Ibid.

28. Interview with former YPSL chair Joel Geier, August 12, 2007.

29. Goodman, *Committee: Extraordinary Career*, 430.

30. Quoted in ibid., 98.

31. Cagin and Dray, *We Are Not Afraid*, 99.

32. Ibid.

33. Nancy Zaroulis and Gerald Sullivan, *Who Spoke Up?: American Protest Against the War in Vietnam 1963–1975* (Garden City, NY: Doubleday, 1984), 25.

34. Fred Halstead, *Out Now! A Participant's Account of the Movement in the U.S. Against the Vietnam War* (New York: Pathfinder Press, 1991), 29.

35. See Robert Caro's multivolume biography of Lyndon Johnson, *The Years of Lyndon Johnson: The Path to Power* (New York: Alfred A. Knopf, 1982).

36. Caro, *Years of Lyndon,* xx.

37. "Dixiecrats" was the label applied to Democrats primarily from the former states of the Confederacy whose best-known political positions consisted of white supremacy and opposition to trade unions and liberalism. After the mid-1960s many of them began to defect to the Republican Party.

38. Quoted in Robert Dallek, *Lyndon B. Johnson: Portrait of a President* (New York: Oxford University Press, 2004), 170.

39. Bernstein, *Guns or Butter,* 317.

40. David Halberstam, *The Best and the Brightest* (Greenwich, CT: Fawcett Crest Books, 1972), 720.

41. For a complete explanation of the Selective Service system and how it benefited the middle class, see Lawrence M. Baskir and William A. Strauss, *Change and Circumstance: The Draft, the War and the Vietnam Generation* (New York: Vintage Books, 1978).

42. Halberstam, *Best and Brightest,* 720.

43. Every major war fought by the United States prior to Vietnam had included a strategy for the home front—concessions to the population to gain support for the war effort. In the First and Second World Wars this meant, among other things, expanding trade-union rights and membership.

44. Quoted in Bernstein, *Guns or Butter,* 526.

45. Ibid., 359.

46. Ibid., 346.

47. Ibid., 346.

48. Bernstein, *Guns or Butter,* 348.

49. Quoted in Halberstam, *Best and Brightest,* 694.

50. Bernstein, *Guns or Butter,* 369.

51. Jimmy Breslin and Barry Farrell, "Strike Fever and the Public," *Life,* August 22, 1966.

52. Quoted in Kim Moody, *An Injury to All: The Decline of American Unionism* (London: Verso, 1988), 86.

53. Bernstein, *Guns or Butter,* 410.

54. Quoted in Zaroulis and Sullivan, *Who Spoke Up?,* 85.

55. *Ramparts* was founded as a liberal Catholic magazine by San Francisco lawyer Edward Keating in the early 1960s. It evolved very quickly into a popular radical magazine of the New Left, which published the early writings of such people as Eldridge Cleaver and exposés of university complicity with the war in Vietnam and the role of the CIA in student politics.

56. Americans for Democratic Action was created in the late 1940s to rally liberal and trade-union support for the Cold War, specifically for the Marshall Plan. Its other goal was to isolate the 1948 Progressive Party presidential campaign of former vice president Henry Wallace, who was campaigning

against Truman's Cold War policies.

57. Halstead, *Out Now!*, 243–44.

58. Tom Wells, *The War Within: America's Battle Over Vietnam* (Berkeley and Los Angeles: University of California Press, 1994), 112.

CHAPTER FOUR: BLACK AMERICA AND VIETNAM

1. Many of the standard histories of the war in Vietnam either completely ignore or underplay the importance of this.

2. For an overview of this subject, see Brenda Gayle Plummer, *Rising Wind: Black Americans and U.S. Foreign Affairs, 1935–1960* (Chapel Hill, NC: University of North Carolina Press, 1996).

3. Mike Marqusee, *Redemption Song: Muhammad Ali and the Spirit of the Sixties* (London: Verso, 1999), 167.

4. Michael Honey, *Southern Labor and Black Civil Rights: Organizing Memphis Workers* (Chicago, IL: University of Illinois Press, 1993), 204.

5. Ibid.

6. Taylor Branch, *Parting the Waters: America in the King Years 1954–1963* (New York: Simon & Schuster, 1988), 171.

7. Quoted in Malcolm X and Alex Haley, *The Autobiography of Malcolm X: As Told to Alex Haley* (New York: Grove Press, 1964), 106.

8. Willie Dixon with Don Snowden, *"I Am the Blues": The Willie Dixon Story* (Cambridge, MA: Da Capo Press, 1989), 54.

9. Thirty-five southern delegates walked out of the 1948 Democratic convention to form the States' Rights Party. Thurmond eventually got one million votes in the election, winning four states: Alabama, Louisiana, Mississippi, and South Carolina, gaining a total of 39 electoral college votes.

10. Martin Duberman, *Paul Robeson: A Biography* (New York: New Press, 1989), 325.

11. Quoted in Philip A. Klinker and Roger M. Smith, eds., *The Unsteady March: The Rise and Decline of Racial Equality in America* (Chicago, IL: University of Chicago Press, 1999), 209.

12. Manning Marable, *Race, Reform and Rebellion: The Second Reconstruction in Black America, 1945–1990* (Jackson, MS: University of Mississippi Press, 1991), 32.

13. John D'Emilio, *Lost Prophet: The Life and Times of Bayard Rustin* (New York: Free Press, 2003), 52.

14. Ibid.

15. Marable, *Race, Reform and Rebellion*, 50. See also Hazel Rowley's *Richard Wright: The Life and Times* (New York: Henry Holt, 2001).

16. Marable, *Race, Reform and Rebellion*, 50.

17. Patrice Lumumba was the radical leader of the movement for Congolese independence from Belgium. He was elected leader of the newly independent country in 1960 and toppled in a U.S.-backed coup soon after. He was assassinated in January 1961 at the behest of the CIA. Castro was the subject of a series of CIA assassination attempts. The most famous of failed U.S. efforts to topple Fidel Castro was the Bay of Pigs invasion in April 1961.

18. Ahmed Shawki, *Black Liberation and Socialism* (Chicago, IL: Haymarket Books, 2006), 187.

19. For a useful discussion of the civil rights movement's relationship to the Democratic Party, see Ahmed Shawki's *Black Liberation and Socialism*.

20. August Meier and Elliot Rudwick, *CORE: A Study in the Civil Rights Movement, 1942–1968* (New York: Oxford University Press, 1973), 375.

21. Ibid.

22. Ibid.

23. Jack M. Bloom, *Class, Race, and the Civil Rights Movement* (Bloomington, IN: Indiana University Press, 1987), 200.

24. Shawki, *Black Liberation*, 206.

25. If Malcolm's comments on Vietnam are sparse, it was due to the fact he was assassinated in February 1965 when the systematic bombing of North Vietnam began and before the large-scale landing of U.S. troops.

26. Malcolm X speech transcribed by *Democracy Now!*, in "Manning Marable on 'Malcolm X: A Life of Reinvention,'" May 21, 2007, http://www.democracynow.org/article.pl?sid=07/05/21/1416224. The Isaac Woodard referred to by Malcolm X was a sergeant in the U.S. Army during the Second World War. On his way home to South Carolina after his discharge from service in 1946 he had his eyes punched and gouged out by the fists and nightsticks of police who had been called by the bus driver after Woodard had made a request that the driver make an unauthorized stop so that he, Woodard, could use a restroom. The case was widely publicized at the time by the NAACP and on Orson Welles' radio show.

27. Quoted in George Breitman, *The Last Year of Malcolm X: The Evolution of a Revolutionary* (New York: Schocken Books, 1967), 10–11.

28. Shawki, *Black Liberation and Socialism*, 176.

29. Malcolm X, "Two Minutes on Vietnam," in *Vietnam and Black America: An Anthology of Protest and Resistance,* Clyde Taylor, ed., (Garden City, NY: Anchor Press Doubleday, 1973), 60.

30. Malcolm X, *February 1965: The Final Speeches* (New York: Pathfinder, 1992), 42.

31. Ibid., 32.

32. Malcolm X, "Two Minutes," 59.

33. *Malcolm X Speaks: Selected Speeches and Statements*, ed. George Breitman (New York: Pathfinder, 1993), 148.

34. Malcolm X, *February 1965: Final Speeches*, 69.

35. Marable, *Race, Reform and Rebellion,* 100. For more figures on casualty rates, see Appy, *Working-Class War*, 19.

36. Gettleman, *Vietnam and America*, 299.

37. Quoted in Gettleman, *Vietnam and America*, 299. The United States invaded the Dominican Republic in the spring of 1965.

38. Clayborne Carson, *In Struggle*, 183.

39. Ibid., 188.

40. Quoted in Taylor, ed., *Vietnam and Black America*, 258–9.

41. Christian Appy, *Patriots: The War Remembered from All Sides* (New York: Viking Press, 2003), 144.

42. Ibid.

43. Quoted in ibid.

44. See Carson, *In Struggle*, 251 and James Westheider, *Fighting on Two Fronts: African Americans and the Vietnam War* (New York: New York University Press, 1997), 27.

45. Westheider, *Fighting on Two Fronts*, 28.

46. David Zirin, "Muhammad Ali and the Revolt of the Black Athlete," *International Socialist Review* 33 (January–February 2004): 61.

47. Marqusee, *Redemption Song*, 167.

48. Westheider, *Fighting on Two Fronts*, 27.

49. Quoted in Marqusee, *Redemption Song,* 162.

50. Marqusee, *Redemption Song,* 163

51. Quoted in Marqusee, *Redemption Song*, 213.

52. Stan Goff, Robert Sanders, and Clark Smith, *Brothers: Black Soldiers in the Nam* (New York: Berkeley Books, 1982), i.

53. Quoted in Appy, *Patriots*, 145.

54. Like many revolutionary organizations from the period, the Panthers' socialism came more from Mao than from Marx.

55. Quoted in Philip S. Foner, ed., *The Black Panthers Speak* (Philadelphia: J.B. Lippincott, 1970), 1–4.

56. Quoted in Taylor, ed., *Vietnam and Black America*, 291.

57. Ibid., 290.

58. Quoted in Marqusee, *Redemption Song*, 193.

59. Quoted in Ward Churchill and Jim Vander Wall, *Agents of Repression: The FBI's Secret Wars Against the Black Panther Party and the American Indian Movement* (Boston, MA: South End Press, 1988), 63.

60. Quoted in Marqusee, *Redemption Song,* 183.

61. Peniel E. Joseph, *Waiting 'Til the Midnight Hour: A Narrative History of Black Power in America* (New York: Owl Books and Henry Holt, 2006), 123.

62. Quoted in Marqusee, *Redemption Song*, 181.

63. All quotes from King's speech are from Taylor, ed., *Vietnam and Black*

America, 310–18.

64. Quoted in Marqusee, *Redemption Song*, 191.

65. Quoted in Shawki, *Black Liberation*, 203–204.

66. Commander George L. Jackson, "Constraints of the Negro Civil Rights Movement on the American Military Effectiveness," Gettleman et. al., eds., *Vietnam and America*, 321–326.

CHAPTER FIVE: FROM THE BIRTH OF THE ANTIWAR MOVEMENT TO 1968

This chapter was written with the assistance of Paul D'Amato.

1. Zinn, *People's History*, 501.

2. Halstead, *Out Now!*, 19.

3. Zaroulis and Sullivan, *Who Spoke Up?*, 10.

4. Ibid., 9.

5. Maurice Isserman, *If I Had a Hammer: The Death of the Old Left and the Birth of the New Left* (Chicago, IL: University of Illinois Press, 1987), 195.

6. Halstead, *Out Now!*, 33.

7. See Halstead, *Out Now!*, 34, for a description of these events.

8. "The Buddhist Crisis of 1963: The View from Washington," in Gettleman, et al., eds., *Vietnam and America*, 217.

9. For a complete account of the Buddhist crisis and the overthrow of the Diem government see Ellen J. Hammer, *A Death in November: America in Vietnam 1963* (New York: E. P. Dutton, 1987).

10. Two years later, three Americans would immolate themselves in protest against the war. The one that received the most attention was Norman Morrison, a Quaker who burned himself to death near the entrance to the Pentagon on November 3, 1965. See Wells, *War Within*, 58.

11. Quoted in Karnow, *Vietnam: A History*, 281.

12. Zaroulis and Sullivan, *Who Spoke Up?*, 15.

13. Halstead, *Out Now!*, 36.

14. Quoted in Zaroulis and Sullivan, *Who Spoke Up?*, 36.

15. Zaroulis and Sullivan, *Who Spoke Up?*, 35–37.

16. Quoted in Wells, *War Within*, 23.

17. Halstead, *Out Now!*, 64; Wells, *War Within*, 24.

18. Norman Mailer, "The Great Society?" in *We Accuse* (Berkeley, CA: Diablo Press, 1965), 22. The book reprints several of the speeches at the Berkeley Vietnam Day event.

19. Isaac Deutscher, "Myths of the Cold War," in *We Accuse*, 52.

20. Quoted in Halstead, *Out Now!*, 66.

21. Quoted in ibid., 67-68.

22. Zaroulis and Sullivan, *Who Spoke Up?*, 38.

23. Geoff Bailey, "The Making of a New Left: The Rise and Fall of SDS," *International Socialist Review* 31 (September–October 2003): 62–72.

24. For a complete history of SDS see Kirkpatrick Sale, *SDS* (New York: Random House, 1973).

25. Membership figures are from Sale, *SDS*, 663.

26. Quoted in Zaroulis and Sullivan, *Who Spoke Up?*, 41.

27. Quoted in Halstead, *Out Now!*, 58–59.

28. Quoted in Zaroulis and Sullivan, *Who Spoke Up?*, 41.

29. Zaroulis and Sullivan, *Who Spoke Up?*, 39.

30. Ibid., 40.

31. Quoted in Jo Freeman, "Student Power: The New Left Is United by a Sense of Outrage," http://www.jofreeman.com/sixtiesprotest/newleft.htm.

32. Quoted in Wells, *War Within*, 38.

33. Ibid., 46.

34. Ibid., 47.

35. Ibid., 61.

36. Ibid.

37. Ibid.

38. Quoted in Halstead, *Out Now!*, 140.

39. Ibid., 53.

40. James Petras, introduction, *We Accuse*, 3.

41. Ibid., 3.

42. Wells, *War Within*, 133.

43. Ibid., 134.

44. Quoted in Wells, *War Within*, 134.

45. Wells, *War Within*, 170.

46. Ibid.,172.

47. Quoted in ibid., 175.

48. Quoted in Halstead, *Out Now!*, 379.

49. Halstead, *Out Now!*, 387.

50. Zaroulis and Sullivan, *Who Spoke Up?*, 138.

51. Halstead, *Out Now!*, 396.

52. Zaroulis and Sullivan, *Who Spoke Up?*, 114.

53. Quoted in Zaroulis and Sullivan, *Who Spoke Up?*, 104.

54. Quoted in Sale, *SDS*, 369.

55. Zaroulis and Sullivan, *Who Spoke Up?*, 106.

56. Quoted in Halstead, *Out Now!*, 403.

57. Zaroulis and Sullivan, *Who Spoke Up?*, 135.

58. Quoted in Halstead, *Out Now!*, 405.

59. Ibid. There was an attempt to repeat the mobile tactics in New York the following month, but the police had learned from the Oakland protest and broke up the protests with mass arrests.

60. Quoted in Sale, *SDS*, 377.

61. Ibid., 664.

62. Quoted in William Pfaff, "History Is Not on Your Side, Mr. Kerry," *Observer* (UK), August 15, 2004.

63. Quoted in Zaroulis and Sullivan, *Who Spoke Up?*, 127.

64. Bernstein, *Guns or Butter*, 484.

65. For an overview of the role of the Democratic Party in modern politics see Lance Selfa, *The Democratic Party and the Politics of Lesser Evilism* (Chicago, IL: International Socialist Organization, 2004), http://www.internationalsocialist.org/resources.html (accessed October 27, 2007).

66. Quoted in Arthur M. Schlesinger, *Robert Kennedy and His Times* (New York: Ballantine Books, 1978), 513.

67. Ibid., 772.

68. See Ronald Steel, *In Love with Night: The American Romance with Robert Kennedy* (New York: Simon & Schuster, 2000).

69. Ibid., 121.

70. Schlesinger, *Robert Kennedy*, 940.

71. Quoted in Schlesinger, *Robert Kennedy*, 798.

72. Schlesinger, *Robert Kennedy*, 797.

73. Todd Gitlin, *The Sixties: Years of Hope, Days of Rage* (New York: Bantam Books, 1987), 323.

74. "Editors' Introduction to Part IV, the Decisive Year: 1968," Gettleman, et al., eds., *Vietnam and America*, 341.

75. Appy, *Working-Class War*, 309–10.

76. Zaroulis and Sullivan, *Who Spoke Up?*, 180.

77. Quoted in Wells, *War Within*, 279.

78. Gitlin, *Sixties: Years of Hope*, 327.

79. Ibid., 326.

80. Red Squads were created as far back as the Haymarket Affair in Chicago in 1886, and became widespread by the 1920s.

81. Zaroulis and Sullivan, *Who Spoke Up?*, 219.

82. Quoted in Zaroulis and Sullivan, *Who Spoke Up?*, 223.

83. Ellen W. Schrecker, "Protectors of Privilege: Red Squads and Police Repression in Urban America," *Monthly Review*, (November 1991).

84. Zaroulis and Sullivan, *Who Spoke Up?*, 202.

85. Ibid.

86. Quoted in Zaroulis and Sullivan, *Who Spoke Up?*, 205.

CHAPTER SIX: THE U.S. WORKING CLASS AND THE WAR

1. Philip Foner, *U.S. Labor and the Vietnam War* (New York: International Publishers, 1989), 105.

2. Barbara Ehrenreich, *Fear of Falling: The Inner Life of the Middle Class* (New York: Harper Perennial, 1989), 98.

3. Peter B. Levy, *The New Left and Labor in the 1960s* (Chicago, IL: University of Illinois Press, 1994), 57–58.

4. Colin Powell with Joseph E. Persico, *My American Journey* (New York: Random House, 1995), 148.

5. Appy, *Working-Class War*, 27.

6. Lawrence Baskir and William Strauss, *Chance and Circumstance: The Draft, the War and the Vietnam Generation* (New York: Vintage Books, 1978), 9.

7. Appy, *Working-Class War*, 37.

8. See Appy, *Working-Class War*, 37, for statistics on National Guard and reserves racial composition.

9. Appy, *Working-Class War*, 35.

10. Baskir and Strauss, *Chance and Circumstance*, 33.

11. Westheider, *Fighting on Two Fronts*, 25.

12. Quoted in Baskir and Strauss, *Chance and Circumstance*, 48–49.

13. Ibid., 123.

14. See Appy, *Working-Class War*, 33.

15. Baskir and Strauss, *Chance and Circumstance*, 123.

16. Appy, *Working-Class War*, 12.

17. John Pilger, *Heroes* (Boston, MA: South End Press, 2001), 108.

18. Quoted in ibid. For 1971 casualty figures, see the Vietnam Veterans Memorial Wall USA website, thewall-usa.com.

19. Vietnam Veterans Memorial Wall USA website; Appy, *Working-Class War*, 15.

20. Baskir and Strauss, *Chance and Circumstance*, 10.

21. Ibid.

22. Quoted in Andrew Levinson, *The Working-Class Majority* (New York: Penguin, 1974), 136.

23. According to the tvland.com website: "It premiered January 12, 1971, to disappointing ratings, but it took home several Emmy Awards that year, including Outstanding Comedy Series. The show did very well in summer reruns, and it flourished in the 1971–1972 season, becoming the top-rated show on TV for the next five years. After falling from the #1 spot, *All in the Family* still remained in the top ten well after it transitioned into *Archie Bunker's Place*. The show was based on the British sitcom *'Til Death Us Do Part*, about an irascible working-class Tory and his Socialist son-in-law."

24. Ehrenreich, *Fear of Falling*, 101.

25. Lipset left the Socialist Party (SP) in 1960 and had previously been chair-

man of the Young Peoples' Socialist League, the youth section of the SP. He ended his days at the conservative Hoover Institute.

26. Seymour Martin Lipset, *Political Man* (Garden City, NY: Doubleday, 1959), 97–130.

27. Ibid., 115.

28. Ehrenreich, *Fear of Falling*, 110.

29. Richard F. Hamilton, *Class and Politics in the United States* (New York: John Wiley & Sons, 1972), 156.

30. Ibid., 457.

31. Quoted in ibid.

32. Karl Marx, *Capital*, vol. 1 (New York: Vintage Books, 1977), 97.

33. See Allan Chase, *The Legacy of Malthus: The Social Costs of the New Scientific Racism* (Urbana, IL: University of Illinois Press, 1980), which documents the history of racism, from the 1880s to WWII, of the academic and scientific establishment toward African Americans and the immigrant working class.

34. Ehrenreich, *Fear of Falling*, 128.

35. Ibid., 101.

36. Foner and Garraty, eds., *Reader's Companion to American History*, 1,127.

37. Quoted in Ehrenreich, *Fear of Falling*, 126.

38. Hamilton, *Class and Politics*, 461.

39. Ibid., 462.

40. Ehrenreich, *Fear of Falling*, 123.

41. Halstead, *Out Now!*, 243–44.

42. Wells, *War Within*, 112.

43. Harlan Hahn, "Correlates of Public Sentiments about War: Local Referenda on the Vietnam Issue," *American Political Science Review* 64 (December 1970): 1,190.

44. Appy, *Working-Class War*, 41.

45. Levy, *New Left and Labor*, 62.

46. Joseph Goulden, *Meany: The Unchallenged Strong Man of American Labor* (New York: Atheneum, 1972), 353.

47. Sharon Smith, *Subterranean Fire: A History of Working-Class Radicalism in the United States* (Chicago, IL: Haymarket Books, 2006), 219.

48. Ibid., 220.

49. Quoted in James R. Green, *The World of the Worker: Labor in Twentieth Century America* (New York: Hill & Wang, 1980), 217.

50. Stan Weir, "USA: The Labor Revolt," *International Socialist Journal* (Rome) 4, no. 20 (April 1967): 279–96.

51. Moody, *Injury to All*, 86.

52. "Strike Fever," *Life*, August 22, 1966.

53. Moody, *Injury to All*, 86.

54. Ibid.

55. Smith, *Subterranean Fire*, 220.

56. See Dan Georgakas and Marvin Surkin, *Detroit: I Do Mind Dying* (Boston, MA: South End Press, 1998).

57. See Leon Fink and Brian Greenberg, *Upheaval in the Quiet Zone: A History of Hospital Workers' Union Local 1199* (Urbana, IL: University of Illinois Press, 1980).

58. Lee Sustar, "Black Militancy in the Unions: The Postal Strike of 1970," (unpublished paper). According to Sustar, "The business press of the day was filled with speculation about the continuing strike wave. See the March 6, 1969, *Wall Street Journal* for the debate on strike legislation; the July, 22, 1969, *Wall Street Journal* on wage settlements and inflation; the January 5, 1970, *Wall Street Journal* for an overview of labor contracts up for negotiation."

59. See James Matles and James Higgins, *Them and Us: The Struggles of a Rank-and-File Union* (Boston, MA: Beacon, 1974), 262–87.

60. Quoted in Foner, *U.S. Labor and Vietnam*, 79.

61. See Levy, *New Left and Labor*, 147–51.

62. Sustar, "Black Militancy in the Unions;" *New York Times*, March 14, 24, and July 20, 1970; the *Militant*, undated paper for the postal strike, probably March 25, 1970. For a left-wing assessment of the pattern of strikes in this period, see Stanley Aronowitz, "General Strike in the Air," *Guardian*, April 4, 1970.

63. Peter Kihss, "Some Will Go Back," *New York Times*, March 23, 1970.

64. Quoted in Stewart Alsop, "Is America a Shay or a Scow?," *Newsweek*, April 6, 1970.

65. "Postal Anarchy," editorial, *New York Times*, March 19, 1970.

66. Homer Bigart, "Military in Post Offices, Begins Handling the Mail," *New York Times*, March 24, 1970.

67. Ehrenreich, *Fear of Falling*, 121.

CHAPTER SEVEN: FROM QUAGMIRE TO DEFEAT

1. Quoted in Jonathan Schell, *The Time of Illusion* (New York: Vintage Books, 1975), 26.

2. Quoted in Karnow, *Vietnam: A History*, 626.

3. Ibid., 577.

4. Young, *Vietnam Wars*, 246.

5. Quoted in ibid., 237.

6. Quoted in Seymour Hersh, *The Price of Power: Kissinger in the Nixon White House* (New York: Summit Books, 1983), 47–48.

7. Quoted in Shawcross, *Sideshow: Kissinger, Nixon*, 214.

8. Though the Nixon administration was unable to keep the Cambodian invasion a secret, all military personnel involved in it were instructed not to talk

about it, and to evade press inquiries about it. For a complete account of the destruction of Cambodia, see Shawcross, *Sideshow: Kissinger, Nixon.*

9.   Gibson, *Perfect War*, 418.

10.   Shawcross, *Sideshow: Kissinger, Nixon*, 211.

11.   Young, *Vietnam Wars*, 238.

12.   Shawcross, *Sideshow: Kissinger, Nixon*, 222.

13.   Quoted in Hersh, *Price of Power*, 126.

14.   Ibid.

15.   Young, *Vietnam Wars*, 239.

16.   Quoted in Zaroulis and Sullivan, *Who Spoke Up?*, 209.

17.   Quoted in Young, *Vietnam Wars*, 245.

18.   Zaroulis and Sullivan, *Who Spoke Up?*, 217.

19.   Wells, *War Within*, 371.

20.   Foner, *U.S. Labor and Vietnam*, 87.

21.   Ibid., 88.

22.   Ibid., 91.

23.   Quoted in Young, *Vietnam Wars*, 240.

24.   Young, *Vietnam Wars*, 213.

25.   Gibson, *Perfect War*, 300.

26.   Karnow, *Vietnam: A History*, 602. The best history of the program is Douglas Valentine, *The Phoenix Program* (New York: William Morrow and Compant, 1990).

27.   Young, *Vietnam Wars*, 213.

28.   Quoted in Gibson, *Perfect War*, 185–86.

29.   Quoted in Young, *Vietnam Wars*, 245.

30.   The United States, of course, had huge "sanctuaries" for prosecuting its war in Vietnam, with bases throughout the Pacific, including in Thailand and Guam.

31.   Quoted in Michael D. Genovese, *The Watergate Crisis* (New York: Greenwood Press, 1999), 7.

32.   Quoted in Wells, *War Within*, 421.

33.   Wells, *War Within*, 421.

34.   Quoted in Wells, *War Within*, 423.

35.   Wells, *War Within*, 425.

36.   Zaroulis and Sullivan, *Who Spoke Up?*, 320.

37.   Quoted in Wells, *War Within*, 424–35.

38.   Quoted in Zaroulis and Sullivan, *Who Spoke Up?*, 321.

39.   Wells, *War Within*, 427.

40.   Quoted in Foner, *U.S. Labor and Vietnam*, 101.

41.   Ibid., 103.

42.   Zaroulis and Sullivan, *Who Spoke Up?*, 331.

43.   Ibid., 331.

44.   Ibid., 155.

45. The term "Chicano" was a popular term of self-description for young Mexican Americans in the 1960s and 1970s, particularly if they were from the Southwestern United States. The term is still used but with much less frequency during the last two decades.

46. Rudy Acuña, *Occupied America: A History of Chicanos* (New York: Harper and Row, 1981), 367.

47. Ibid.

48. Ibid., 368.

49. Ibid.

50. Ibid. 368–69.

51. Ibid., 370.

52. Quoted in Wells, *War Within*, 475.

53. Ibid., 491.

54. Quoted in Wells, *War Within*, 491.

55. Wells, *War Within*, 491.

56. Wells, *War Within*, 496.

57. The antiwar demonstrations of the 1960s and 1970s were surpassed in size by the many immigrant rights demonstrations throughout the United States during 2006 and 2007.

58. Wells, *War Within*, 503.

59. Quoted in Wells, *War Within*, 504.

60. Ibid., 512.

61. Ibid.

62. Quoted in Halstead, *Out Now!*, 367.

63. Quoted in Wells, *War Within*, 471.

64. Quoted in Halstead, *Out Now!*, 338.

65. Halstead, *Out Now!*, 399.

CHAPTER EIGHT: FROM WATERGATE TO THE FALL OF SAIGON

1. Richard Moser, *The New Winter Soldiers: GI and Veteran Dissent During the Vietnam Era* (New Brunswick, NJ: Rutgers University Press, 1996), 41.

2. Appy, *Working-Class War*, 207.

3. Quoted in ibid., 255.

4. Appy, *Working-Class War*, 208.

5. Quoted in Zinn, *People's History*, 492–3.

6. Donald Duncan, "The Whole Thing Was a Lie!," *Ramparts* (February 1965).

7. Quoted in Zinn, *People's History*, 493.

8. For a thorough treatment of the bizarre nature of the Levy trial, see Robert Sherrill's *Military Justice Is to Justice as Military Music Is to Music* (New

York: Harper Perennial, 1971).

9.   Zinn, *People's History*, 493.

10. Quoted in Moser, *New Winter Soldiers*, 41.

11. Quoted in Appy, *Working-Class War*, 224.

12. Quoted in Young, *Vietnam Wars*, 231.

13. Ibid.

14. David Cortright, *Soldiers in Revolt: GI Resistance During the Vietnam War* (Chicago, IL: Haymarket Books, 2006), 55.

15. Ibid.

16. Halstead, *Out Now!*, 495.

17. See Andrew E. Hunt, *The Turning: A History of Vietnam Veterans Against the War* (New York: New York University Press, 1999), 22–54.

18. Franklin, "Antiwar Movement We," 61.

19. Quoted in Colonel Robert D. Heinl, "The Collapse of the Armed Forces," in Gettleman et. al., eds., *Vietnam and America*, 335.

20. Appy, *Working-Class War*, 231.

21. Ibid.

22. Franklin, "Antiwar Movement We," 63.

23. Ibid., 64.

24. See Joel Geier, "Vietnam: The Soldiers' Rebellion," *International Socialist Review* 9 (Fall 1999), 45.

25. Quoted in Hunt, *Turning: A History*, 133.

26. Ibid., 134.

27. Quoted in Young, *Vietnam Wars*, 256.

28. See Gerald Nicosia, *Home to War* (New York: Three Rivers Press, 2001), 84–97.

29. Quoted in Young, *Vietnam Wars*, 256.

30. Nicosia, *Home to War*, 111.

31. Quoted in "Vietnam Veterans Against the War: Testimony to the U.S. Senate Foreign Relations Committee," in Gettleman et. al., eds., *Vietnam and America*, 455–62.

32. Quoted in Nicosia, *Home to War*, 141.

33. Ibid., 142.

34. Ibid.

35. Quoted in Appy, *Patriots*, 395.

36. Heinl, "Collapse of Armed Forces," 326.

37. Quoted in Max Elbaum, *Revolution in the Air: Sixties Radicals Turn to Lenin, Mao and Che* (London and New York: Verso, 2002), 1.

38. The President's News Conference of May 8th, 1970, The American Presidency Project, americanpresidency.org, http://www.presidency.ucsb.edu/ws/print.php?pid=2496.

39. Cited in Elbaum, *Revolution in the Air*, 43; Todd Gitlin in *The Sixties: Years of Hope, Days of Rage*, cites the Yankelovich Survey findings in Seymour Martin Lipset, *Rebellion in the University* (Boston, MA: Little Brown, 1972).

40. Jack Weinberg and Jack Gerson, *SDS and the Movement in the New Left of the Sixties* (Berkeley, CA: Independent Socialist Press, 1972), 181.

41. Ibid.

42. Elbaum, *Revolution in the Air*, 17.

43. Celia Petty, Deborah Roberts, and Sharon Smith, *Women's Liberation and Socialism* (Chicago: Bookmarks, 1987), 46–7.

44. Quoted in Elbaum, *Revolution in the Air*, 18.

45. See Sale, *SDS*.

46. Simon Leys, *The Chairman's New Clothes: Mao and the Cultural Revolution* (London and New York: Allison and Busby, 1981), 13.

47. Chris Harman, *The Fire Last Time: 1968 and After* (London: Bookmarks, 1998), 35.

48. Quoted in Elbaum, *Revolution in the Air*, 98.

49. The Bay Area Revolutionary Union would soon call itself the Revolutionary Union and eventually the Revolutionary Communist Party, becoming one of the largest Maoist organizations on the U.S. left in the 1970s.

50. Quoted in Elbaum, *Revolution in the Air*, 98.

51. Quoted in Ron Jacobs, *The Way the Wind Blew: A History of the Weather Underground* (London and New York: Verso, 1997), 51.

52. Sale, *SDS*, 598–99.

53. Weinberg and Gerson, *SDS and the Movement*, 208.

54. Quoted in Weinberg and Gerson, *SDS and the Movement*, 203.

55. Jacobs, *Way the Wind Blew*, 75.

56. Quoted in Jesse Lemisch, "Weather Underground Rises from the Ashes: They're Baack!," *New Politics* XI, no. 1 (Summer 2006): 8.

57. A detailed description of these various groups can be found in Elbaum, *Revolution in the Air*.

58. Karnow, *Vietnam: A History*, 626.

59. "Twenty-seven months of bombing of North Vietnam," noted a CIA report, "have had remarkably little effect on Hanoi's overall strategy in prosecuting the war," quoted in Shawcross, *Sideshow: Kissinger, Nixon*, 210. Yet as the war progressed, U.S. B-52 air strikes increased massively.

60. See Gibson, *Perfect War*, chap. 15.

61. For the full story about the Pentagon Papers, see Ellsberg, *Secrets: A Memoir of Vietnam and the Pentagon Papers*.

62. Quoted in Fred Emery, *Watergate: The Corruption of American Politics and the Fall of Richard Nixon* (New York: Touchstone, 1994), 8.

63. Quoted in Karnow, *Vietnam: A History*, 577.

64. Ibid., 634.

65. Quoted in Young, *Vietnam Wars*, 260.

66. Ibid., 270.

67. For a complete account of the peace negotiations, see Gareth Porter, *A Peace*

Denied: The United States, Vietnam, and the Paris Agreement (Bloomington, IN: Indiana University Press, 1975).

68. Appy, *Patriots*, 396.
69. Quoted in Nguyen Tien Hung and Jerrold L. Schecter, *The Palace File: Vietnam Secret Documents* (New York: Harper Perennial, 1986), 146.
70. Young, *Vietnam Wars*, 280.

CONCLUSION: THE LEGACY OF VIETNAM

Major Stephen D. Wesbrook, "The Potential for Military Disintegration," in *Combat Effectiveness*, Sam Sarkesian, ed. (Beverly Hills, CA: Sage, 1983), 270–71; Will quoted in Dominick Cavallo, *A Fiction of the Past: The Sixties in American History* (New York: Palgrave, 1999), 1; Rumsfeld quoted in Eric Schmitt, "After the War: Detainees; U.S. Releases 5 Syrians Hurt in Convoy Attack," *New York Times*, July 1, 2003.

1. In 1995, Agence France-Presse reported that the government of Vietnam had issued statistics citing that throughout the twenty-one years of the U.S.-backed war in Vietnam (1954–1975), five million Vietnamese died. For a partial translation of the report, see http://www.rjsmith.com/kia_tbl.html#press.
2. Young, *Vietnam Wars*, 302.
3. Victor Mallet, "America Meets the Ghost of the Tet Offensive," *Financial Times*, March 27, 2003.
4. Quoted in Wells, *War Within*, 53.
5. See David Zeiger's documentary *Sir! No Sir!* particularly the testimony of former Green Beret Master Sergeant Donald Duncan.

FURTHER READING

GENERAL HISTORIES

The Vietnam Wars 1945–1990 by Marilyn B. Young

Patriots: The Vietnam War Remembered from All Sides by Christian G. Appy

Working-Class War: American Combat Soldiers in Vietnam by Christian G. Appy

The Perfect War: Technowar in Vietnam by James William Gibson

Intervention: How America Became Involved in Vietnam by George Kahin

Sideshow: Kissinger, Nixon and the Destruction of Cambodia by William Shawcross

Vietnam and Other American Fantasies by H. Bruce Franklin

A People's History of the Vietnam War by Jonathan Neale

Vietnam and America: The Most Comprehensive Documented History of the Vietnam War by Marvin E. Gettleman, Jane Franklin, Marilyn B. Young, and H. Bruce Franklin

The Politics of Heroin in Southeast Asia by Alfred McCoy

VIETNAMESE NATIONAL STRUGGLE

Vietnamese Anticolonialism 1885–1925 by David G. Marr

Vietnamese Tradition on Trial 1920–1945 by David G. Marr

Vietnam 1945: The Quest for Power by David G. Marr

Vietnam: A Portrait of Its People at War by David Chanoff and Doan Van Toai

A Viet-Cong Memoir: An Inside Account of the Vietnam War and Its Aftermath by Truong Nhu Tang

Victory at Any Cost: The Genius of Vietnam's General Vo Nguyen Giap by Cecil B. Currey

Last Night I Dreamed of Peace: The Diary of Dang Thuy Tram

U.S. ANTIWAR MOVEMENT

The War Within: America's Battle Over Vietnam by Tom Wells

Who Spoke Up?: American Protest Against the War in Vietnam 1963–1975 by Nancy Zaroulis and Gerald Sullivan

Out Now! A Participant's Account of the Movement in the United States Against the Vietnam War by Fred Halstead

Vietnam and Black America: An Anthology of Protest and Resistance by Clyde Taylor

Fighting on Two Fronts: African-Americans and the Vietnam War by James E. Westheider

Berkeley at War: The 1960s by W. J. Rorabaugh

Lynch Street: The May 1970 Slayings at Jackson State College by Tim Spofford

THE GI MOVEMENT

Soldiers in Revolt: GI Resistance During the Vietnam War by David Cortright

The New Winter Soldiers: GI and Veteran Dissent During the Vietnam Era by Richard Moser

Winter Soldier: An Oral History of the Vietnam Veterans Against the War by Richard Stacewicz

The Turning: A History of Vietnam Veterans Against the War by Andrew E. Hunt

Born on the Fourth of July by Ron Kovic

Home to War: A History of the Vietnam Veterans' Movement by Gerald Nicosia

Soldados: Chicanos in Vietnam by Charley Trujillo

The New Legions by Donald Duncan

Busted: A Vietnam Veteran in Nixon's America by W. D. Ehrhart

Homefront: A Military City and the American Twentieth Century by Catherine Lutz

THE DRAFT AND DRAFT RESISTANCE

Chance and Circumstance: The Draft, The War, and the Vietnam Generation by Lawrence Baskir and William Strauss

Confronting the War Machine: Draft Resistance During the Vietnam War by Michael S. Foley

Hell No We Won't Go: Resisting the Draft During the Vietnam War by Sherry Gershon Gottlieb

Desertion in the Time of Vietnam by Jack Todd

Our War: What We Did in Vietnam and What It Did to Us by David Harris

The Trial of Doctor Spock by Jessica Mitford

Redemption Song: Muhammad Ali and the Spirit of the Sixties by Mike Marqusee

U.S. WAR CRIMES

Against the Crime of Silence: Proceedings of the Russell International War Crimes Tribunal edited by John Duffet

The Phoenix Program by Douglas Valentine

The Real War: The Classic Reporting on the Vietnam War by Jonathan Schell

Four Hours in My Lai by Michael Bilton and Kevin Sim

Nuremberg and Vietnam: An American Tragedy by Telford Taylor

Son Thang: An American War Crime by Gary D. Solis

My Lai 4: A Report on the Massacre and Its Aftermath by Seymour M. Hersh

Heroes by John Pilger

AGENT ORANGE

GI Guinea Pigs: How the Pentagon Exposed Our Troops to Dangers More Deadly than War: Agent Orange and Atomic Radiation by Michael Uhl and Todd Ensign

Waiting for an Army to Die: The Tragedy of Agent Orange by Fred A. Wilcox

Agent Orange on Trial by Peter H. Schuck

The Wages of War: When America's Soldiers Came Home: From Valley Forge to Veitnam by Richard Severo and Lewis Milford

MILITARY INJUSTICE ISSUES

Military Justice Is to justice as Military Music Is to Music by Robert Sherill

Long Binh Jail: An Oral History of Vietnam's Notorious U.S. Military Prison by Cecil B. Curry

The Unlawful Concert: An Account of the Presidio Mutiny Case by Fred Gardner

"The Case of Billy Dean Smith" by Mark Allen, *The Black Scholar*, October 1972

INDEX

303 Committee, 37

AFL-CIO, 153, 162
ARVN. *See* Army of the Republic of Vietnam
Abrams, Creighton, 186, 199
Acheson, Dean, 58, 81–82
Acuña, Rudy, 169, 170
ads, antiwar, 162–163, 168
Afghanistan, 1
African-American soldiers, 79–80, 82, 180, 183–184
  protest and rebellion, 127–128, 179
  statistics, 89
African-American veterans, 94–95, 219n26
African Americans, 79–100
  antiwar movement and, 111, 173
  See also civil rights movement
African troops, 23
AFSCME, 148
Agent Orange, 49
agents provocateurs, 132
Agnew, Spiro, 166–167
airline mechanics' strikes, 75, 151
Algeria, 84, 88, 110
Ali, Muhammad, 92–95
Alien Registration Act, 66, 67
All in the Family, 142, 224n23
alternative press
  GI newspapers, 180–181
  See also *Ramparts*

ambassadors, South Vietnamese, 106
American Friends of Vietnam, 65
American Independent Party, 145
American Legion, 63–64
American Revolution, 114–115, 180, 184
Americans for Democratic Action, 76, 217n56
Anderson, John, 76, 147
Annam, 6, 7
anticommunism, 24, 25, 27, 31, 66
  antiwar movement and, 101, 103, 107, 112–114 passim
  Duong Van Minh and, 33
  Nixon and, 158
  Truman and, 64
  twenty-first century replacement for, 208
  See also HUAC; McCarthyism
antinuclear movement, 103
antiwar movement, 59, 61–77, 101–133
  African-American roots, 79–100
  American public opinion, 147–148
  labor movement and, 117, 136–137, 148
  twenty-first century, 206
  Vietnam, 33
  World War I, 11
antiwar speeches, 97–99
Appy, Christian, 48, 95, 138, 140, 177, 178
  on enemy "body counts," 47, 183
Armies of the Night (Mailer), 119
arms-control agreements, 198

Army of North Vietnam. *See* North Vietnamese Army

Army of the Republic of Vietnam, 35, 196, 199

army surveillance of civilians, 131

arrogance, 41

assassinations
  CIA and, 84, 106, 164
  Malcolm X on, 87
  of Diem and Nhu, 29, 106
  of JFK, 87
  of Lumumba, 84
  of MLK, 59, 126–127
  of Malcolm X, 88
  of Robert Kennedy, 59, 127
  Operation Mongoose and, 125

athletes
  military conscription and, 139
  See also boxers

atrocities, 27, 42, 43, 48–49, 178

Ayers, Bill, 191–192

B-52s, 46, 160, 199

Badilo, Gilbert, 142

Baker, Mark, 164

ballot-box tampering, 71

Baltimore Colts, 139

"Ban the Bomb" march, 104

Bao Dai, 17, 18, 22, 26

Bardacke, Frank, 122

Barry, Jan, 181, 185

Baskir, Lawrence, 138, 140–142 passim

Battle of Ia Drang, 44

Battle of Kontum, 199

Bay Area Revolutionary Union, 191, 193, 229n49

Bay of Pigs invasion, 39, 84, 125

Beallsville, Ohio, 140–141

Becker, Norma, 167

Belafonte, Harry, 117

Belgium, 5–6, 84

Ben Tre, 57

Berkeley, California, 68, 69, 115

Bernstein, Irving, 72

Bidaut, Georges, 22

"Big Minh," 33

bigotry
  against working-class people, 144–145
  George Wallace and, 145
  mass media and, 142, 143

Black Americans, 79–100
  antiwar movement and, 111, 173
  See also Black soldiers; Black veterans; civil rights movement

Black Muslims. *See* Nation of Islam

Black Panther Party, 86, 95–96, 184
  police infiltration, 132

Black Power movement, 85
  labor movement and, 151–152

Black soldiers, 79–80, 82, 180, 183–184
  protest and rebel, 127–128, 179

Black veterans, 94–95

Bloom, Jack, 86

blue-collar workers
  Vietnam War and, 77
  See also construction workers

Blum, Léon, 14

bombing, xi
  of Cambodia, 160, 198
  of North Vietnam, 35, 42, 43, 46, 161, 230n59
    "Christmas bombings," 1972, 200
    Hongai, ix
    "Iron Triangle," 49
    Operation Rolling Thunder, 73, 108
    stopped just before 1968 election, 133
  of South Vietnam, 46–47, 57–58, 199

Bond, Julian, 91, 92, 95

Booth, Paul, 113

Bosnia, 1

"Boulwarism," 153

boxers (athletes), 92–95

Brennan, Peter, 135, 136

Britain. *See* Great Britain

Brown Berets, 169

Buchanan, Pat, 174

Buddhists, 27, 33, 102, 105–106

bulldozers, 49

Bundy, McGeorge, 32, 132–133

Bundy, William, 108
Bush, George H. W., 1, 2
Bush, George W., 72, 138, 208
business press, 187, 225n58
Buttinger, Joseph, 65

CIA, 17, 26, 28, 33, 44
  anticommunism and, 64
  Castro assassination attempts and, 218n17
  Catholic flight from North Vietnam and, 105
  Diem assassination and, 29, 32
  domestic protest and, 131
  Lumumba assassination and, 84, 218n17
  Nguyen Cao Ky and, 34
  Operation CHAOS, 131
  Operation Phoenix, 164
  Tonkin Gulf incident and, 37
Cagin, Seth, 68, 69
Calley, William, 48
Cambodia, 25, 159–161 passim, 198
  coup, 1970, 165
  U.S. invasion, 165–166, 226n8
Campaign for Nuclear Disarmament (CND), 104
"cannon fodder," 137
Cao Bang, 17
capitalism, 112, 144
Carmichael, Stokely, 117
Caro, Robert, 71
Carson, Clayborne, 90
Castro, Fidel, 126, 218n17
Catholic Church, 26–27, 105
Catholic Worker, 105–106
Central Intelligence Agency. See CIA
Chance and Circumstance (Baskir and Strauss), 138, 140–142 passim
CHAOS Operation, 131
Charlie Company, 48
Chávez, César, 162
Chiang Kai-shek, 13
Chicago, 103, 117, 142
  "Days of Rage," 1969, 192

Democratic national convention, 1968, 59, 127–132
"Chicano" (word), 227n45
Chicanos, 169–171
child war victims, ix, x
Chin Tan, 51
China, 13, 23–25 passim
  British in, 6
  Cultural Revolution, 190–191
  recognizes Ho Chi Minh's government, 23
  Soviet Union and, 193–194, 198
  U.S. and, 193–194
  Vietnam and, 10, 13, 19, 24–25, 40, 51
    occupation, 211n33
  World War II and, 16
Chomsky, Noam, 46
Chou En-lai, 24
Civil Rights Act (1964), 72, 84
civil rights movement, 67–69 passim, 71–72, 83–100
  antiwar movement and, 111
  communism and, 112
civilian casualties, 47, 201
  murder of civilians, 184–185
  See also My Lai massacre
class anger and resentment, 147–148
class revolt
  Watts rebellion as, 97
class solidarity, 155
class struggle, 109
class war, 53
class bias
  in mass media, 142–143
  in Selective Service Administration, 137–138, 140
  in sociology, 143–146
  South Vietnam, 35
"Clean for Gene," 124
client leaders. See "puppet" leaders
Clifford, Clark, 58
Clinton, Bill, 1
Cochinchina, 6, 7, 19, 21
Cohelan, Jeffrey, 76
COINTELPRO, 131
Colby, William, 164

Cold War, 39–41 passim, 64–69 passim
collaboration, 15, 16, 18
    See also "puppet" leaders
colleges and universities, 68–70, 106
    "being systematically destroyed," says
        Nixon, 165
    State Department "truth team" and,
        109–110
    student draft deferments, 72
    See also student strikes; teach-ins
colonialism, 5–12 passim
    African Americans and, 83
    Algeria, 110
    fosters nationalism, 9
    genocide and, 17
    put to an end in Vietnam, 17–18
    resumed in Vietnam, 26, 63, 64
Colts (football team), 139
communism, 9–15 passim, 21
    Isaac Deutscher on, 109
    See also anticommunism; Marxism
Communist International (Comintern), 12,
    13, 16–17, 210n20
Communist Party of China (CCP), 13
Communist Party of France, 12
    supports first war in Vietnam, 22
Communist Party of Russia, 13
Communist Party of the United States
    (CPUSA), 66, 190, 194
Communist Party of Vietnam, 11, 28. *See
    also* Indochinese Communist Party
complacency, 55–56
confirmed kills, 48
Congo, 84, 88
Congress, 38, 74
    antiwar demonstration support, 172
    armed forces desegregation and, 80–81
    HUAC, 66–69, 92, 112
    LBJ and, 72, 97, 108
    McGovern-Hatfield amendment, 168
    postal workers and, 154
    war funding and, 125, 168
    See also Dewey Canyon III
Congress of Racial Equality (CORE), 69, 83
Conlon, Thomas, 109–110

conscription. *See* draft
construction workers
    rampage in New York City, 135–136
corruption in politics
    China, 13
    Democratic Party, 70–71, 125
    Kennedy family and, 125
    South Vietnam, 26–27, 52, 196
    Texas, 70–71
Corson, William R., 35
Cortright, David, 180–181
counterdemonstrations, 135–136
coups, 20, 21, 29, 32–34 passim, 126
    Cambodia, 165
    Congo, 218n17
courts-martial, 178, 179
Cousins, Norman, 103
covert operations
    against Cuba, 125–126
    against North Vietnam, 37
    justification for, 64
Crawford, Jeanette, 92
credibility, 36, 39–41 passim
criminalization of dissent, 66
Cronkite, Walter, 54, 59
Cuba, 190
    U.S. and, 125–126
Cuban missile crisis (1962), 40
    See also Bay of Pigs invasion
"cult of personality," 191
Curry, Dave, 142

Daley, Richard J., 125
Danang, 108
Davidson, Carl, 113
Davis, Ed, 171
"Days of Rage," 1969, 192
Dearborn, Michigan, 76–77, 147
Declaration of Independence, 18, 98
Decoux, Jean, 16
defoliants, 28, 49
De Gaulle, Charles, 39
dehumanization of Vietnamese, 46, 185
Dellinger, Dave, 118, 174

Delson, Robert, 63, 64–65
D'Emilio, John, 83
Democratic Party, 71–72, 75–76, 111
    Dixiecrats, 71, 81, 216n37
    George Wallace and, 145–146
    headquarters break-in, 198
    national convention, 1948, 218n9
    national convention, 1964, 85
    national convention, 1968, 59, 127–132
    1968 elections and, 123–133
    Vietnam War funding and, 74
Democratic Republic of Vietnam, 18, 22, 61
demonstrations. See protests, demonstrations, etc.
Depression (1929), 14
desegregation
    of armed forces, 80–81
    of defense industries, 81
desertion by U.S. soldiers, 182–183
destroyers, 37
destroying a town "to save it," 57
Detroit, 49, 86, 152, 184–185
Deutscher, Isaac, 109
Dewey Canyon III, 182, 185–186
Dewey, Peter, 19, 20
Dewey, Thomas, 81
dictatorships, 26, 98
Diem Chuy, 51
Diem, Ngo Dinh. See Ngo Dinh Diem.
Dien Bien Phu, 23, 24, 55, 63, 64
Dies, Martin, 66
dikes, bombing of, 161
direct action, 67–68
Dixiecrats, 71, 81, 216n37
Dixon, Willie, 80
Dohrn, Bernardine, 191–192
Dong Loc, x
Doumer, Paul, 5, 6–7
Dow Chemical Company, 119–122
Dowd, Douglas, 130
draft, 73–74
    African Americans and, 80, 91–93 passim, 139
    deferments, 72, 137–139 passim
    intelligence tests and, 93, 140

local draft board demographics, 139
    resistance, 80, 91
        draft card burning, 117
        draft evasion convictions, 93, 94
        "Stop the Draft Week," 121
Draper, Hal, 115–116
Dray, Philip, 68, 69
drugstore sit-ins, 216n25
Duberman, Martin, 81
Du Bois, W. E. B., 83–84
Duck Hook Operation, 161, 163
Duffy, James, 48–49
Dulles, John Foster, 24
Duncan, Donald, 178–179
Duong Van Minh, 33

Easter Peace Walks, 104
Edison High School, Philadelphia, 141
Ehrenreich, Barbara, 136, 142–143, 144, 146, 155
Ehrhart, Bill, 179–180
elections and referendums, 25, 76, 147
    California, 76
    Georgia, 91
    sham, 26, 52
    U.S. midterm (1966), 75
    U.S. presidential (1948), 81
    U.S. presidential (1960), 71
    U.S. presidential (1964), 36, 58, 59, 107
    U.S. presidential (1968), 75–76, 123–133, 145
    U.S. presidential (1972), 145–146
    See also ballot-box tampering
Ellsberg, Daniel, 197, 198
emperors, 6, 9, 10, 17, 18, 22, 26
enemies, political, 197–198
executions, 15

FBI, 128, 131
FTA, 180–181
famine, 17, 18
farming, 7
farmland destruction, 204
fascism, 26

Federal Employees for Peace, 173
films, 2
Foner, Philip, 135–136
Fort Hood, Texas, 127–128, 181
Fort Hood Three, 179
"fragging," 50, 183
France
  bans uses of Chinese ideographs, 8
  collaboration, 15, 16, 18
  Communist Party, 12
  Foreign Legionnaires, 22–23, 62
  Paris protests, May 1968, 188
  Popular Front government, 14
  Socialist Party, 11, 12
  Vietnam conquest and colonization, 5–16
    passim
      end of, 17–18
      recolonization attempt, 19–23, 31,
      62–64 passim
  Vietnamese in, 11
  World War II and, 15–16
  See also Dien Bien Phu
Franco, Francisco, 26
Franklin, H. Bruce, 61–62, 65, 182
Free Speech Movement, 69–70
freedom of movement, 67
freedom of religion
  claimed in South Vietnam, 106
  disproved in South Vietnam, 105
freedom of speech
  restricted by Smith Act, 66
  See also Free Speech Movement
Freedom Summer, 69
Freeman, Jo, 112–113
Fulbright, William, 36, 74, 76, 197

GIs. See soldiers.
Gandhi, Mohandas, 83–84
Gelson, George, 139
General Electric, 153, 193
Geneva Accords, 1954, 23–27 passim, 31
genocide, 17, 51
  Cambodia, 160
Georgia, 91, 92

Germany, 5–6
  World War II and, 15, 16
Gerson, Jack, 188, 192
Gibson, James, 9, 35
Gilligan, John, 129
Gitlin, Todd, 128
Goldwater, Barry, 36
"gook" and "gooks" (labels), 46, 47, 49, 185
Gottlieb, Stanford, 114
Goulden, Joseph, 148
Gracey, Douglas, 20
Great Britain
  Asia and, 5–6, 16
  Vietnam and, 19–20
  World War II and, 16
"Great Society" (LBJ concept), 70, 71, 75
  MLK on, 97–98
Green Berets, 126, 178, 179
Grenada, 1
Gruening, Ernest, 61, 111
guerrillas and guerrilla war, 16, 29

Haiphong, 22
Halberstam, David, 72
Haldeman, H. R., 171, 197
Halstead, Fred, 61, 102, 118, 175, 176, 194
Ham Nghi, 10
Hamer, Fanny Lou, 85
Hamilton, George, 139
Hamilton, Richard F., 144, 146
Hanoi, 21, 22
  bombing of, 1972, 200
hard-hat demonstrations, 135–136
Harman, Chris, 190
Harper, Steve, 137
Harvard University, 138
Hatfield, Mark, 168
Heinl, Robert D., Jr., 177, 186
helicopters
  torture and, 164–165
Heller, Lennie, 117
Helms, Richard, 173
Henderson, William, 25
Henry, Jamie, 184–185

herbicidal warfare, 28, 49, 204
Herr, Michael, 180
Herrick, John J., 37–38
Hersh, Seymour, 163
Hershey, Lewis B., 138
history
    "historical amnesia," x
    historiography, 2–3
Hitler, Adolf, 15
    Ky's hero, 34
Ho Chi Minh, 9, 11–16, 21–25 passim, 27–28
    as "spiritual father," 50
    known as Nguyen Ai Quoc, 11
    Tet Offensive and, 54
    Vietnam independence and, 18
Ho Chi Minh Trail, 42, 159, 196
Hodgson, Godfrey, 161
home-front concessions, 217n43
Honey, Michael, 80
Hongai, ix–x
Hoover, J. Edgar, 96
hospitals
    bombed by U.S. in North Vietnam, 200
    Veterans Administration, 181
House Committee on Un-American Activities (HUAC), 66–69, 92, 112
Hubbard, Al, 182, 184
Hue, 56–57, 105
Humphrey, Hubert, 59, 74, 85
    1968 elections and, 124, 128–129, 132–133
Hunt, David, 57
Huntsman, Jon, 171

Ia Drang, Battle of, 44
illiteracy
    fostered by French colonization, 8–9
images of war, 41–42
Independent Socialist Club, 69, 115
imperialism, American, 39, 41, 51
    Black Panther Party on, 95–96
    college students' opinion, 187
    defeatable, 207–208
    Malcolm X on, 88
    Norman Thomas on, 63
        protested by merchant marine, 62
        Weather Underground on, 192–193
imperialism, British, 6
imperialism, French, 5–12 passim, 14, 16
imperialism, Japanese, 15
indentured workers, 7
India, 6, 20
    African Americans and, 83–84
"Indian Country," 53
Indochinese Communist Party, 14–15, 210n20
    dissolution into broad National Front, 16
inflation, 75, 151
informers, 132
Inter-University Committee for a Public-Hearing on Vietnam, 110
International Association of Machinists, 75, 151
International Communist League, 21
International Volunteer Services, 53
internationalism, 12, 13
    African Americans and, 84, 88, 90
    Muhammad Ali and, 94
interventionism, 1
    denounced by American Legionnaires, 63–64
    denounced by Black Panther Party, 95
    U.S. public opinion, 1954, 64
Iraq Syndrome, 2
Iraq War, 2003, 1, 72, 206–208
    Vietnam government on, 205
"Iron Triangle," 49
Isserman, Maurice, 104

Jackson, George L., 99–100
Jackson State College, police killings, 1970, 166
Japan, 10
    World War II and, 15–18 passim
        rearmed to suppress Vietminh, 62
Jim Crow. See segregation
Johnson, Ed, 64
Johnson, Lyndon, 32, 70–74 passim, 125
    calls airline mechanics to return to work, 151

calls Vietnam "raggedy-ass little fourth-rate country," 2
declines to seek reelection, 59, 124
doesn't want "any damn Dinbinphoo," 55
elected president, 107, 123
feels like "a hitchhiker caught in a hailstorm," 123
Humphrey and, 128–129, 132
MLK and, 97
public support for war and, 108
Robert Kennedy's hatred for, 127
"seemingly bottomless capacity for deceit," 71
Tonkin Gulf incident and, 36, 38, 39
U.S. public opinion, 58
Junction City Operation, 44

Karnow, Stanley, 23, 56, 196
Keating, Edward, 217n55
Kennedy, John F., 26–28 passim, 65, 125
  assassination
    Malcolm X on, 87
    supposing he had survived, 212n2
Kennedy, Robert F., 58, 76
  African Americans and, 126–127
  assassination, 59, 127
  1968 elections and, 123–127
  supporters go over to George Wallace, 146
  wishes he'd "been born an Indian," 126
Kent State University, National Guard killings, 1970, 166–167
Kerry, John, 182, 185
Khe Sanh, 55, 56
Khmer Rouge, 160
killed in action, 48
King, Coretta Scott, 117, 162
King, Martin Luther, Jr., 67, 84–86 passim, 91, 96–100, 116
  assassination, 126–127, 180, 183–184
  Memphis sanitation workers' strike and, 152
  New York City antiwar march (1967) and, 117
Kissinger, Clark, 117

Kissinger, Henry, 158–161 passim, 163, 199–200
Klonsky, Mike, 191–192
Kolko, Gabriel, 44
Komer, Robert, 53
Kontum, Battle of, 199
Korean War, 23–25 passim, 63, 108
Kovic, Ron, 182
Krogh, Egil, 198
Kruschev, Nikita, 39–40
Kuomintang, 13
Ky, Nguyen Cao, 34

labor movement, 75, 143, 149–155
  antiwar and, 117, 136–137, 148
  student movement and, 153
  See also strikes; unions
Laird, Melvin, 163
Lam Son 719, 196
land expropriation, 7
landlords, 35, 52
Lansdale, Edward, 26, 39
Laos, 25, 159, 185
  invasion of, 196
laws, 72, 84. See also Alien Registration Act; Postal Reorganization Act
Le Duc Tho, 199, 200
League for Industrial Democracy, 110
Leclerc, Philippe, 20, 21
LeMay, Curtis, 145
Lenin, Vladimir, 12, 13
Levy, Howard, 179
Levy, Peter, 136, 147
Leys, Simon, 190
liberal reform, 71–72
Lipset, Seymour Martin, 143, 224n25
lobbies and lobbyists, 65
Lodge, Henry Cabot, 32
Long An, 57–58
Los Angeles, 170–171
Los Angeles County Sheriff's Department
  attacks Chicano antiwar protest, 170–171
Louisiana, 92

Louisville, Kentucky, 92–93
loyalty oaths, 66–67
Lumumba, Patrice, 84, 218n17
lynching, 80
Lynd, Staughton, 110–111

machine-gunners, 48–49
Maddox, 37–38
Mailer, Norman, 109, 119
Malcolm X, 80, 86–89, 93, 99
mandarins, 9, 10, 11
Mansfield, Mike, 74
Mao Zedong, 23, 190–91
Maoism, 190–91, 193–94
marches, 115
    New York City (1967), 116–17
    San Francisco (1968), 132
    Washington, D.C. (1965), 110–13 passim
    Washington, D.C. (1969), 162
Marqusee, Mike, 93
Marr, David, 11
Marable, Manning, 83, 89
Marx, Karl, 144
Marxism, 12, 84
massacres
    Chiang Kai-shek and, 13
    My Lai, 48, 184
May Day parades, 14
McCarthy, Eugene, 58, 123–25 passim, 128, 181
McCarthy, Joseph, 66–67
McCarthyism, 63
    African Americans and, 82–83
McCloy, John J., 58
McCone, John, 73
McGovern, George, 128
McGovern-Hatfield amendment, 168
McNamara, Robert, 32, 40, 58, 73, 206
    commissions Pentagon Papers, 197
    hides and falsifies costs of war, 74
    is father of son with differing politics, 166
    says "they could hang people for what's in [Pentagon Papers]," 195
McNaughton, John, 40, 206

Meany, George, 148, 153, 167
medals
    returned to the government in protest, 185–186
    thrown away in anger, 93
media
    on Nixon pledge to end war, 161
    on working class, 135
    propaganda and, x–xi
    Yippies and, 120
    See also news media; press; television
Medina, Ernest, 48
Meier, August, 85
Memphis sanitation workers' strike, 152
mercenaries, 164
merchant marine, 62
Mexican Americans, 169–71
Mexican immigrants, 63
Michelin, 7
military advisers, 28, 29, 35
military aid
    to France, 22
    to Greece and Turkey, 64
    to South Vietnam, 27
Military Assistance Command—Vietnam, 33
military conscription. *See* draft
military police, 118–119
military reserves, 72, 137, 138
military spending, 42, 74
miners and mining, 7–8
Minh, Duong Van, 33
mission civilisatrice, 8
Mississippi Freedom Democratic Party, 85, 89–90
Mitchell, Clarence, 91
"Mobe," 117–118
Mobilizer, 118
monarchy
    abolition of, 18
Mongoose Operation, 125
Moody, Kim, 151
moratorium movement, 162, 163, 169–170
Morrison, Norman, 221n10
Morse, Wayne, 61
Moscow, 12

Moser, Richard, 177
Moses, Robert, 79, 111
Moyers, Bill, 72
Muhammad, Elijah, 80
Muller, Bob, x
murders
    Alabama, 90–91
    of Vietnamese civilians, 184–185
    See also massacres; state murders
Muslims, 86–87
Muste, A. J., 104–105, 112
"My Lai from the Sky," 58
My Lai massacre, 48
    "not an isolated incident," 184

NAACP, 83, 85, 91
NLF, 28–29, 32–35 passim, 39, 40, 42–45 passim
    attacks U.S. air base in Pleiku, 108
    CIA and, 164
    declines Huey Newton offer to raise troops, 95–96
    resilience of, 50–57
    "search and destroy" missions and, 47–48
    sweeps ARVN in 1972, 199
    Tet Offensive and, 54–57 passim
    "Viet Cong" (label) and, 28, 34
    Vietnamese public opinion, 53
NVA. See North Vietnamese Army
napalm, 119–120
Nation of Islam, 80, 86–88 passim, 93
National Association for the Advancement of Colored People, 83, 85, 91
National Chicano Moratorium Committee, 169–171 passim
National Committee for a Sane Nuclear Policy. See SANE
National Guard, 64, 72, 128, 166
    African Americans and, 139
    draft avoidance and, 137–139 passim
    kills four students at Kent State, 166
    mobilized to deliver mail, 155
National Liberation Front of South Vietnam. See NLF

National Mobilization Committee to End the War in Vietnam, 117–118
nationalism, 9–15 passim
    civil rights movement and, 84
navy nurses
    court-martial of, 179
Neal, Edward, 139
Negroponte, John, 200
Nelson, Gaylord, 74
neutrality, 33, 34, 39
New Left, 104, 107, 112
New York Graphic, 136
New York Times
    complains about "defiance" of striking postal workers, 154
    publishes Pentagon Papers, 197
Newark, New Jersey, 67
news media
    working class and, 142–143
Newton, Huey, 95–96
Ngo Dinh Diem, 26–29, 31–33 passim, 51–52, 102–103
    American Friends of Vietnam and, 65
    assassination, 32, 106, 126
    Buddhist repression and, 105
    Lansdale and, 39
    MLK on, 98
    Malcolm X on, 87
    Robert Kennedy on, 126
Ngo Dinh Nhu, 26, 29, 32, 87
Ngo Vinh Long, 8
Nguyen Ai Quoc. See Ho Chi Minh
Nguyen Cao Ky, 34
Nguyen Chanh Thi, 34
Nguyen Khanh, 33–34
Nguyen Van Thieu, 34, 200
Nhu, Madame, 106
Nhu, Ngo Dinh, 26, 29, 32, 87
Nixon Doctrine, 163
Nixon, Richard, 75–76, 157–175 passim
    as "peace candidate," 157
    as vice president, 63
    calls protesters "bums," 166
    elected president, 59, 133, 157
    reelected, 199

mobilizes National Guard to deliver mail, 155

says "if you can't lie, you'll never get anywhere," 198

says "this country is not headed for revolution," 187

visits China, 193–194, 198–199

withdraws from presidency, 201

Nol, Lon, 165

nonviolent direct action, 67–68

North Vietnam

flight of Catholics from, 26–27, 105

Henry Kissinger and, 160–161, 199–200

negotiations with U.S., 199–200

partition and, 31

North Vietnamese Army, 42, 43, 159

Khe Sanh and, 55

sweeps ARVN in 1972

Tet Offensive and, 55–57 passim

nuclear disarmament movement, 103

nuclear testing, 103, 107

nurses

court-martial of, 179

OSS, 15, 17, 19

Oakland, California, 95, 121–122

Oberdorfer, Dan, 45, 55–56

O'Connor, Carroll, 142

October League, 193

Office of Strategic Services, 15, 17, 19

Office of Economic Opportunity, 71

officers killed by own troops, 183

Oglesby, Carl, 113–114

oil industry, 70, 207

strikes, 153

Oklahoma City sit-ins, 216n25

Oleo Strut (GI coffeehouse), 181

Olson, Gail, 186

Operation Abolition, 69

Operation CHAOS, 131

Operation Duck Hook, 161, 163

Operation Junction City, 44

Operation Mongoose, 125

Operation Phoenix, 164

Operation Ranch Hand, 28

Operation Rolling Thunder, 73, 108

Operation Speed Express, 50

Operation Starlight, 43–44

Operation Sunshine, 29

Osborne, K. Barton, 164

Out Now! (Halstead), 61, 194

PAVN. *See* North Vietnamese Army

Pachaug Victory, 62

Paine, Tom, 184

Paris

peace accords, 1973, 200

protests, May 1968, 188

Patton, George S., III, 47

Peace Corps

headquarters occupation by former volunteers, 167

Malcolm X calls "neo-missionaries," 88

peace movement. *See* antiwar movement

peace negotiations, 199–200

Paris accords, 1973, 200–201

Pearl Harbor, 15, 16

peasantry, 11, 34, 35, 49, 52

armed, 21

landlessness of, 7

organized, 13, 16, 17

rebelliousness of, 6, 13

Vietminh allegiance, 22

"Pentagon Coup" (1964), 33

"Pentagon Papers," 105

"they could hang people for what's in there," says McNamara, 195

Pentagon protest, October 1967, 118–119

People's Army of Vietnam. *See* North Vietnamese Army

People's Liberation Armed Forces (PLAF), 44

Persian Gulf War, 1

Pétain, Philippe, 15

Petras, James, 115–116

Phan Boi Chau, 9–10

Phan Chu Trinh, 10

Philadelphia, 141
Phillips, Kevin, 146
Phoenix Operation, 164
Pickus, Robert, 115–116
Pilger, John, 140–141
"plumbers" (intelligence unit) 197–198
polarization (U.S. society), 158, 206–207
police
    arrest Jack Weinberg in Berkeley, 69
    attack protesters in Oakland, 121
    break up New York protest with mass arrests, 222n59
    chant "Kill, Kill, Kill" in Chicago, 130–131
    face challenge by Black Panther Party, 95
    gouge eyes of Black WWII veteran, 219n26
    guard Pentagon from flower-wielding students, 118–119
    kill students at Jackson State, 166
    photograph people at demonstrations, 131
    use fire hoses on students in San Francisco, 68–69
    use tear gas on students in Madison, 120–121
    wiretap 1,000 people in New Haven, 132
    See also military police; Red Squads
police, French, 11. See also sûreté
police informers, 132
police, South Vietnamese, 26
Political Man (Lipset), 143–144
political corruption. See corruption in politics
political enemies, 197–198
political prisoners, 14, 27, 92, 93
    Fort Hood Three, 179
polls, 80, 147, 171, 187
Postal Reorganization Act (1970), 155
postal workers' strike, 1970, 149, 154–155
Potsdam conference (1945), 19
Potter, Paul, 107, 111
Poulo Cordone, 8, 10
poverty, 85, 140
Powell, Colin, 137–138
press
    White House and, 45
    See also alternative press; business press

pretexts for war, 212n14. See also Gulf of Tonkin incident
Price of Power (Hersh), 163
prisons and prisoners, 8, 10, 14, 16, 20
prisoners of war, 20
    See also political prisoners; torture
Progressive Labor Party, 190
Progressive Party, 81
Project 100,000, 140
propaganda, x, 31, 45, 167,
    leafleting of North Vietnam, 119
    Success Offensive, 54
protectorates, 6
protests, demonstrations, etc., 14, 113–114, 162, 194, 228n57
    African-American, 127–128
    Agnew on, 167
    Buddhist, 33, 105, 106
    Chicano, 169–170
    civil rights, 67
    diversity of protesters, 116
    Eugene McCarthy on, 123
    G.I., 167
    hard-hat pro-war, 135–136
    labor-union antiwar, 148–149
    medal-returning ceremonies, 185–186
    merchant marine, 62
    personal effect of, 175
    political effect of, 163, 174–176
    pro-war, 135–137
    self-immolation, 105, 106, 221n10
    student, 68–70
    supporting Muhammad Ali, 94
    women, 189
    Chicago, 1968, 59, 129–130
    New York City, 63, 116, 135–136, 148
    Paris, 1968, 188
    San Francisco, 132, 172
    South Vietnam, 33, 105, 106
    Washington, D.C.
        1965, 110–113 passim, 118–119
        1967, 176
        1971, 172–173
    See also counterdemonstrations; marches

Psychological Strategy Committee, 45
Puerto Rico, 141
"puppet" rulers, 9, 15, 17, 18
    United States and, 25–29, 31, 35, 39, 51,
        195–196

Quang Ngai, 53

ROTC buildings
    attacked and burned, 165–166
racism, 8, 47, 85
    Selective Service Administration and,
        138–139
    social class and, 144
    U.S. military and, 82, 183
radar stations, 37
Rader, Gary, 117
Ramparts, 76, 120, 178, 217n55
Ranch Hand Operation, 28
Randolph, A. Phillip, 81, 83
Raskin, A. H., 142
Rauh, Joseph, 85
Reagan, Ronald, 1, 75, 122
rebellions, 14
    of African Americans, 86, 96–97
    of soldiers, 59, 127–128, 158, 177–186 pas-
        sim
    "fragging," 50, 183
red-baiting, 69
Red Papers, 191
"Red Scare," 66, 82
Red Squads, 131–132
reformism, 71–72
refugees, Catholic, 26–27
religious freedom
    claimed in South Vietnam, 106
    disproved in South Vietnam, 105
repression, 8–9
    against Buddhists in South Vietnam, 27,
        105, 106
    against Indochinese Communist Party, 14
    against Vietminh supporters, 27, 28
    Japanese, 15
    See also police

Republic of Vietnam. *See* South Vietnam
Republican Party, 75–76, 146–147
reserves (military forces), 72, 137, 138
Resistance (organization), 117, 121
Reuther, Walter, 85, 162, 167
revolution, 11, 13, 114–115, 189–195 passim.
    See also Revolutionary War
Revolutionary Communist Party, 193
Revolutionary Union, 191, 193, 229n49
Revolutionary War, 114–115, 180, 184
rice farming, 7
Riverside Church speech (MLK), 97–99
Rolling Thunder Operation, 73, 108
Roosevelt, Franklin, 66, 70–71, 81
Rostow, Walt, 32, 39, 41, 45
ROTC buildings
    attacked and burned, 165–166
rubber industry, 7
Rubin, Jerry, 118
Rudd, Mark, 193
Rudwick, Elliot, 85
Rumsfeld, Donald, 1, 203, 205
Rusk, Dean, 32, 109
Russell, Bertrand, 104, 105
Russia. *See* Soviet Union
Russian Revolution, 11
Rustin, Bayard, 80, 83, 85, 104–105

SDS, 110–114, 120, 174
    growth, 122
    radicalization, 188–189
    ultimate collapse, 191–192
SS *Winchester Victory*, 62
Saigon, 20, 26, 27
Sainteny, Jean, 21
Salazar, Ruben, 170–171
Sale, Kirkpatrick, 192
San Diego, 171
San Francisco, 68–69, 175
SANE, 103, 104, 112–115 passim
Sanders, Robert, 95
sanitation workers' strike, 152
Savio, Mario, 69
Scheer, Robert, 65, 76

Schlesinger, Arthur, 65, 127
Schnall, Susan, 179
schools
  China, 13
  France, 9
  Philadelphia, 141
  Vietnam, 8, 10
  See also colleges and universities
Schultz, George, 153
Scranton, William, 158
Seale, Bobby, 95
"search and destroy" missions, 47–48
Second International, 12
secret bombing of Cambodia, 160, 198
secret committees, 37
secret police, 26
segregation, 79, 92–93. See also desegregation
Selective Service System, 92
  class and racial biases, 138
self-determination, national, 12, 16, 114
self-immolation, 105, 106, 221n10
Sellers, Cleveland, 92
Sewell, William, 120
Shapen, Robert, 57
sharecropping, 7
Shawki, Ahmed, 84
Sheehan, Neil, 198
sheriff's deputies
  attack Chicano antiwar protesters, 170–171
Sherry, Michael, 40, 41
ships, 37–38
Shrade, Paul, 162
Shrecker, Ellen, 131–132
Shriver, Sargent, 71
Sihanouk, Norodom, 159
sit-ins, 67, 120, 216n25
situation comedies, 142
SLID, 110
slogans, 110, 114, 189, 194
  striking postal workers', 154
  Weather Underground's, 193
Smith Act, 66, 67
Smith, Jack, 185
Smith, Sharon, 149, 180
SNCC, 67, 83, 85, 90–92, 112

social class, 53
  tolerance and, 144
  Vietnam War public opinion and, 76–77
  See also class anger and resentment; class
    revolt; class solidarity; class struggle;
    class war
socialism, 109
Soviet Union, 12–13
Socialist Party of France, 11, 12
Socialist Party USA, 68, 104. See also Young
  People's Socialist League
Socialist Workers Party, 66, 194
socialists, 63–66 passim, 68, 76
sociology
  class bias in, 143–146
soldiers
  antiwar movement and, 176
  coffeehouses, 180–181
  morale, 186
  newspapers, 180–181
  resistance and rebellion, 50, 59, 127–128,
    158, 177–186
    desertion, 182–183
    "fragging," 50, 183
  See also African-American soldiers; African
    soldiers; military police
South Africa, 88
South Vietnam, 25–29
  army (ARVN), 35, 196, 199
  partition and, 31
  surrender of, 201
  See also Ngo Dinh Diem; Saigon; Viet-
    namization
Southern Christian Leadership Conference
  (SCLC), 83
southern states, 145. See also Dixiecrats
Soviet Union, 12–13
  China and, 193–194, 198
  desegregation and, 81
  recognizes Ho Chi Minh government, 23
  U.S. and, 39, 107, 193–194
  World War II and, 16–17
Speed Express Operation, 50
Spellman, Francis Cardinal, 26, 65
Spock, Benjamin, 117, 173

Stalinism, 12–13, 191, 193
Starlight Operation, 43–44
state murders
    Jackson, Mississippi, 166, 170
    Kent, Ohio, 166–167, 170
    Los Angeles, 170–171
States' Rights Party, 81, 218n9
Steinke, Richard, 178
stereotype of workers, 142–143, 146
Stettinius, Edward, 19
Stone, I. F., 111, 127
"Stop the Draft Week," 121–122
"strategic hamlet" program, 28–29, 34–35
Strauss, William, 138, 140–142 passim
street theater, 117
strikes, 13–14, 75, 149–155. See also student strikes; wildcat strikes
student draft deferments, 72
Student League for Industrial Democracy (SLID), 110
student movement, 68–70, 118–121 passim
    Cambodia bombing and, 165–167
    "Clean for Gene," 124
    labor movement and, 153
Student Peace Union, 103–104, 106, 107
Student Nonviolent Coordinating Committee, 67, 83, 85, 90–92, 112
student strikes, 165–166
Students for a Democratic Society. See SDS
Success Offensive, 54
suicide as protest, 105, 106
Sullivan, Gerald, 61, 103, 112, 118–121 passim, 123
    on antiwar movement after Chicago 1968, 132
    on Army surveillance of civilians, 131
Sunshine Operation, 29
Supreme Court, 67, 91, 94, 197
sûreté, 9, 10
surrender
    LBJ on, 39
surveillance, 131
Sustar, Lee, 153, 154
Swados, Harvey, 150

Taylor, Maxwell, 32, 34, 40
teach-ins, 108–110, 115, 116
teachers, 53
    Dean Rusk on, 109
    fired for protesting against Dow Chemical, 121
    subpoenaed in Bay Area, 68
tear-gas canisters
    cause two deaths in L.A., 170–171
television, 161, 165
    McGovern-Hatfield amendment and, 168
    working-class people and, 142
television reporters
    murdered by sheriffs in L.A., 170–171
tenant farming, 7
Terry, Wallace, 184
Tet (holiday), 54
Tet Offensive, 1968, 54–59, 157
    Kissinger on, 159
    LBJ and, 124
Texas, 66, 70–71, 127–128
    Chicano war casualties, 169
theft of land, 7
Thi, Nguyen Chanh, 34
Thich Quang Duc, 105
Thieu, Nguyen Van, 34, 200
Third International. See Comintern
Third World, 83, 90, 187, 190
Thomas Edison High School, Philadelphia, 141
Thomas, Norman, 63, 65, 112
Thorez, Maurice, 22
303 Committee, 37
Thurmond, Strom, 81, 185, 218n9
Ticonderoga, 37
'Til Death Us Do Part, 224
Tonkin, 6, 7, 17, 19, 22
Tonkin Gulf incident, 36–38, 123
torpedo boats, 37
torture, 126, 164
treaties, 107
    Paris peace accord, 1973, 200–201
troop withdrawals, 162, 163, 165, 171, 173
troopships, 62
Trotskyists, 21, 194

truces, 23–24
Truman Doctrine, 64
Truman, Harry S., 64, 66, 125
  desegregates armed forces, 80–81
Truong Nhu Tang, 50, 52
Tu Duc, 6
tunnels, 49
Turn Toward Peace, 103, 115
Turner Joy, 37

UN. *See* United Nations
U.S. *See* United States
USSR. *See* Soviet Union
USS *Maddox*, 37–38
USS *Ticonderoga*, 37
USS *Turner Joy*, 37
unions, 150, 151, 167–168
  antiwar protests and, 162–163
  See also labor movement
United Nations, 19
United States
  drops leaflets on North Vietnam, 119
  military spending, 42, 74
  surveillance of civilians, 131
  Vietnam and, 17–19 passim, 21, 31
    Truman administration, 22, 61–66 passim
    Eisenhower administration, 23–28, 65
    Kennedy administration, 28–29, 35,
      38–40, 65, 103, 106
    Johnson administration, 32–59, 70–75,
      109, 132–133
    Nixon administration, 157–201 passim
  World War II and, 16–18 passim, 62
United States Congress. *See* Congress
United States Department of State, 109
  Senior Informal Advisory Group, 58–59
United States Navy, 37
United States Supreme Court, 67, 91, 94, 197
universities and colleges, 68–70, 106
  "being systematically destroyed," says
    Nixon, 165
  State Department "truth team" and,
    109–110
  student draft deferments, 72

  See also student strikes; teach-ins
University of California, Berkeley, 68, 69, 109
University of Michigan, 108
University of Wisconsin, 110, 120
Urban League, 91

VA hospitals, 181
VVAW. *See* Vietnam Veterans Against the War
values, 99
Versailles peace conference (1919), 11–12
veterans, 171
  denounce U.S. intervention, 63–64
  experience ill treatment at VA hospitals, 181
  march against war, 117
  testify about war crimes, 184–185
  throw away medals, 185–186
  See also African-American veterans; Viet-
    nam Veterans Against the War
Vichy government, 15
Viet Cong. *See* NLF
Viet Nam Friendship Association (VNFA),
  62–63
Vietminh, 16–18, 20–25 passim
  return of (as NLF), 51
  See also Workers' Party
Vietnam
  Chinese occupation, 211n33
  education, 8–10 passim
  French occupation, 5–18 passim
  French recolonization attempt, 19–23, 31,
    62–64 passim
  "First Vietnam War," 34
  independence declaration, 18, 61
  Japanese occupation, 15–17
  partition, 25, 31
  reunification, 35
  Revolution (1945), 18
  U.S. invasion of, 38, 42, 50, 51
  See also Annam; Cochinchina; North
    Vietnam; South Vietnam; Tonkin; Viet-
    nam War
Vietnam GI, 181
"Vietnam Lobby," 65
Vietnam Moratorium Day, 162, 163

Vietnam Syndrome, 1, 205
Vietnam Veterans Against the War, 172, 181–182, 184–185. *See also* Winter Soldier Investigation
Vietnam War
  casualties, 141
    African-American, 89
    Chicano, 169
    civilian, 47, 201, 184–185
    demographics, 142
    statistics, xi, 57, 201, 204, 230n1
    See also killed in action; massacres
  civil rights movement and, 85–86
  Congress and, 38, 74, 125, 168, 172
  costs, 74, 133, 168
  herbicidal warfare, 28, 49, 204
  historiography, 3
  iconography, 41–42
  in films, 2
  Malcolm X on, 86–88 passim
  Martin Luther King Jr. on, 98
  Muhammad Ali on, 94
  statistics, 57
  torture and, 164–165
  U.S. public opinion, 76–77, 147, 168, 171
Vietnamese language, 8–9
"Vietnamization," 159, 165, 195–196
villagers, 48, 52–53
Vo Nguyen Giap, 14, 23, 42
voter registration, 90
Voting Rights Act, (1965), 84

Wallace, George, 136, 145–146
Wallace, Henry, 81, 217n56
war crimes investigations, 184–185
"war on poverty," 71
"war on terror," 208
war, pretexts for, 212n14. *See also* Gulf of Tonkin incident
War Resisters League, 121
War Shipping Administration, 62
War Within, The (Wells), 61
Washington Post, 99
Watergate scandal, 198, 201

Watts rebellion, 1965, 96–97
Washington, D.C.
  "citadel of imperialism," says Malcolm X, 88
"We Shall Overcome," 69
Weather Underground, 191–192
Weinberg, Jack, 69, 188, 192
Weir, Stan, 150
Wells, Tom, 61, 116–117, 130, 166, 167, 172
Wesbrook, Stephen D., 203
West Virginia, 141
Westheider, James, 92
Westin, Av, 165
Westmoreland, William, xi, 41–45 passim
  Khe Sanh and, 55
  on Black servicemen, 79
  says "[the] Oriental doesn't value life," 47
  Tet Offensive and, 56
  U.S. tour, 1967, 54
Weyand, Fred C., 41
Wheeler, Earle, 73
White House
  committees, 37, 45
  "plumbers," 197–198
  press relations, 45
White, Walter, 83
Who Spoke Up? (Zaroulis and Sullivan), 61
Wichita sit-ins, 216n25
wildcat strikes, 150–151, 166
Wilkins, Roy, 91
Will, George F., 203
Wilson, Woodrow, 12
Winchester Victory, 62
Winter Soldier Investigation (1971), 49, 182, 184–185
Wisconsin
  George Wallace support, 146
  See also University of Wisconsin
"wise men" (State Dept. advisory group) 58–59
withdrawal of troops, 162, 163, 165, 171, 173
women's movement, 189
Woodard, Isaac, 87, 219n26
workers, 135–155
  blamed for fascism and communist "totalitarianism," 143–144

death of, 7
frustration of, 149–150
starvation wages of, 8
stereotyped as "reactionary," 142–143, 146
See also blue-collar workers; labor move-
ment
Workers' Party, 27
World War I, 11
World War II, 15–19 passim
African-American public opinion, 80
French recolonization of Vietnam and, 62
Tet Offensive and, 56
Vietnam bombings and, 47, 160, 204
Wright, Richard, 84

X, Malcolm, 80, 86–89, 93, 99

Yippies, 118, 129–130
Young, Marilyn, 17–18, 31, 53, 57–58, 160,
201, 204
Young People's Socialist League, 68, 104
Young Socialists of America, 194
Young, Whitney, 91
Younge, Sammy, 90–91

Zaroulis, Nancy, 61, 103, 112, 118–121 passim, 123
on antiwar movement after Chicago 1968,
132
on army surveillance of civilians, 131
Zinn, Howard, 101, 102, 179
Zirin, Dave, 92
Zumwalt, Elmo R., Jr., 183

ABOUT HAYMARKET BOOKS

Haymarket Books is a nonprofit, progressive book distributor and publisher, a project of the Center for Economic Research and Social Change. We believe that activists need to take ideas, history, and politics into the many struggles for social justice today. Learning the lessons of past victories, as well as defeats, can arm a new generation of fighters for a better world. As Karl Marx said, "The philosophers have merely interpreted the world; the point, however, is to change it."

We take inspiration and courage from our namesakes, the Haymarket Martyrs, who gave their lives fighting for a better world. Their 1886 struggle for the eight-hour day, which gave us May Day, the international workers' holiday, reminds workers around the world that ordinary people can organize and struggle for their own liberation. These struggles continue today across the globe—struggles against oppression, exploitation, hunger, and poverty.

It was August Spies, one of the martyrs who was targeted for being an immigrant and an anarchist, who predicted the battles being fought to this day. "If you think that by hanging us you can stamp out the labor movement," Spies told the judge, "then hang us. Here you will tread upon a spark, but here, and there, and behind you, and in front of you, and everywhere, the flames will blaze up. It is a subterranean fire. You cannot put it out. The ground is on fire upon which you stand."

We could not succeed in our publishing efforts without the generous financial support of our readers. Many people contribute to our project through the Haymarket Sustainers program, where donors receive free books in return for their monetary support. If you would like to be a part of this program, please contact us at info@haymarketbooks.org.

Order online at www.haymarketbooks.org or call 773-583-7884.

ALSO FROM HAYMARKET BOOKS

Beyond the Green Zone:
Dispatches From an Unembedded Journalist in Occupied Iraq

Dahr Jamail with a foreword by Amy Goodman • As the occupation of Iraq unravels, the demand for independent reporting is growing. Since 2003, unembedded journalist Dahr Jamail has filed indispensable reports from Iraq that have made him this generation's chronicler of the unfolding disaster there. ISBN: 978-1-931859-47-9.

Welcome to the Terrordome: The Pain, Politics, and Promise of Sports

Dave Zirin • This much-anticipated sequel to *What's My Name, Fool?* by acclaimed sportswriter Dave Zirin breaks new ground in sportswriting, looking at the controversies and trends now shaping sports in the United States—and abroad. Always insightful, never predictable. ISBN: 978-1-931859-41-7.

Road from ar Ramadi:
The Private Rebellion of Staff Sergeant Camilo Mejía

Camilo Mejía • A courageous personal account of rebellion within the ranks of the U.S. military in wartime—written by the first soldier to publicly refuse to return to fight in Iraq. ISBN: 978-1-931859-553-0

In Praise of Barbarians: Essays Against Empire

Mike Davis • No writer in the United States today brings together analysis and history as comprehensively and elegantly as Mike Davis. In these contemporary, interventionist essays, Davis goes beyond critique to offer real solutions and concrete possibilities for change. ISBN: 978-1-931859-42-4.

Sin Patrón: Stories from Argentina's Worker-Run Factories

The lavaca collective, foreword by Naomi Klein and Avi Lewis • The inside story of Argentina's remarkable movement to create factories run democratically by workers themselves. ISBN: 978-1-931859-43-1.

Diary of Bergen Belsen:
The Story of How One Woman Survived the Holocaust

Hanna Lévy-Hass, foreword by Amira Hass • A unique, deeply political survivor's diary from the final year inside the notorious concentration camp. ISBN: 978-1-931859-48-6.

Soldiers in Revolt: GI Resistance During the Vietnam War

David Cortright, introduction by Howard Zinn • "An exhaustive account of rebellion in all the armed forces, not only in Vietnam but throughout the world."— *New York Review of Books*. ISBN: 978-1-931859-27-1.

Oranges in No Man's Land

Elizabeth Laird • Since her father left Beirut to find work, and her mother was tragically killed in a shell attack, ten-year-old Ayesha has been living with her granny and her two younger brothers. But when Granny's medicine runs out, she must cross the war-torn city to find help. ISBN: 978-1-931859-56-1.

No One Is Illegal:
Fighting Racism and State Violence on the U.S.-Mexico Border

Justin Akers Chacón and Mike Davis • Countering the chorus of anti-immigrant voices, Davis and Akers Chacón expose the racism of anti-immigration vigilantes and put a human face on the immigrants who risk their lives to cross the border to work in the United States. ISBN: 978-1-931859-35-3.

History of the Russian Revolution

Leon Trotsky • This detailed history, written by one of the revolution's central participants, offers the most vivid and inspiring account of the upheavals of 1917, which overthrew the tyranny of tsarism in February and by October established the most radically democratic society in world history. ISBN: 978-1-931859-45-5.

The Essential Rosa Luxemburg

Edited by Helen Scott • This insightful new presentation of Rosa Luxemburg's two most important works presents the full text of *Reform or Revolution* and the *Mass Strike* with explanatory notes, appendices, and introductions. ISBN: 978-1-931859-36-3.

A Little Piece of Ground

Elizabeth Laird • Twelve-year-old Karim and his family are trapped in their Ramallah home by a strict curfew. Meanwhile, Karim longs to play soccer with his friends. When Israeli soldiers find him outside during the next curfew, it seems impossible that he will survive. ISBN: 978-1-931859-38-7.

Subterranean Fire:
A History of Working-Class Radicalism in the United States

Sharon Smith • Workers in the United States have a rich tradition of fighting back and achieving gains that previously seemed unthinkable, but that history remains largely hidden. In *Subterranean Fire*, Sharon Smith brings that history to light and reveals its lessons for today. ISBN: 978-1-931859-23-3.

The Bending Cross: A Biography of Eugene V. Debs

Ray Ginger, introduction by Mike Davis • The classic biography of Eugene V. Debs, one of the most important socialist thinkers and organizers in U.S. history. ISBN: 978-1-931859-40-0.